Whistleblo
Social Serv

P ublic Accountability and
P rofessional Practice

—

Edited by

Geoffrey Hunt

Director
European Centre for Professional Ethics
University of East London
London
and
National Co-ordinator, Freedom to Care

ARNOLD

A member of the Hodder Headline Group
LONDON • SYDNEY • AUCKLAND

in Great Britain in 1998 by
ber of the Hodder Headline Group
ad, London NW1 3BH

noldpublishers.com

ry *Cataloguing in Publication Data*
ecord for this book is available from the British Library

ongress *Cataloging-in Publication Data*
:ord for this book is available from the Library of Congress

65245 4

ing Editor: Clare Parker
ditor: Wendy Rooke
Controller: Priya Gohil
n: Julie Martin

0/11pt Times by Phoenix Photosetting, Chatham, Kent
bound in Great Britain by J W Arrowsmith Ltd, Bristol

Contents

iv   *Contents*

Notes on the contributors

Sue Amphlett is the Director of PAIN – Parents Against INjustice.

Don Brand is Director of the General Social Care Council Implementation Project and Honorary Fellow of the National Institute for Social Work.

Diana Campbell is the editor of *Caring Times*, a magazine for social care sector workers.

Mike Cox is a member of the British Association of Social Workers' Mental Health Special Interest Group.

Eileen Fairweather is a freelance journalist. She has written for many national newspapers and magazines, and is a former winner of the Catherine Pakenham Award for women journalists. She is co-author of *Only The Rivers Run Free: Northern Ireland, the Women's War* (published by Pluto, 1984), and has contributed to two anthologies and written two popular comic novels for young people.

Mike Feintuck lectures in law at Hull University.

Geoffrey Hunt is the Director of the European Centre for Professional Ethics, University of East London, and the founder and co-ordinator of Freedom to Care, a corporate responsibility and ethics campaign. He has edited *Whistleblowing in the Health Service* (published by Edward Arnold, 1995), *Ethical Issues in Nursing* (published by Routledge, 1994) and, with Paul Wainwright, *Expanding the Role of the Nurse* (published by Blackwell Science, 1994).

Caroline Keenan lectures in law at Bristol University.

Susan Machin was a social worker at Ashworth secure hospital, was the Chair of Freedom to Care, and is currently studying for a degree in law.

Roland Powell was parliamentary officer for the British Association of Social Workers. He is currently a social work manager and a visiting researcher at Queen Mary & Westfield College, London University.

Daphne Statham is the Director of the National Institute for Social Work and has been instrumental in drawing up the plans for a regulatory body for social work and social care.

Alison Taylor has MA qualifications in social work and probation, and specialist experience in psychiatric social work, child care and work with young offenders. She has recently published two novels and remains actively involved in children's rights.

Ron Thomson has a senior managerial position in a mental health organization in the voluntary sector.

Stuart Vernon lectures in law at the University of East London.

Foreword

This is by any standards an important book. It demonstrates public interest disclosure in action in the context of organizational accountability. It also makes an overwhelming case for why whistleblowing makes a vital contribution to attempts to achieve public accountability for organizational failings, some of which have been on the grand scale.

By analysis the book provides remedies and hopes for the future. We urgently need, for instance, to stem the tide of child abuse which apparently has been, and may still be, endemic in some of our children's homes. Indeed, a child in care in the 1990s may well be a child in danger. We must not make the mistake of concluding that everything occurred in the 1970s and 1980s. Other no less pressing problems are considered by the contributors.

Stuart Vernon in Chapter 11 charts what he describes as 'the significant transformation of whistleblowing from a vice to a virtue' and the recognition of the advantages of the practice for employers, employees, service users and carers. Whistleblowing has a history of being regarded as sneaking or telling tales – of being viewed as a breach of confidentiality or as evidence of disloyalty. It has not infrequently led to the employee facing disciplinary and legal action and dismissal. Vernon concludes, however, that we are a long way from there being a *general* right to disclose information concerning wrongdoing, let alone a legal duty to do so. Parliament and the courts have, at the time of writing, only protected some special situations. This is to be contrasted with the more progressive position in the USA, where the Whistleblower Protection Act 1989 and individual legislation in some of the states provide a significant measure of protection.

In the UK we urgently need a legal framework that provides for (1) internal structures that permit employees to notify employers of matters of concern and (2) an external procedure for whistleblowing which, in the public interest, discloses wrongdoing.

Geoffrey Hunt, in his Introduction, notes that 'whistleblowing is a symptom of a shortfall in the organizational systems we have to provide for the new expectations of accountability'. He rightly refers to the 'crisis of accountability'. The book throws new and welcome light on why organizational failures continue to occur. In particular, one could well refer to 'the crisis of management', whether on a national or a local level. Much convincing detail is provided. However, we must not ignore the fact that we already have many suggestions and recommendations from exhaustive inquiries. Why have these not been put into practice? Why are the same mistakes being made, and why is a great deal of avoidable suffering and damage still occurring? It must be a high priority to ensure that the political and organizational will is found to put the detailed lessons into practice.

Allan Levy QC
October 1997

Preface

This book is conceived as a companion volume to my earlier book, *Whistleblowing in the Health Service* (published by Edward Arnold, 1995). It may usefully be read together with that book, in the preface to which I explain how I came to be personally involved in the issue of whistleblowing. It is intimately situated in the activities and experience of Freedom to Care's growing campaign for corporate responsibility and ethics. (However, readers should not assume that every contributor has some connection with Freedom to Care. This book is not a publication of that organization.)

It is my hope that we may achieve some answers to the questions posed by catastrophic organizational failures by examining these failures *through the experience of some of those involved*, particularly professionals and other employees. I see this book as a small part of Freedom to Care's continuing social project to bring the inside stories of such failure together, learn from them and develop recommendations and strategies for long-lasting reform. Readers who wish to share their experiences, make comments or criticisms, or inquire about Freedom to Care should write to the following address: Freedom to Care, PO Box 125, West Molesey, Surrey KT8 1YE.

I apologize to purists for using the term 'social services' (not capitalized) rather loosely in some places. Some of the contributors are much more careful in their usage than I am. Social services proper cover state provision in relation to disabilities, mental health problems, special educational needs, drug abuse problems, AIDS sufferers, and so on, and the carers of those with these conditions. Our focus in this book is on child protection, which is of course a multi-agency function. Both in my introduction and elsewhere, illustrations are sometimes drawn from areas which are not strictly speaking in the social services – but the same general point is being made, and nearly always there is a special interest in the role of social workers. I understand that not all social workers are employed by social services departments.

I am grateful to all social services members of Freedom to Care for sharing their experiences. In the social services and related areas I especially thank Susan Machin, Ron Thomson, Flo Watson and Yvonne Rosier for the support they have given me in completing tasks other than compiling and editing this book. My wife Beverley and children William and Laura have to be thanked for their support, and for always managing to unglue me from the keyboard when I appeared to be hypnotized by the screen. I also acknowledge the patience of my colleagues at the University of East London, particularly Sarah Beeston, my Head of Department.

Geoffrey Hunt

Introduction: Whistleblowing and the crisis of accountability

Geoffrey Hunt

Why does it go on and on?

Time after time catastrophic failures in social services, in which children and vulnerable adults are seriously harmed by some of the very people meant to protect them, carry on for years without thorough investigation, without rectification, and without redress. There may be client complaints, professional warnings, revelations by brave whistleblowing social workers, official inquiries, high-level recommendations, police investigations – but still it goes on. Why?

'Why did Hackney take so long to act?' asks one newspaper headline, following the revelation that for 10 years children in care in a London borough council's home had been exploited by a paedophile social worker who later died of AIDS (*The Evening Standard*, 1997). Over the period at least two children had complained, the council had been warned six times by police and others, some councillors had demanded action and there had been some council 'investigations', but still the social worker remained in his post. In another London borough a similar story was unfolding: for years children were subjected to abuses and neglect in Islington council's homes. No less than *13* inquiries, the whistleblowing of a social worker who personally risked everything, and a 3-year newspaper campaign were necessary in order to bring a stop to the evil.

The organizational failure is not limited to inner-city London. It is national. In rural North Wales, more than a decade of abuses of children in care is now coming to light through a public inquiry. In the last 8 years there have been major police investigations into long-standing abuse in child care settings in Leicestershire, Staffordshire (the so called 'pindown' case), Wales, Cheshire, Merseyside and elsewhere. Is anything being learnt?

While abuses continue on the very doorstep of social services departments, elsewhere they may be over-zealous. The frustration and anger experienced by the 'users' of social services have reached almost unbearable proportions. Sue Amphlett of Parents Against Injustice, which provides advice and support for people who say that they have been mistakenly involved in investigations of alleged child abuse, confirms from her files (see Chapter 3) that official recommendations are often not effected:

> The local authority upheld their [a family's] complaint and wrote them a letter thanking them for pointing out the failures within the system. They reassured them that these failures would not occur again. Three and five years later a second and third family made identical complaints. Their complaints were also upheld with similar reassurances being given that things would change.

Amphlett reminds us that Lord Justice Butler Sloss said of the report on abuses in Orkney: 'The report reveals a depressing and disturbing resemblance four years on, to many of the criticisms made in the Cleveland Report'.

Child care is not the only context in which persistent abuse goes on and on. Abuses of the elderly and the learning disabled in residential care must now be recognized as persistent and endemic (Ogg and Bennett, 1992; *The Guardian*, 1992; *Nursing Times*, 1995; *Child Care Forum*, 1996). Other institutions in which social workers have a role have failed to meet professional and public expectations. A 1992 public inquiry, headed by Louis Blom Cooper QC, into abuses at Ashworth Secure Hospital reported brutality and serious malpractice, and made sweeping recommendations which were followed up by a government task force. Yet only four years later new allegations about ongoing abuses and professional misconduct were made and another public inquiry began (*The Independent*, 1997; *The Times*, 1997). Within weeks discoveries were being made of child pornography videos in Broadmoor Secure Hospital (*The Sunday Times*, 1997). It goes on and on.

This persistence is generating a public crisis of confidence. How can public services which show themselves to be incapable in many instances of properly investigating and correcting their own operations be entrusted by the public to carry out the task of properly monitoring, investigating and preventing the abuse of the vulnerable?

Common sense?

We can deal at once with some rather obvious, 'common-sense' responses to my question as to why it goes on and on. People often say that at the root of the problem is one of the following. It is a local aberration; there is insufficient evidence to act; it is human nature; this field of work has peculiar difficulties; there are always 'bad apples' (negligent managers, paedophiles, etc.); there is chronic under-resourcing of social services and social work.

If enough has not been said already to scotch the idea that it is a local aberration, then the national surveys presented in Chapter 7 should be persuasive. This is not to deny that some social services departments and public welfare organizations are far better than others, or that some may be as good as they can be under existing organizational culture and structures.

Although there is often insufficient evidence for an employer or the police to act on a 'beyond reasonable doubt' basis, this does not explain why there is often so little effort to obtain the evidence in a balanced manner by keeping proper records, to consult community groups, to liaise properly with other official agencies and bodies, to monitor and follow up, to take greater care with recruitment and promotion, and so on. And I am not speaking here of what cannot be explained in even minimal procedural terms, such as why records 'go missing' and clear leads are 'dropped'.

'Human nature' is a perennial premise of cynicism and defeatism. That workers and managers in social services should appeal to it so often is itself a symptom of their malaise, and it is precisely that which stands in need of explanation. Human nature is not a part of the problem, but a widespread *belief* in an ever-evil human nature is. Since absolutely anything can be explained from human nature, whether good, bad or indifferent, it really has no general explanatory power whatsoever. It is worth keeping in mind that one is not seeking perfection, whatever that may be, but rather one is seeking considerable improvement. Even if true, the claim that if all of the recommendations in this book were implemented thoroughly abuse of the vulnerable would still occur provides no basis whatsoever for concluding that some (or even immense) reform is not possible.

In important respects the burdens and difficulties of social services and social work are no different from those of other areas of work which have a very intimate engagement with people's lives. The potentially harmful consequences of getting things wrong are just as grave in, for example, medicine, policing and the judicial system. Indeed, I would argue that these areas suffer from similar problems because they have similar outmoded cultures, structures and processes. They are hierarchical, they exclude significant stakeholders, they have introverted and sometimes arcane discourses and perceptions, and they are secretive and defensive (see Hunt, 1995, Introduction).

The failures presented in this book are *organizational*. Even if we can identify 'bad apple' individuals in management or social work or elsewhere in the organization, this is generally not sufficient to explain the extent, fundamental nature and persistence of failure. Indeed, it explains neither why 'bad apples' (for example, a paedophile care worker or a bullying and negligent manager) are in post in the first place, nor why they stay there, sometimes for decades. What this means is that even if we were able with a wave of a magic wand to remove from social services everyone who is negligent or inclined to abuse, we would still be left with a tendentially negligent and abusive *system*. People who work in the system are 'trained' and constrained by it. I think the illustrations in this book show that the problem in many ways is precisely that we have a 'system', a closed hierarchy of 'posts' and 'procedures' rather than a decentralized network of stakeholders (communities, families, representative groups, agencies, professionals, employers, etc.) continually evolving a consensus through mutual checks and balances.

It is also hard to believe that the persistence of failure has anything specific to do with resource shortages when there always appear to be resources available on a daily and ubiquitous basis for social service-type organizations to defend themselves from openness, scrutiny, criticism and reform.

Crisis of accountability

I am willing to assert that the problem of organizational failure is not confined to abuse in care settings – the problem is one of the need for the reform of accountabilities *throughout* our national life – in the public, private and voluntary sectors. Whistleblowing is a symptom of a shortfall in the organizational systems that we have to provide for the new expectations of accountability. The conscientious employee who has nowhere to turn may decide to cut through the maze of procedure, especially when it is turned against him or her, and take the simple and direct path, saying, in effect, '*I'll* hold you to account. I'll tell *the world* about it'. Unfortunately, whistleblowing does not stop it from going on and on. It only provides us with the signs and symptoms of the disease, which are the proper starting point for a diagnosis.

Alison Taylor, who says that years ago she lost her job as a social worker in North Wales for 'refusing to ignore persistent and widespread allegations about the abuse of children in council care', believes that there is 'too little impetus in the [social work] profession towards accountability' (Chapter 2). London newspaper journalist Eileen Fairweather, who played a major role in exposing abuses in Islington homes, says (Chapter 1) that there will be more child abuse scandals in children's homes 'until publicly accountable child protection becomes a true national priority'. Other contributors to this book emphasize accountability.

Of course they are right, but what are *accountable* child protection services and social services in general? What is accountability? How does accountability work? How is it effected? What are its mechanisms? How is it sustained? How do we close the gulf between what we know as individuals to be right and good, and the everyday realities of the social services workplace? In order to answer these questions we first have to acknowledge and understand the nature and gravity of the problem we face, which is the point of this book.

Accountability is about a preparedness to give an explanation and justification to relevant others for one's acts and omissions. It is about responsibility to one another, and is therefore a recognition of social duties as well as rights. It is tied up with questions of authority and power because it leaves open the following questions. Accountable to whom, and why? Accountable for what, and why? Accountable under what circumstances and in what manner? What is the proper content and form for the account one gives? These are questions which delineate a contested area, an area in which claims for an account by one group may be denied as a legitimate or authorized claim by another. We have a crisis of accountability because the traditional and settled authorities can no longer claim a monopoly over accountability, and can no longer say with complete conviction, 'You cannot claim an account from me; I am claiming one from you'. In social services, so-called 'users' are demanding an account, and social services authorities are often saying, in one way or another, 'We have no obligation to give you one' (see Chapter 3 by Amphlett). Of course, others are reconsidering, while a few may be starting to take a lead.

Organizations which are unaccountable, in terms of new expectations, will not only fail to ascribe blame where it is due, but will equally demoralize staff and misrepresent matters to the public by wrongly ascribing credit to the organization or its executives when it properly belongs elsewhere. The whistleblower is caught in this contest of accountabilities – a hero to the public and a trouble-maker, even a deviant, to the organization. The whistleblower shows us that this is a time when accountabilities are shifting, or can be shifted, to encompass a wider arena of stakeholders and to challenge the 1990s initiative of managerialism to maintain control through intensified forms of quantifying or calculating accountabilities (quality assurance, performance indicators, etc.). The whistleblower insists on a common discourse, an exchange of personal stories: 'This is what the organization is doing to people, this is what it is doing to me for objecting to it. Would *you* like to be on the receiving end of this practice, whoever you are – doctor, patient, manager, social worker, corporate executive?'

There are some recurring themes in the contributions to this book which throw light on our question of why specific organizational failures go on and on, that is, they show us how and why accountabilities are misdirected, in conflict, distorted or absent. These themes concern deficiencies in:

- management;
- the status of 'employee';
- professional autonomy and standards;
- procedures;
- the voice and power of 'users';
- organizational defences;
- the law.

Management

Deficiencies in management figure in nearly every account of social services failure. Amphlett finds inadequacies in strategic management at government level. In Chapter 1, Fairweather speaks of an 'unworkable management structure' and quotes the White Report into Islington's homes, which refers to 'an organization lacking the culture, philosophy and managerial infrastructure to work in and intervene in highly sensitive child care matters'. One of the anonymous contributors in my Chapter 4 raises the question of how a manager's judgement can be laid open to fair challenge and scrutiny. In Chapter 5, Susan Machin states that 'any challenge to an individual manager's competence, or to that of management as a whole, may be seen not only in terms of a possible threat to their [the employee's] current employment, but also as a source of potential damage to future career prospects'. A survey of social workers conducted by Diana Campbell and myself (see Chapter 7) revealed widespread dissatisfaction, not to say disaffection, with management. Many social workers seem to have little faith that managers actually understand the objectives and difficulties of their work. Managers, particularly at a senior level, are rather too often seen as potential perpetrators of bullying, cover-up, buck-passing and victimization. Although one should not overlook the fact that many social workers are quite satisfied with management, it is surely worrying that victimization is mentioned by almost a quarter of respondents and inhibits the raising of concerns which might stop abuses.

In Chapter 8 Roland Powell links the growth of the new managerialism with social work whistleblowing: 'The imposition on social work of standardized procedures is one factor which leads to whistleblowing, as bad professional practice can continue as long as it remains within the procedures'.

The status of 'employee'

As I have argued elsewhere, the status of 'employee, bound up as it is with the privileges of management embedded in the law of contract and employment, sits very uneasily with that of professional and citizen

(Hunt, 1996). The public service professional, especially the one working under the new 'market'-style managerialism, may find that public interest standards of competence and codes of conduct promoted by professional associations and self-regulatory bodies will have little weight in the objectives and methods of market-oriented service provision. The person as citizen – one who has civil and human rights and duties – will find that these are not necessarily expressible in the workplace. The neophyte social worker who has concerns about vulnerable children, inequality and deprivation may be disappointed to find that neither the social work profession as a whole nor the workplace is, rather paradoxically, a vehicle designed to express those concerns.

The contemporary status of employee is in many ways structured in dependency, morally disempowering the professional and citizen residing in one and the same person. The years of silence and inaction among Islington workers are in part explained by this conflict of accountabilities and the ascendancy of accountability to employer. As Fairweather puts it: 'But I suspect that most of those covering up just wanted to shield their professional, or political, careers and their pensions'. Ron Thomson (Chapter 6) describes how the cards are stacked against the employee who refuses to acquiesce in the face of wrongdoing, and how this employee can be blighted for life by an unfair reference. Linking workplace acquiescence with holocaust bystanders, he makes a plea for reforms in employment law and elsewhere to facilitate speaking up. While Mike Cox speaks of 'an unequal balance of power in favour of the employer' (Chapter 9), Daphne Statham and Don Brand of the National Institute of Social Work emphasize that social work needs a regulatory body because we can no longer rely on the employer to protect the public from incompetence and misconduct (Chapter 10).

Professional autonomy and standards

Roland Powell's chapter implies that traditional social work values, and ample space for professional autonomy and discretion, are a bulwark against organizational failure. If I understand him correctly he would argue that even social work failures are at least in part due to the constraints and pressures placed on them by the new managerialism and its narrow procedural idea of accountability: 'Procedures as sources of power have created a situation where it is increasingly difficult for social workers to be accountable for their professional practice legitimated by a professional knowledge base'. He adds, 'It is the professional element of *discretion* which is a problem for the new managerialism'. Machin, too, asks what the role of social workers in a secure hospital can be, pointing out that at Ashworth 'social workers are now directly accountable to and managed by non-social-work professionals'.

Mike Cox follows a similar line of argument. He discusses the training and education of social workers and bemoans the undermining of the traditional advocacy role and the 'dilution of the values of professional social work'. He says that 'the professional obligation to speak out against malpractice and adverse social welfare policies ... now has no dedicated place in social work education'. In his view, whistleblowing is 'an essential social work function'. It seems, according to Cox's argument, that one obstacle to the persistence of institutional failure – the advocate-cum-social worker – has been eroded. He goes on to criticize the failure to interlink the accountabilities of professional, employer and employee to the public, through the law and one's moral conscience.

Against this one has to consider a more pragmatic issue. How do we know that social work is achieving its stated goals? How do we know that social services on the whole do more good than harm? These are serious questions. I have spoken to a few social workers who entertain the idea that society might be better off if the state's social work/social care provisions and institutions, including child protection, were abolished. People, including children, would certainly be harmed as a consequence – but on the whole would there be more harm or less than there is now? When we consider the statistics and the stories provided in Amphlett's chapter we cannot dismiss these questions as fictions of the overworked and demoralized social worker. They require some sort of answer. Taylor points out that social work's mode of thought tends to 'preclude for the most part quantifiable evidence of negligence or ineptitude in the way in which iatrogenesis indicates medicine's failures'. This is changing, of course, and the government is now funding research studies into the effectiveness of social service provisions. However, the question remains – by what methodology are these studies aiming to establish the degree of effectiveness? What are they measuring?

While many social workers are not very impressed by managers, it has to be said that many are not very impressed by each other. Our survey (see Chapter 7) reveals an unacceptable level of misconduct in social work practice, ranging from sexual abuse and physical abuse to breaches of confidentiality and falsifying or omitting records. Statham and Brand remind us that social workers 'are the only remaining unregulated professional and occupational groups in the publicly funded caring services'. They make a very strong case for a regulatory body – now on the horizon – to play a part in 'establishing, developing and enforcing standards, and provide a vital additional route for staff, service users, carers or members of the public to use when other systems fail'. Social work now operates in a much changed society. There has been radical legislation of children and community care, the care sector has become a much stronger mix of state, private and voluntary providers, service users are playing a different kind of role, and the work-force is quite different from what it was.

Procedure

While some might argue that social work, as an occupation which has never been fully professionalized, always depended to an unacceptable degree on procedure – on rules, regulations and guidelines – Powell argues that any space for professional discretion which may have existed is rapidly receding under the impact of mechanically imposed procedure. He compares contemporary social work procedure to the rules followed by benefits agency workers. There is a great deal of form-filling and the check-list has become a decision-making tool. Of course, many public sector professionals are complaining of the same thing – academics, doctors, nurses and police officers all find themselves continually involved in a kind of bureaucratic origami.

Amphlett is deeply concerned about procedure, in particular the 'investigative system of alleged abuse', and finds it seriously deficient. I think that there are two points here. First, social workers and others in social services and related agencies tend to follow procedure blindly and, secondly, there is a need for more and better procedure – procedures which involve and empower families, for example. She makes a convincing case for a series of reforms, including the provision of information for families, better gatekeeping, ethically informed guidance for those carrying out investigations, a better complaints and appeals system, and enhanced accountability of social workers and other professionals. 'One reason why there is such a large investigative trawl is that many local authorities have not established effective gatekeeping policies', she says.

The voice and power of 'users'

When one reads some of the accounts in this book it is sometimes hard to believe that the real stakeholders in social services – those who provide it with its *raison d'être* – are its 'users'. Amphlett is surely quite right, for example, to question the lack of support given to families following an investigation. While we can all understand the ethical rationale behind the investigation of child abuse allegations, it is also right for the public, in the form of groups such as PAIN, to question the manner and extent of such investigations. Social services do not have a *carte blanche* from society to investigate as they please. 'PAIN has always maintained', says Amphlett, 'that there are more families being subjected to the process of investigation when, in reality, the child has not been abused, than there are families being investigated when the child does require protection or is at significant risk of abuse'. Empirical evidence for this proposition is now building up. There is something radically wrong, even perverse, about a system the rationale of which is to protect the vulnerable but which, on the one hand, generates an unbalanced proportion of unnecessary investigations and enormous consequent distress and, on the other, actually provides new environments for abuse of the vulnerable to continue unchallenged.

Organizational defences

The contributions in this book are dotted with assertions about the defensiveness of social service organizations, their political 'supervisors', and related agencies. Fairweather describes the Islington council at the time of the abuses as 'defensive', when she and her media colleagues were doing their damnedest to find out the truth in the interest of children past, present and future. Questions are evaded with the stock responses: 'There's no point in delving into the past', 'You can't prove anything', 'It would be too much effort to find out', 'The person who knows has moved on', 'Why don't you ask X?', 'I don't know where the files are', 'People always complain, don't they?', 'The whole thing has been exaggerated', 'Children invent things – you can't take them too seriously', 'I can't tell you, it's confidential'.

'Gwynedd County Council maintained a stance of denial throughout the then largest police investigation of its kind in British history', says Taylor. Machin reports that at Ashworth, 'staff placed loyalty to each other as a paramount value, to the extent of protecting staff who had abused patients'. A putative 'breach of confidentiality' may be used by the employer to batter the employee who speaks up to protect the vulnerable (see the case of R in Chapter 4; Hunt, 1995, pp. xxii–xxiv, 145–153).

The obstructiveness encountered by employees who question incidents, practices and policies is not necessarily based on malice, but on a different cultural perception in which defensiveness and denial are constructed as loyalty, defence of reputation, being nice to colleagues, etc. (Argyris, 1990). While in terms of public concern it is the failing organization which is 'deviant' (deviating from the public interest which it was set up to protect), executives and managers, and many workplace peers, will project the whistleblower as the deviant.

The law

Several contributors mention legal aspects of accountability and whistleblowing, and Stuart Vernon (Chapter 11) and Mike Feintuck and Caroline Keenan (Chapter 12) focus on the law. How far can we ascribe social services catastrophes to deficiencies of the law? It seems that there are a number of areas. Not only is the law inaccessible – for example, legal aid is now very inadequate, as Amphlett points out – but it does not always provide a safety net or an instrument for redress and justice. Thus the whistleblower is very much alone from the legal point of view: 'We are a long way from any notion of a general *right* to disclose let alone a legal *duty* to disclose information concerning wrongdoing', says Vernon. He argues that whistleblowers should have protection under the law.

Feintuck and Keenan present the general legal position on access to information in relation to local government's role in the social services and examine 'the position of those involved in child sex abuse investigations, especially parents of children at the centre of investigations'. Taking up the challenges presented by Amphlett's chapter, they propose principles of practice for the disclosure of information and 'mechanisms of challenge' to social service decisions not to disclose.

Blocked accountabilities

All of the themes outlined above are, no doubt, real aspects of the organizational failure of social services. But is there any coherence here, or just an unconnected collection of disparate 'factors'? Are they symptoms of a deeper and systemic disorientation or dislocation? Is there something which brings them all together, some 'principle' if you like, which enables us to understand what is wrong in all its manifestations? My own thought about this is that at bottom there is a crisis of accountability. This points to the need for a shift to what I call 'networked accountability', which I can only outline here.

The deficiencies boil down to blockages and dislocations in stakeholder accountability: management, given its remit and interests, tendentially puts itself and its organization before other considerations; the employees have limits put on their expression of social conscience by the power relationships implicit in the employment relationship; the professionals have their public service ethic (public interest concerns) constrained by managerial priorities and employee status, and the 'users' or clients are constructed by the foregoing constraints as the raw material of 'the system' rather than its human rationale and motive force. In this rigidified mechanism of human relationships the organization takes on a wooden life of its own – one which suffocates conscience and initiative – and the law emerges passively from this wooden life with its 'contract', 'confidentiality' and 'fidelity to the employer' and the like, unable truly to challenge it.

Without a consensus-evolving network of ordinary-language accountabilities based on checks and balances, every effort to improve 'the system' by adding to it another procedure (a public inquiry, 'equal opportunities', an ombudsman, etc.) will tend to result in new frustrating failures and new defeats. Not that there is anything intrinsically wrong with new procedures – it is rather a matter of new procedures taking on a real significance and becoming more than just 'procedures' if they are aspects of a cultural change. A cultural change is a change in assumptions and perceptions. For example, if people who come into contact with social service are 'consumers' this signals a market-place culture, as 'users' an instrumental or manipulative culture, and as 'clients' a professional expertise culture.

Without networked accountability there is no moral fulcrum to make wise decisions. The following points illustrate this.

- In Islington and Hackney well-intentioned 'equal opportunities' procedures grafted on to a system of blocked accountabilities resulted in new opportunities ('political correctness') for some to exploit the vulnerable.
- A report on a 'user' is wrongly destroyed at her request in one scenario (case P in Chapter 4) and wrongly withheld from 'users' in other scenarios (Amphlett, in Chapter 3, suggests that records should be destroyed in unfounded cases).
- Actual abuses go unchallenged, and are even protected and covered up, while unfounded or trivial allegations leave behind a huge investigatory swathe of public distress.
- In the case of S in Chapter 4 we have a social worker who quite understandably feels affronted and hurt at being accused through the 'normal functioning' of a system he has in his own small way been (again, quite rightly) helping to administer to others for many years.
- In a number of social or public service 'scandals' we turn to the 'ultimate' device of a 'public inquiry', only to find that a few years down the road the same thing happens again.

This system of blocked accountabilities does not sufficiently encourage ethical (socially responsible, beneficent) behaviour, nor does it sufficiently discourage or inhibit unethical (socially irresponsible, maleficent) behaviour. To put it more strongly, it facilitates unethical behaviour, and inhibits ethical behaviour. We have begun to answer the question with which we began. This is why it goes on and on. (To show this with detailed argument and illustration is the subject of another project – another book in the making.)

Networked accountability

What networked accountability would look like, as a model, is perhaps becoming clearer. Its essential elements are:

- stakeholders;
- networking;
- checks and balances;
- narrative discourse;
- evolving consensus and trust;
- projects.

It is premised on the acknowledgement that those who have a stake in social services (as in any organization) are much wider than, say, employers and managers, professionals and other employees, and 'users' and 'carers'. *Stakeholders* are individuals and communities, families, special interest groups, friends and concerned citizens, official agencies (police, housing, benefits, probation, healthcare, etc.), professional associations, unions, campaign groups, media interests, suppliers and contractors, voluntary bodies, insurance companies, churches, regulatory and self-regulatory bodies, and others.

The stake that people have differs in kind and weight. Ethically this requires a form of relationship between stakeholders which recognizes and facilitates these differences. Put simply (rather too simply, no doubt) a hierarchical bureaucracy is not such a form, but *networking* is. A network is a form of connection in which each unit has free access to every other unit, directly or indirectly depending on the importance of the other units to any particular unit, and no unit is prioritized.

The connection between each unit is that of vehicles of mutual voice and control, i.e. *checks and balances*. For example, communities and community groups are allowed and encouraged to participate in policy discussion and decision-making through representative organs such as 'consumer' (citizen) councils, public hearings, local committees and focus groups, and to take their own initiatives (informed by and balanced against other stakeholders), e.g. in relation to the vulnerable and crime. The Department of Health's concept of 'partnership' between families and professionals is also relevant here (Royal College of Nursing, 1994).

A network of stakeholder checks and balances would undermine the dominance of any form of discourse, so that forms which legitimize bureaucratic control (such as the quantitative 'cost-effectiveness' language and practice of the new managerialism) could not predominate and would have to change and incorporate themselves in a wider social consensus. The currency of networked communication could only take a *narrative* form, in which each stakeholder tells 'their story' as they experience it and enters into an exploratory dialogue with every other stakeholder. Given the networked nature of interaction, any stakeholder would have an interest in listening and endeavouring to understand what the others have to say. Of course, there would still be disagreement, misunderstanding and conflict, but at least it would be out in the open and negotiable.

An open and networked discussion would facilitate the evolution of *consensus*, necessarily partial and shifting as this may be. *Trust* would become a possibility denied in bureaucratic forms of 'welfare'. Instead of a fixed and programmed structure, in which responsiveness, innovation and change are problematic, networked accountability would allow activities primarily to take the form of *projects*. For example, a forum of stakeholders might discuss and work to some consensus and implementable plan on the issue of paedophiles in the community.

The recommendations of the contributors – such as a regulatory body for social workers (Statham and Brand), information and follow-up support for families in which there is a social services investigation (Amphlett), or internal procedures and external whistleblowing facility for employee concerns (Vernon) – if situated in the context of networked accountability, may all be seen as elements in a programme of unblocking accountabilities, of shifting the balance of voice and power of the stakeholders in social services. By de-centring the social services organization one would be preventing the growth of institutionalized generalizations in which there is little scope for treating carers and those being cared for, exploiters and those being exploited, and victimizers and victims, as unique *individuals*. One also prevents one interest (careerism, the 'politically correct', financial gain or whatever) taking over and subverting the original ethical aim to care for the vulnerable and hurt. Even the question of what, for example, 'sexual abuse' is – how it is to be defined – would not then be left to those who have an interest in creating and sustaining a 'sex abuse industry'.

If everyone is keeping everyone else in check then it might just stop going on and on.

The myth of Sisyphus

In a Greek myth, Sisyphus blows the whistle on Zeus's rape of Aegina. He is punished for this public interest disclosure by being made to roll a heavy rock to the top of a hill only to watch it roll down, so that he had to push it up again and again, on and on. If Sisyphus had stopped and thought, he might have first dug a hole at the top of the hill for his rock to sit in. He would also, of course, have to contend with the fact that he might encounter some resistance to this from those who had an interest in punishing him.

References

Argyris, C. (1990) *Overcoming organisational defences*. Englewood Cliffs, NJ: Prentice-Hall.

Child Care Forum (1996) Unite behind Karen. **Issue 19**, 1. Children weeping. **Issue 19**, 16.

The Evening Standard (1997) Why did Hackney take so long to act? 24 July, p. 7.

The Guardian (1992) Social worker sacked as police investigate disabled abuse case. 26 August, p. 4.

Hunt, G. (ed.) (1995) *Whistleblowing in the health service*. London: Edward Arnold.

Hunt, G. (ed.) (1996) Professional, employee or citizen? Walker Martineau Seminar on Conflicts within the Professional Role, London Chamber of Commerce, 26 February, unpublished.

The Independent (1997) Catalogue of horror prompts inquiry. 8 February, pp. 1, 8.

Nursing Times (1995) Supplement on elder abuse. 18 October 1995. **91**, 26–32.

Ogg, J. and Bennett, G. (1992) Elder abuse in Britain. *British Medical Journal* **305**, 998–9.

Royal College of Nursing (1994) *Nursing and child protection: an RCN survey*. London: Royal College of Nursing.

The Sunday Times (1997) News digest. 16 February.

The Times (1997) Psychiatrist at Ashworth Hospital suspended. 11 February, p. 3.

Part One

The Actors

1

Exposing the Islington children's homes scandal: a journalist's view

Eileen Fairweather

In 1992, as a freelance journalist I learned that desperate Islington social workers wanted to blow the whistle on widespread sexual abuse in the borough's children's homes. With the *London Evening Standard*, I began a lengthy investigation. The *Standard*'s reports were initially dismissed by the Labour council as 'politically motivated . . . a sensationalist bit of gutter journalism', and based on bribes. However, the newspaper and its sources persisted for 3 years, provoking 13 government-ordered inquiries. These proved increasingly critical, and eventually led to the forced resignation of Islington's social services directors, numerous reforms, and apologies by the council to the young people abused in its care. Some victims have received therapy and compensation, and a major police inquiry was launched.

In 1993, *Standard* staff reporter Stewart Payne and I were commended in the 'Reporting Team of the Year' category of the prestigious British Press Awards, and won its Team Award in 1996. The judges said that 'The *Standard* refused to be deflected by the misplaced attacks of Islington Council. The team stuck to its guns (and) showed that investigations by the press, properly conducted and painstakingly researched, can still make a huge difference to the world.'

Why was it so difficult to expose?

An appalling regime of sexual abuse and management cover-ups is over, and one look at my crammed, much-thumbed address book for Islington 'contacts' explains why. Scores of people secretly assisted the *Evening Standard*'s long investigation – field and residential social workers, middle managers, police officers, parents and young people.

I find it terrifying, however, that ultimately this nightmare was ended only thanks to the determination of one key whistleblower, who tirelessly evidence and persuaded others to talk. I also have no doubt that, *Standard* not constantly pushed the agenda, in the face of coun- and an initially half-hearted response by the Department of Health (DoH) and police, Islington's children's homes would still be controlled by paedophiles, pornographers and pimps. This, too, is frightening, given that the *Standard*'s commitment was of a kind probably unique within today's media. The press is an inevitably commercial animal, driven by fierce competition not just to inform but also to entertain and to be the first with scoops. We ourselves often nearly gave up on Islington, that 'old' and budget-devouring story.

Abused children should not have to rely for help upon a heroic whistleblower and a peculiarly bloody-minded news team. If the Islington scandal taught me anything, it was that adequate *national* structures to protect the acutely vulnerable children in the UK's care system – and to respond immediately, when injustice is exposed – do not yet exist.

Our current legal system makes child abuse one of the hardest crimes to prove, and consequently most police forces earmark few resources to investigation. This, too, makes the care system attractive to paedophiles. Islington is not unique, and its problems were not merely local ones. There have been numerous children's home scandals across the UK, in authorities of all political persuasions, and there will be more until publicly accountable child protection becomes a true national priority.

In May 1995, after 12 government-ordered independent inquiries into the *Evening Standard*'s allegations, another one (the fifth which could be called a major inquiry) finally confirmed what we first described two and a half years previously. Why did establishing the truth prove so difficult?

In October 1992, we told the stories of four girls and four boys who were abused and prostituted while supposedly under the protection of the North London Labour Council. They were just sample cases. For well over a decade traumatized children and concerned staff reported brutal abuse throughout the borough's 12 care homes – and management did nothing or actively covered up. The first independent inquiries ordered in the wake of our revelations avoided looking at the abuse allegations. Eventually, in frustration, we submitted an 118-page dossier to the DoH. In 1995, Ian White CBE, the director of Oxfordshire social services, and his assistant Kate Hart studied it and confirmed that of 32 'extremely serious' allegations against Islington staff, only four staff were subjected to disciplinary action, and two were sacked. These were just the ones we knew about; others continue to come to light (White and Hart, 1995).

The allegations centred on sexual abuse and child pornography. Others included cruelty, acute neglect, dealing heavy drugs, and abducting a child. But whatever the strength of the evidence, most accused staff – including some who admitted guilt – were simply allowed to resign. Many took medical or early retirement, with enhanced benefits. Others were given good references, enabling them to obtain work with children elsewhere.

Crucial social services files, requested by police investigators, went missing. A total of 26 children, mainly at two care homes, were believed to be caught up with pimps, but no appropriate action had been taken. A further 61 children known to social services were feared to be involved with local child sex rings.

The White Report became big news in the national media, which until then had only patchily reported the *Standard*'s allegations. At last the council put up its hands, pledged real reform and apologized. The question remains – why did it have to take 60-plus articles, 3 years and a total of 13 independent inquiries and inspections to reach this point?

An unworkable management structure, a defensive council and a demoralized and under-supported work-force all contributed to the Islington 'malaise', but so did political correctness. White finally addressed a key issue which previous inquiries had avoided. Of 19 sexual abuse allegations, 13 allegations involved men and boys, four involved men and girls, and two involved women and boys. Most reported abuse was by supposedly gay men who, to the detriment of children and the majority of ordinary decent gays, cynically exploited Islington's naïve, rigid interpretation of equal opportunities. This was to escape both proper vetting and investigation.

In the late 1970s and early 1980s, Islington adopted what White called the 'very laudable' aim of ending discrimination in child-care employment. It attracted numerous homosexual staff because, as one of the *Standard*'s many lesbian sources recalled, 'It was a safe place to come out in'. However, zealotry allowed a well-intentioned policy to be hijacked. In the interest of 'positive discrimination', Islington became lax about demanding professional experience, qualifications or even proper references of any self-declared gay man who applied to work in or run its children's homes. Mere friends could supply references, and the council could not query their backgrounds. Yet at least three men who were featured in our investigative work and the White Report were 'networkers' directly linked to convicted child abusers who pool victims and pornography.

As in many authorities today, interviewers were also discouraged from asking questions about the personal life and attitudes of those wanting responsibility for disturbed children. To combat discrimination, identical questions had to be asked of every candidate. Any give-away remarks by interviewees could not be followed up. When allegations did arise in Islington against 'gay' men, those making them, including traumatized children, were written off as 'homophobes'. The 'pro-gay' lobby achieved influence in key areas, for example, on Islington's fostering panel, within training, policy advice and an agency which supplied a high proportion of staff. The politically naïve unwittingly assisted those with a more sinister agenda as Islington gradually became a 'classic case study', said White, of 'an organisation lacking the culture, philosophy and managerial infrastructure to work in and intervene in highly sensitive child care matters' (White and Hart, 1995, p. 37).

After his devastating report was published, the council at last apologized to the children in its care, vowed to review its equal opportunities policies, and even thanked the *Evening Standard* for its 'significant part in revealing the truth.' Alan Clinton, the new leader of Islington Council, said that 'the publishing of this report marks a point of no return – no return to the appalling conditions and disgraceful service in our children's homes of a few years ago. I am sorry that this was ever allowed to happen'.

Yet a full year before this report, Islington was aware of all of the allegations which, Ian White said, 'should have been investigated with vigour'. However, council-chosen investigators recommended against further investigation because 'too much delving into the past ... would be counterproductive'.

White's appointment was *forced* on Islington by the DoH, who finally lost patience with the inadequate, 'independent' inquiries which Islington had set up. Although all were critical, most dodged or minimized the central issue of large-scale child abuse. The sole Islington-appointed investigator who challenged this, after the first inquiry, was sacked. Why did the DoH allow *Islington* to appoint those running the inquiries, decide their remit and agree what should be published? This has never been adequately explained.

Islington's interpretation of equal opportunities was only part of the problem; girls also suffered terribly under its care system. In common with many authorities, it mainly attracted only unqualified staff to this neglected and stressful 'Cinderella' service. The various inquiries rightly noted a host of contributory factors, including poor management, administrative chaos, an over-reliance on agency staff, and lack of training and supervision. Staff relationships were also bad, and social workers were on their second strike in recent years when the *Standard* first published. They were striking not only over pay and conditions but also to preserve services under threat. It was widely felt, even by dissidents within the Labour Party, that council leader Margaret Hodge was attentive to housing (in which the borough was sometimes truly innovative) but quite inattentive to social services. The objections of senior managers to the experimental decentralized and de-specialized system that she imposed were dismissed; they felt that she did not perceive social workers as having any real expertise.

By the time the White Report was published, Hodge was a Labour MP, a close friend of leader Tony Blair, and had responsibility for the party's policy on children under five. Yet still she downplayed the child-care disgrace during her 10-year reign, or shifted the blame. A leader article in

The Independent newspaper warned, 'Unless she is prepared to take full responsibility for what went wrong it will be impossible for Tony Blair to justify her future promotion'. Hodge's attitude to social services meant that ambitious, bright councillors avoided involvement with it. The 1993 secret appendix report recorded that managers felt that they had few 'heavy-weight champions' on the council.

On the ground, in the borough's children's homes, the maι.y caring staff who were struggling to cope with deeply damaged children, and to fend off pimps, drug-pushing and abuse by colleagues, simply felt abandoned – no one was listening. This seemed to include the inquiries. The first, for example, lambasted one home as a dirty, cheerless, unsafe, 'disgusting dump', but drew no conclusions about a more serious issue – were children within it being abused and sold? Such a question was not allowed, under its terms of reference. Subsequent inquiries were also barred from examining much of the evidence given to them by us, as well as children, staff and two unions (the British Association of Social Workers (BASW) and Unison).

Eventually the *Evening Standard* wrote up a dossier of the most serious allegations and submitted it to the DoH's watchdog, the Social Services Inspectorate (SSI), indicating that it would stay on the case until they were properly investigated. The White Report was the result. After we wrote up White's devastating vindication in the *Standard*, I went home and cried from relief and exhaustion. No wonder Islington staff had to blow the whistle – if it had been so difficult for the media, with all its independence and power to get things out into the open, what had it been like for them? And then there was the unimaginable suffering of the young victims, disbelieved or ignored for so long.

The closed circle: why staff had to blow the whistle

In this chapter, I want to look at why reform within Islington could only be achieved through the media, the forces which made it possible for mass child abuse to be tolerated for so long, and the fear, the political wishful thinking or the isolation which for years kept concerned social workers silent.

Many of those involved with exposing Islington believe that, at some level, a conspiracy existed to protect the paedophiles who infiltrated its child-care system. How deep that went, and why, will probably never be proven. A few people undoubtedly covered up because they, too, were paedophiles or had other 'skeletons in the cupboard'. However, I suspect that most of those who were covering up just wanted to shield their professional or political careers and their pensions. As one manager told us, abusers were given good references because the departmental ethos was,

'Lord, if there's going to be a scandal, please let it break elsewhere'. Many otherwise decent staff and councillors simply turned a blind eye, fearful of seeming 'reactionary'. The main conspiracy, therefore, was a pernicious, unconscious one of moral and political laziness. If you did not see evil you did not have to do anything about it; readjust your world view or risk the wrath of colleagues.

Some Islington staff were silenced by genuine fear – for their jobs or even their physical safety. Two male workers who reported child sex rings and drug dealers targeting their homes, with apparent collusion by some staff, were ignored by management and threatened with violence by colleagues. One worker was so frightened, after anonymous phone calls saying his legs would be 'blown off', that I took him to Scotland Yard. Islington was 'off their patch', they said. However, their advice was to 'Go for it, publish the story'.

Sharing dangerous knowledge provided some protection, and was the motive for many whistleblowers to come forward. By the time the *Standard* came on the scene, three workers believed that they had already been victimized by management after raising serious concerns (two were subsequently cleared). Other Islington social workers really did not know what was going on, or only noticed the odd disconcerting incident. Client confidentiality reinforced the partial nature of their knowledge. It *needed* outsiders, journalists with the power to ask questions of everyone, to piece together this complex, disturbing jigsaw. The staff's fear, in some cases, appeared to transmute into a disabling, counter-productive paranoia – some felt that no one could be trusted and that everyone was bent including, possibly, the *Standard*'s reporters, and even the SSI inspectors and police whom we said could be trusted. Paranoia made some feel totally helpless, unable to see that Islington's problems were not all attributable to a single pervasive conspiracy, but that they were multiple in origin and therefore *solvable*.

I am glad, looking back, that the *Standard* rejected the whistleblowers' initial suggestion that we deal with them as a group. I had learned that lesson the hard way, having previously worked with staff in another authority on a group basis. They ended up constantly challenging my motives and methods, and I finally gave up. The tendency of groups which feel powerless to find internal scapegoats, rather than uniting against those about whom they are complaining, is well known. It means that a lot of corruption and malpractice goes unchallenged and unexposed. With the Islington whistleblowers we instead negotiated individually. That protected them, too, since only one or two ever knew for sure who was telling us what.

In 1991 the council, despite union opposition, finally forced through complete decentralization. Social workers were divided between 24 Neighbourhood Offices, where social work and housing were jointly run. Often staff dealing with life-or-death child protection issues were now answerable to an office manager from a housing background, with no social work experience or training. Such managers also assumed control of children's homes on their patch. The Director of Neighbourhood Services was also a housing administrator, without social work expertise, but was the social workers' manager.

The council, heady on its 'innovative' democratic experiments, had long been moving towards completely generic social work. In the late 1980s it cut back child guidance and other work with sexual abuse victims, believing that self-help groups were preferable to experts (the need for *both* was not considered). By 1992 the borough had no child protection specialists other than one Child Protection Co-ordinator and an assistant. Co-ordination between the 24 Neighbourhood Offices was minimal, as was clerical support. In some offices, social workers were expected, despite having heavy case-loads, 'democratically' to take turns on reception. Filing and record-keeping became a shambles.

Social workers who were aware of paedophiles active across the borough had no mechanism for comparing notes with and warning the other 23 Neighbourhood Offices. Their repeated pleas for joint meetings were rejected both by the Child Protection Co-ordinator and by Islington's Assistant Director with responsibility for children and families. Many letters to the latter about urgent child protection issues did not even receive replies. Social workers felt despair and had good reason to believe that the Area Child Protection Committee (ACPC) could not do its job. Alarmed health workers joined in assisting the *Standard*'s inquiry.

Staff blew the whistle because they had nowhere else to go. Islington NALGO (now Unison) feared 'homophobia' and did not want to appear to be undermining hard-pressed care staff – it was committed to addressing poor pay and under-investment. Important as these were, they were not the only issues. Worried staff therefore secretly turned to councillors and MPs. However, they invariably responded that there was no cause for concern, after consulting the Assistant Director and the police. It was a closed circle.

Meanwhile, concluded Ian White, Islington social services was in 'a deplorable state'. By the time the *Standard* published it had disintegrated 'from top to bottom'. In 1989, after the Islington child Liam Johnson was battered to death, a judicial review condemned the social services' management structure as a 'time-bomb waiting to go off' (London Borough of Islington, 1989). However, the council ignored the review's recommendations for reforms, as well as union pleas for change. The children's home scandal was the inevitable time-bomb.

All activity with children is vulnerable to take-over by paedophiles. Churches, leisure centres, schools, charities, scouts, sports groups and children's homes – none of these are exempt. It is not a reflection upon these organizations if they are targeted. Paedophiles, of every sexual orientation, are often extremely plausible, determined and patient. However, it reflects badly if, like Islington, they refuse to heed increasingly disturbing evidence, and abolish child protection specialists. Ian White's report concluded that the borough's 'positive bias towards certain groups' became 'unfair protection and a great danger'. At the same time, 'there was no strong ethos of promoting children's rights and protecting children at risk.'

Boys' tearful and angry disclosures flew in the face of council politics. Gay men were oppressed (true), ergo all gay men were good (false). A 1980s policy group, run by feminists I once knew, who were nice and well-meaning women, even categorically advised the council that gay men were less likely than heterosexuals to abuse children. Intelligent and knowledgeable analysis was rendered impossible in Islington. Ian White's report concluded that 'in the late 1980s and early 1990s, the equal opportunities environment, driven from the personnel perspective, became a positive disincentive for challenge to bad practice' (White and Hart, 1995, p. 32). The 'overprotection' afforded minority groups meant that even 'Managers believed they would not be supported if they triggered disciplinary investigations'. A manager among our sources put this more pithily. He had not pushed harder for full investigation of a children's home worker (later arrested during a child sex-ring investigation) because 'in Islington you were always scared of being dragged off to some mind-control workshop'.

Breaking out of the closed circle

The newspaper investigation began following the abortive Old Bailey trial, in March 1992, of a former Islington residential worker, Tom Yeomans, aged 43. He was charged with the buggery of a 14-year-old boy in care, but was acquitted. We eventually established that files requested from Islington by the police had gone missing, and this led to the resignation of Islington's Assistant Director at the time. Yeomans, a gay militant, became the key worker in 1989 for the child, Steven (not his real name), but within weeks was ordered to end contact. A worried supervisor recorded that Yeomans was 'identifying too closely' with the 'vulnerable' boy. At a meeting with managers, Yeomans' resignation was agreed. Yeomans maintained contact with Steven, took him away overnight, and 1 year later applied to foster the boy. Yeomans' allies within Islington's children's homes, the fostering panel and the advocacy organization, *Voice for the Child in Care* (VCC), supported his fostering bid, and at meetings field social workers who feared that abuse was taking place were criticized for being 'anti-equal opportunities'. The Assistant Director rejected these social workers' appeal to make Steven a ward of court, VCC reported them to the local ombudsman, and the pressure led Steven's social worker to stand down.

Yeomans' fostering application was about to be approved when the boy broke down and tearfully alleged months of sexual abuse. The police asked Islington for the boy's social work and residential files, which noted the long-standing concerns about Yeomans. They were told that these were unavailable. The prosecution was only given the social work files the day before the trial began. This was after police implied that secret photocopies had been made, for fear that the originals would be withheld, and Islington would not look good if this emerged in court. However, the residential files remained 'missing'. Steven, an illiterate and disturbed boy, crumbled and contradicted himself under aggressive and humiliating cross-examination. The trial collapsed without Yeomans having to face questioning. Judge Mitchell QC ordered the jury to find him not guilty, because Steven's evidence was uncorroborated and 'it is dangerous to convict on the alleged victim's evidence if that evidence stands alone'. However, he added that he was halting the trial 'reluctantly', branded Yeomans a liar, and said that his behaviour was 'irresponsible . . . it displayed at the very least poor judgement.'

Was this case an isolated one or, as social workers claimed, part of a pattern? In May 1992, we learned that another former Islington children's home worker was under arrest, following a boy's allegation of abuse, and that Islington had again withheld vital file material from the police. Nick Rabet, aged 47, worked at an Islington children's home for 15 years until 1989. As deputy superintendent he then opened an expensively equipped private children's activity centre on a friend's country estate in Sussex. He was arrested in 1991, after police had raided the homes of his friends, Neil Hocquart, aged 40, and Walter Clack, aged 73, in Cambridgeshire. They found hundreds of obscene photos of children, and videos. They also discovered that Hocquart had invested £13 000 in Rabet's centre, abused one of his boy helpers, and regularly visited it with Clack.

Hocquart took a fatal overdose while in police custody, and Clack was subsequently fined £5000 for possessing child pornography. The police believed that they were looking at a child sex ring, raided Rabet's home and found hundreds of suggestive photos, including one of Rabet with a boy who had formerly been in his care. When traced by police, the boy alleged abuse by Rabet over many years. While working for Islington, Rabet had showered the boy with gifts and regularly taken him for weekends at his Sussex home. A concerned manager had tried to ban this. A psychiatrist and the boy's mother had also registered acute concern about Rabet's interest in the boy. All of this was documented. However, when Sussex police asked Islington management for any relevant material in the boy's files, they were told that none could be found. Rabet's personnel file had also supposedly disappeared. Yet the *Standard* had recently accessed it and, because our sources feared a cover-up, passed on its details to police. Management only produced material handed to it by staff, weeks earlier, after guessing that Sussex police was finding out about it anyway, via the newspaper.

The *Standard*'s interest was now heightened. Two possible cover-ups, in the Yeomans and Rabet cases, seemed more than coincidence. Staff reporter Stewart Payne and I were paired full time and we spent the next 3 months tramping Islington's streets, and hours late at night on the phone persuading staff to talk to us. At first, we could scarcely believe what we heard. Frantic, frightened residential staff told us, for example, that armed pimps regularly stayed the night with (sometimes under-age) girls in the children's homes, and forced them to service customers there. (Islington is a deprived inner London borough, close to the red-light district of King's Cross, and children in its care are inevitably vulnerable to pimps.) What was most shocking of all was management's inaction – they repeatedly rejected staff's pleas for greater security, Child Protection Conferences and police investigation.

Young people, with surprising openness, confirmed what desperate staff told us, as did hundreds of pages of documentation. Islington ordered staff not to talk to us, but by October 1992, when we published our 8-page account, the borough was leaking like a sieve. Confidentiality is, rightly, a prime professional obligation for social workers. However, as journalists we could only 'stand up' the story if we got to 'first base'. Persuading staff that we could not depend on hearsay was our hardest task.

The paper instructed Stewart and me only to interview young people over 16 years of age, and wherever possible with their parents' permission. We never told young people how we learned about them, and few pushed us – most were furious with Islington and desperate to tell their stories. Some families had become involved with social services not because they were abusive or neglectful but because they were fragile. For example, the mother of the boy who alleged abuse by Rabet had only asked for brief respite care when she had a breakdown, after divorcing a violent, alcoholic husband. She felt that she then lost her increasingly disturbed child to the care system and Rabet's influence.

By the time police found the boy he was an angry and hurt young man who already had a criminal record, which made him an 'unreliable' witness (a recurring problem for child abuse investigators). Rabet was released from arrest just before we published. None the less, on the basis of a balance of probabilities, East Sussex social services instructed its staff no longer to use his activity centre. Rabet's solicitor told us that he set it up to help problem children, and added, 'The allegation was untrue. Our client co-operated fully with the police inquiry which he believes has totally cleared him'.

After 3 months of research, we published an 8-page report on eight young people. Some lonely boys had tolerated abuse from workers who subtly befriended them, because they longed for father figures. Their abusers' eventual loss of interest as the boys turned to men was yet another rejection, and seemed more profoundly wounding than the abuse itself, as they now realized that they had never been valued for themselves. Others had been violently terrorized by paedophiles. D, at 9 years of age, was shown a spade and told that he would be killed with it if he told. He was suicidal when we found him, a drug addict, with his arms heavily scarred from the self-mutilating cuts which are a recognized symptom of sexual abuse. However, his abuser, Roy Caterer, a volunteer at a now closed special school used by Islington and other London boroughs, was only arrested after a despairing Islington social worker bypassed management and took her suspicions about five young people directly to the police. (In child abuse investigations, social services should be the lead agency.) Police raided and found huge amounts of home-made pornography, including pictures of D, and Caterer received a seven and a half year prison sentence for offences against seven boys and two girls. D, like all of the Islington victims we found, had never been given therapy, despite social workers' and families' pleas.

We also described how social workers in one office were visited by a stream of tearful, apparently drugged children caught up with a local man. Staff discovered that he had twice been imprisoned for running child brothels, and once for supplying drugs. Despite probation service warnings, Islington had upon release housed him opposite a children's playground, and close to a unit for vulnerable homeless families. The children, mostly known to social services or in care, dropped hints about a place called the 'Hot House', but were too scared to say much.

The office social services manager begged for funds for further investigation, but was sternly rebuked in writing by council leader Margaret Hodge: 'Given the state of the social services budget, I expect more appropriate responses'. This was two years before the children scandal – which Hodge later claimed that managers hid from her – erupted. The girl whom we featured had been taken into care after proven or suspected sexual abuse. K, of African origin and unknown age, had simply been abandoned at around 12 years of age. In care, she became pregnant by a married man she met at the 'Hot House', who slept with the probably under-age girl on council premises.

Islington, which insisted on such thorough grounding in equal opportunities, gave staff almost no training in the complex needs of sexually abused children. Specialists know that such girls and boys will, without therapy, loving support and clearly drawn boundaries, remain vulnerable to re-abuse. Promiscuity and prostitution are common, due to low self-esteem and the feeling that this is all that they deserve. However, Islington had no specialists to help such children become abuse survivors. When girls at Islington units brought back violent older men, streetwise staff who judged them to be 'pimps' were, extraordinarily, rebuked by managers for not understanding that young people, too, had a right to 'sexual self-expression'. The dudes with mobile phones were just 'boyfriends'.

Shoot the messenger?

After the *Standard* published, we were inundated for days with telephone calls and further disturbing information from staff and young people (who sometimes began by sobbing uncontrollably). We printed several case studies, but Islington continued to deny everything. On television and radio, council leader Margaret Hodge denounced our work as 'politically motivated . . . a sensationalist bit of gutter journalism'. She claimed, 'there is neither neglect nor incompetence', and suggested that we had bribed children to invent allegations. Indeed, social services somehow persuaded two children to sign statements to this effect, and the council reported us to the Press Complaints Commission (PCC). Fortunately, we had taped most of the interviews. Some parents and children had asked for payment, and the tapes included our voices explaining that we could not pay anyone, because this would compromise a serious investigation. We offered these tapes to the PCC, which in March 1993 threw out Islington's complaint. However, Islington's 'shoot the messenger' response had the desired effect – with the exception of BBC television and radio, the other media shied away from the horrors we had unearthed.

None the less, ministers expressed alarm, and the *Standard* swiftly dispatched a dossier to the SSI. We described the breadth and sometimes seniority of our anonymous professional sources and, after the SSI had promised confidentiality, we provided photocopies of supporting documentation. We always had far more than we published – by agreement, we only quoted in print those documents to which many professionals had access, so that the source of the 'leak' could not be proven. Other documents, of more limited circulation, none the less served to reassure our exacting editors and lawyer.

Had Islington taken legal action, demanding that we reveal our sources, we had an immensely strong 'public interest' defence. In the unlikely event that it won, the paper would refuse to comply and would, Stewart assured me cheerfully, 'visit us in prison'. However, we accurately calculated that Islington, with so much to hide, would not dare to risk a court confrontation. The council proposed to investigate our allegations internally. The SSI rejected this and ordered an inquiry by outsiders. It was an unsatisfactory compromise – Islington would still be allowed to choose who ran it and its terms of reference. The council appointed Jo Tunnard, former director of the Family Rights

Group charity, and Brian McAndrew, former chief executive of the London Borough of Enfield. The remit of their 'interim' inquiry was to investigate whether the homes in our stories had been 'out of control', and whether the eight young people we described were now safe.

Islington's choice of Brian McAndrew to interview distraught families and children, and concerned social workers, seemed unsatisfactory to many, as he was a professional administrator with no child protection expertise. Inevitably, the interim inquiry did not go far enough. When its interim report was published, in February 1993, we had to present as our headline their condemnation of a key Islington home as a 'disgusting dump'. Decor, not abuse, provided the strongest quote.

Stewart and I had never visited the homes, as our editors, fearful of trespass accusations, forbade this. However, a few days before McAndrew and Tunnard reported, three young people at the 'dump' home rang and begged us to visit it. We were wary of being 'set up', but the young people were adamant that we should see how they lived. They smuggled me in and I was stunned – it was like a workhouse. The kids in this 'towards independence' unit slept on stained mattresses, which looked as though they had been scavenged from skips, on bare, filthy floorboards, and used torn sheets as curtains. Cockroaches infested the kitchen – they had kept some fat corpses to show us. Innocently they mentioned in passing that they liked the cook because 'she sometimes gives us left-overs'. She was only meant to cook for the staff – the kids were judged to be old enough to be self-catering. The youngest was 15 years of age, their food allowance was just £20 per week, and mostly, the kids admitted with disconcerting honesty, they lived on toast, cigarettes and the odd treat of crack cocaine, funded by muggings and someone they referred to as a pimp named 'Fat Alan'. They had two chairs, between six of them, for 'mealtimes'.

The inquiry (which was only shown the relatively cleaner reception area and living room) termed the unit, 'disgusting . . . nothing could have prepared us fully for what we encountered inside. We were devastated to find that young people were living, and staff working, in what we can best describe as a dump'.

These youngsters had been briefly questioned by the inquiry team, but kept quiet about the abuse, drugs and pimps. They told us that the staff said the truth would lead to their home being closed down. It was all that they had. The inquiry did interview the young people featured in our original article, and believed them: 'All eight young people have been abused physically, sexually or both . . . some have been abused sexually for long periods whilst in the care of the local authority. . . . It is striking how little specialist counselling seems to have been provided'. Three, it confirmed, were homeless, while another was working as a prostitute. However, it was not within the inquiry's remit to confirm who had abused these young people, whether their abuse had been properly investigated by social services, or whether files had been withheld from the police, as the *Standard* alleged. The report described Islington social services as being in a state of 'deep malaise', but could not say which managers were responsible. Nor did it comment on whether the men who had sex with children in care were pimps and customers. It simply confirmed that 'Staff were aware of men/boyfriends staying over but felt powerless to deal with it. The lack of security made their job a nightmare. There is no agreed approach on how staff will approach the young people's sexuality.' Repeated staff pleas for minimal security measures had, it confirmed, been ignored by management. 'Net curtains were delivered the day after the Press articles'.

The inquiry confirmed that the two units we mainly highlighted were sometimes 'out of control', and expressed 'great concern' about a 'perceived tradition' of allowing accused staff 'to move on quietly'. Islington grudgingly agreed that a 'number of improvements need to be made', and ordered refurbishment. However, said Neighbourhood Services Director Martin Higgins, the inquiry report was 'questionable and often very misleading'.

Who really misled whom? Key evidence disappeared from files that the inquiry requested – for example, a photograph of the injuries to 'Mary', who was knifed in the neck by her pimp. When Mary spoke to the inquiry she even denied that this attack had taken place. We soon established that, within a few days of our story about her, an Islington manager rang Mary and offered to arrange criminal injuries compensation for this injury. Was she pressured, in return, to wrong-foot us? Tunnard and McAndrew had also asked Islington for reports by its recently appointed Children's Homes Inspector, and were told that none existed. However, they did exist, and the *Standard*, at the last minute, was sent them. Inspector Mike Betts' reports were so critical that director Martin Higgins, and social services chairwoman Sandy Marks, even withheld them for months from the social services committee. Betts had demanded urgent improvements. Soon the long-serving manager was removed from the post and replaced by a young former Labour councillor with no social services experience. The *Standard* tipped off the inquiry, which hastily interviewed Betts, obtained his scathing reports and indignantly rewrote their own to ask why 'we had neither seen them nor known they existed'. Two weeks later, Betts was demoted. For the first time the union weighed in. Betts' reports, stated NALGO, 'were suppressed because they supported serious allegations made in the *London Evening Standard*'.

Following publication of the interim report no heads rolled – except Jo Tunnard's. Tunnard, the inquiry's child-care expert, was due to head a second-stage inquiry with Brian McAndrew, but was suddenly sacked. A high-ranking council source told us that this was because she wanted the second-stage report to name responsible individuals, and 'felt that specific allegations needed further investigation, because of discrep.. cies in people's accounts'. The council had expected the inquiry team to produce an anodyne report which found in its favour. 'It didn't like the criticism and Ms Tunnard has been made to carry the can'.

The media began to pay attention. In May 1993, the *Standard* won a prize for investigative journalism in the national British Press Awards, and was specifically praised for continuing to dig in the face of council denials and condemnation. If we were going to get anywhere, we needed the other media on our side.

Jo Tunnard was replaced by Emlyn Cassam, former director of Norfolk social services. Abuse victims no longer had the option of speaking to a woman, as many prefer. But the 100 or more people who gave evidence to these men swiftly realized that abuse was not, in any case, on the agenda of their 'management review'. Published in July 1993, the review concentrated on problems of organization (Cassam and McAndrew, 1993). While its criticisms and 37 detailed recommendations for change were needed, it referred to abuse only in the vaguest way. Cassam and McAndrew branded Islington social services' structure 'unworkable', the quality of child care 'unacceptable', and working relationships 'hostile and untrusting'; staff were 'dispirited and apprehensive'. It continued, 'many times we were told that the services are not safe and that staff are fearful of the consequences – a view with which we concur'. The inquiry blamed Islington's decentralized social services – the system 'almost guarantees failure'. With regard to the *Standard*'s abuse allegations, 'we have drawn no detailed conclusions', and it would be 'premature to call for disciplinary action'. Yet long after the review was published, the *Standard* discovered that Cassam and McAndrew met Islington's request for a secret appendix on our allegations. What the council dubbed their 'missing chapter' described violence, drugs and neglect in care, and Islington's treatment of the boy who alleged abuse by Tom Yeomans, as 'a travesty of child care'. The extreme secrecy surrounding the case, said Cassam and McAndrew, was 'a mystery we cannot fathom'. However, they recommended that further inquiries be of 'the minimum required to allay public concern' (Cassam and McAndrew, 1993).

At least our allegations were looked at. Two BASW solicitors drew up a 96-page dossier documenting members' abuse concerns. However, when the BASW met Cassam and McAndrew, they had not even read it. Worse, the eight young people featured in the *Standard*'s reports had still received no help. One child's stepmother described him as a 'time-bomb', enraged and tormented by flashbacks. The mother of another told us, 'He is so far over the edge now only psychiatric care can save him'. At Islington's crowded press conference for the review, we challenged the council to apologize to these young people, but we were angrily told that no abuse had been proven. The inquiry report instead urged that 'councillors, managers and staff divest themselves of the baggage of the past and make a fresh start in giving the best service possible in the present financial climate'. So that was that.

Islington created a new post – head of children's homes – but that was the only substantial immediate reform. The council remained adamant when we waved social services documents that had just been faxed to us by a new whistleblower. These confirmed that at least 10 named children, mainly in care, were believed to be involved with three paedophile pimps. The council had known for the past 30 months – long before the *Standard* first published – but had done nothing. One of the pimps was Fat Alan. None of the men, claimed the Islington police child protection team in the documents, could be identified. However, knowing that the police can trace an address from a telephone number, we had persuaded young people to give us Fat Alan's number, and had passed it months before to Scotland Yard's Obscene Publications Branch. Apparently, the Yard had met Islington and area police chiefs about the allegations, but had not passed the number on and took no appropriate action about Fat Alan. Throughout our investigation, we were struck by the minimal trust, co-ordination and co-operation between sections of the police.

That evening, Stewart and I felt very tired and became very emotional together in a pub. We and our sources had by now given evidence of sexual abuse and child prostitution to two inquiries, and spent hours with the police. What more would it take?

The tide turns

We passed the 'Fat Alan' documents to the SSI, which promised another inquiry on organized abuse – by Cassam. We were not optimistic, but we perked up on learning that Jo Tunnard, the sacked inquiry member, had made her own secret report to the SSI. This included information from children's home workers who were still at that stage too frightened to talk to us. They described a colleague dealing crack cocaine, drug deals openly stored in the fridge, and strange men picking up the kids at night in vans. In autumn 1992 they begged management in vain for an investigation. One worker secretly taped a telephone call specifically instructing him not to speak to police.

In March 1993 the home closed after a riot, when five youngsters were led away in strait-jackets.

Our sources told us that one of the home workers also had key information which could finally topple Islington's house of cards. We badgered and she 'came over'. She said that she had received repeated veiled threats concerning her job security from management, who knew what she knew, but that she was by now more angry than scared. If necessary, she said bravely, she was prepared to be sacked. She agreed that we could give the SSI her name and offer to sign an affidavit. We urged this because we trusted that the SSI was, if initially slow, by now deeply alarmed and on the side of the angels. It was time to break the circle of fear and identify some sources – we could not hide them for ever behind our reassurance that they were 'reliable'.

In October 1993, Stewart Payne and I met the SSI and told our source's story. About 2 weeks before Yeoman's trial, she was instructed to bring Steven's residential files to the office of the Assistant Director (I am referring to the same Assistant Director throughout). She delivered them by hand, and it was after this that they disappeared. By now we also knew that files had gone missing in another disturbing case involving a boy at Nick Rabet's Islington children's home.

At the October SSI meeting, we also explained why we suspected that Islington withheld information from Sussex officers who were investigating Nick Rabet. The SSI knew our high-placed council source and seemed stunned. This revelation, plus the courage of the social worker who knew what had happened to the Yeomans' files, directly led to the forced resignation of Islington's Assistant Director. After our meeting the SSI had descended upon the council.

When I heard the news I again cried with relief, and a whistleblower threw a party. Until then, some sources had not even known that close colleagues were also confiding in us. They 'came out' and celebrated because they felt safer. The Assistant Director's settlement forbade her to speak to the press. Whatever pressures she may have been under from the council remain unknown.

The SSI ordered another inquiry, into the missing files, and we were invited to write up the so far ignored abuse and drugs allegations. We submitted an 118-page dossier to the SSI in December 1993, after being assured that we could do so under 'legal privilege'. In print we had only published what we could legally prove, but we did not have the time or necessary access to files to investigate all of the other allegations put to us – we just knew that someone should. This became the basis of the White Inquiry.

First, however, Emlyn Cassam was supposed to look at the abuse allegations. He submitted a draft report to the council in March 1994. It was, in my opinion, a whitewash and was never published. Cassam had, with Jo Tunnard's permission, access to her secret report to the SSI. He did not have our dossier – Islington had asked both the SSI and the *Standard* for it, but we felt so little trust that we only gave permission for the council to see a brief summary, from which all identifying sources, as well as indications as about the extent of our knowledge of 'networkers', had been removed. I do not believe that Cassam saw this either, but no matter – Tunnard's report included some of the same disturbing information as our dossier, and Cassam's draft report informed the council that he was aware of 31 serious allegations. However, he concluded, 'we do not see the need for further investigation(s). . . . They can be demoralising', but he did concede that 'the number and nature of the allegations does give rise to concern. . . . Some people may be disappointed that we have not commented in detail. . . . So be it . . . enough lessons have been learned'.

Cassam's covering letter reassured the Chief Executive, Eric Dear, that 'a line should be drawn under the past. Some people will disagree and claim a "white-wash". To counter this to some extent I have referred to a few "nasties", but not, I hope, in too negative a way'. This report never saw the light of day. We understand that it was shown to the health minister, and to the SSI who finally lost patience, met the council and ordered it to accept a fully independent inquiry by *their* appointee. Islington could 'choose' between White or 'a bunch of lawyers'.

The SSI had begun hammering Islington from all directions. It sent in independent children's homes inspectors, and in November 1993 their report on four homes confirmed that little had changed. Buildings were in poor repair, safety standards alarming, staff morale low, there was a high rate of absconding and little attention was being paid to children. A principal inspector said, 'We found reasons for serious concern and a clear lack of management responsibility and accountability. But we are confident there is a will for change'. Behind the scenes the SSI had warned the recalcitrant council that it could face an unprecedented government take-over of its children's homes.

Within Islington there was pressure for an *internal* replacement for the now vacant Assistant Director's post. The union resisted this and, in January 1994, Hannah Miller moved from Croydon into a newly created post as Chief Social Services Officer. At last Islington social work would be managed by a specialist. Much of the credit for reforms within Islington since then goes to Miller.

Also in January 1994 two SSI inspectors published a scathing condemnation of Islington's complaints procedures – 'a vital element in combating abuse and malpractice'. Set against SSI standards of good practice, Islington failed to meet the optimum 'well met' bench-mark against all 16 criteria, and completely failed in nine, indicating 'serious shortcomings with no evidence that the department was attempting to improve its performance'.

In March 1994, Brian McAndrew's 'missing files' inquiry was published. It confirmed that crucial files in the Rabet, Yeomans and New Barns cases had gone missing. He attributed this to 'carelessness, confusion, poor communication, poor standards, and neglect of administrative support'. We thought that McAndrew's report was hopelessly muddled, told the SSI why, and Ian White later re-studied our evidence. He found the same administrative chaos, a trail gone cold and no proof of collusion. However, he confirmed, the files had become lost 'at assistant director level', where 'many confidential files were destroyed by mistake'.

That March, Islington hit the national headlines in a new child-care scandal when a couple whose youngest child literally rotted to death in its rarely changed nappies were imprisoned. SSI inspectors studied Islington's social work files and, in July 1994, judged council promises of reform to be hollow. Islington provided 'a very low quality of service' riddled with 'serious flaws', and gave 'grave cause for concern'. After internal wrangling, seven specialists were appointed in late 1994, and the number of Neighbourhood Offices was reduced from 24 to 12 (new director Hannah Miller had wanted just six).

Meanwhile new whistleblowers passed on their concerns about an Islington Family Centre manager. The SSI made a swoop inspection, condemned the unit as dirty and uncaring, and ordered yet another case review after we made certain revelations in July 1994.

The White Report

In May 1995 Ian White's 60-page report was published. It was the thorough, unflinching analysis that had been needed from the start. He had systematically compared our dossier with Islington's files, and confirmed that the borough knew of but mostly failed to investigate 32 grave allegations. Worse, by allowing suspects to resign with good references, the council had dumped probable paedophiles on other unwitting authorities. According to White:

> Islington did not in most cases undertake the standard investigative processes that should have been triggered. . . . It is possible, therefore, that some staff now not in the employment of Islington could be working elsewhere in the field of Social Services with a completely clean disciplinary record and yet have serious allegations still not investigated in their history.
>
> (White and Hart, 1995, p. 31).

The White Report received comprehensive media coverage, and one Labour councillor told us that she burst into tears after reading it, and said 'I felt so ashamed'. New director Hannah Miller accepted White's unprecedented recommendation that she invite local authorities throughout the UK to check the background of former Islington employees, given how many left by what White called the 'back door'.

Two former employees who recently quit Islington were soon traced. One was working at a hostel for homeless young people, and resigned after proving unable to explain his relationship with a girl in Islington's care. Another had a key post in another London borough and also resigned following an interview by the council. Hannah Miller believed that there was sufficient evidence for 12 former Islington staff to be added to the Department of Health's Consultancy Register, which warns authorities nationally against suspect staff (*The Independent*, 1995).

Others named in White's confidential annexe are working in unregulated fields such as psychotherapy, in certain Third World countries, or remain untraced. A children's home superintendent, whose widespread abuse was the cause of one under-age girl becoming pregnant, is now dead. However, White's confirmation that this terrible abuse took place still meant a great deal to the victims. At the time of writing no prosecutions have resulted.

Controversially, White called for a Home Office initiative to pool nationally the police and social services concerning suspects in children's homes, education and the youth service. Currently, police are unable to pass on their intelligence about unconvicted men. While acknowledging that this has civil liberties implications which need careful thought, White pointed out that 'a large number of men involved in paedophile rings have clean records' despite 'very serious' information held by police. (A joint conference for all London boroughs on the theme of pooling information is, at the time of writing, under discussion.)

In March 1996, Islington launched a helpline run by the National Society for the Prevention of Cruelty to Children (NSPCC), both to support abused children and adult survivors, and to encourage evidence.

Currently, Islington Police Child Protection Team, which came under new leadership in 1995, has obtained witness statements concerning sexual abuse from several young people formerly in Islington's care. Some came forward voluntarily, following the publicity given to the White Report, and Islington has co-operated fully in helping police to trace others. Their evidence may, however, be judged to be legally 'out of time' and never reach court. One Islington abuse survivor, Demetrious Panton, went public in March 1996, both on television and in print. He has rejected Islington's apology and offer of compensation and, at the time of writing, he is taking a QC's advice on suing former council leader, Margaret Hodge, and Chief Executive, Eric Dear.

Many social workers were disappointed that White's otherwise painstaking and perceptive inquiry uncritically reported reassurance from senior police officers that there was no failure to investigate organized network abuse in Islington, or to seek proof that it existed. How hard was anyone really allowed to look?

For some time following these events Islington predictably faced problems in recruiting staff, but it has improved training, appointed a

Children's Rights Officer, and has a well-publicized complaints procedure for children in care. No staff were victimized for assisting the
Evening Standard (we never admitted who they were, and they never
said), and the new administration reinstated former children's home
inspector, Mike Betts, as a manager.

Ian White concluded that 'What happened in Islington was a tragedy
for its children. The credit for exposing this situation must go to the
Evening Standard and the social workers who had the courage to speak
up'.

Personal conclusions

I wish to acknowledge the frighteningly large role that personal agendas
and chance also played in this dreadful story. Would those who fought
for 3 years to expose the truth have carried on, if we had not on some
level identified with the children in Islington's indifferent care?

The key whistleblower had suffered heart-breaking personal tragedies,
which left them fearlessly protective of other children. I myself left an
unhappy home at 16 years of age for bed-sits. Throughout the Islington
campaign, the *Standard* was edited by Stewart Steven, who was orphaned
at 9 years of age and himself grew up dependent on charity. Others central
to the investigation had no such personal experience, but we all felt anger
at the truth being branded a cheap journalistic lie. Genuine concern, not
just professional skill or the usual media egos, kept our unusually close
team digging.

I mention this because it is yet another lesson. Child protection is far
too important to depend on the right people colliding at the right time.
How many other child abuse scandals remain unexposed, for want of
this?

Acknowledgements

It is indicative of the risks which whistleblowers take that the social
workers, police officers and others who helped the *Standard*'s investigation still do not want to be named – but they know who they are, and
we thank them. I also thank Stewart Payne for being a superb colleague, and executive editor Phillip Evans for guiding us so well. They
brought not just skill but good humour to an often grim campaign.
Maureen Davies of the Beacon Foundation helpline for ritual abuse victims receives numerous brickbats from a sceptical media, so deserves
special thanks: she alerted us to the Islington scandal. This chapter is
dedicated to the memories of Kamala and Jay, whose brief lives
inspired so much.

References

Cassam, E. and McAndrew, B. (1993) *Report for London Borough of Islington on the Management of Child Care Within the Neighbourhood Services Department.* London: London Borough of Islington.

The Independent (1995) Child abusers escape the net, by N. Timmins. 1 May, p. 3. Abuse case man given child care job and Care agencies are 'black hole', by N. Timmins. 2 August, p. 5.

London Borough of Islington (1989) *Liam Johnson Review: Report of Panel of Inquiry.* London: Islington Area Child Protection Committee.

White, I. A. and Hart, K. (1995) *Report of the Inquiry into the Management of Child Care in the London Borough of Islington.* A report commissioned by Islington Council following serious allegations about child care practices in the borough. London: London Borough of Islington.

2

Hostages to fortune: the abuse of children in care

Alison Taylor

> I know of no more sacred duty than ... the care and education of a
> child.
>
> (Ludwig van Beethoven, 1770–1827)[1]

In 1987 I was dismissed from a senior childcare post with Gwynedd
County Council because I refused to ignore persistent and widespread
allegations about the abuse of children in care[2]. Public disquiet about the
welfare of children in care in North Wales continued to grow, particularly after a major investigation by North Wales Police in 1991 led to the
conviction of several former social workers. The North Wales Child
Abuse Tribunal of Inquiry, established in 1996 under the chairmanship
of Sir Ronald Waterhouse, was the direct outcome of this disquiet. At the
time of writing (November 1997) the Tribunal is still sitting, and matters
relating to some of my own experiences in North Wales therefore remain
sub judice. However, references can be made to other areas of my professional experience, and to the recently published report by Sir William
Utting, former head of social services inspectorates in England and
Wales[3].

Introduction

Children in state care are accommodated in local council residential
homes, foster homes, hostels, and in the private sector (which offers, at
least on paper, resources which many councils can no longer afford). The
childcare population is a mix of young offenders, persistent truants,
orphans, abuse victims, those removed for their own protection from
disordered, dangerous and dysfunctional families, and those exhibiting
serious behavioural problems[4].

Major police investigations into the alleged abuse of such children are
now almost commonplace, and a significant number of social workers in

the UK are now convicted child abusers. Whilst the childcare industry is not necessarily rife with sadists and paedophiles, our previous complacency about the integrity of people attracted to the work allowed abuse to become, if not the norm, very far from extraordinary. For instance, Peter Righton, a government adviser and policy-maker, enjoyed the trust of senior figures at the heart of social work in the UK, and is now exposed as a paedophile who used that trust to procure children. Frank Beck, who wielded power in Leicestershire for so long, and Peter Howarth, former deputy head of Bryn Estyn in Clwyd, both died in prison. John Allen and Steven Norris are serving long sentences for their crimes against children in Wales, but there will always be other Rightons and Becks and Howarths and Allens and Norrisses waiting in the wings. At times, they erupt on to centre stage, like Thomas Hamilton in Dunblane and Fred and Rosemary West in Gloucester, and instead of acting out their savage fantasies behind the closed doors of an institution, do so in full view of a horrified world.

The moral and political climate

> As some day it may happen that a victim must be found,
> I've got a little list – I've got a little list
> Of society offenders who might well be under ground
> And who never would be missed – who never would be missed!
> (Sir W.S. Gilbert, 1836–1911, *The Mikado*)

The quality of our civilization and collective conscience is measured by the way in which we treat the least powerful, and usually the most alienated, members of our society. Conscience is a fragile thing, often underdeveloped or poorly perceived, and prone to collapse in the face of pressure, or to desertion in the face of wayward pleasure. From the days of Herod to the days of Hitler and beyond, profound failures of conscience have bloodied history.

Ethics are born of conscience, but face an uphill struggle for survival in a world that is increasingly making choices between one lesser evil and another. Market forces and capitalism have undermined the professional independence of medicine, law and social work, creating a money-dominated environment which leaves little room for considerations beyond expediency. In this new reality, practitioners become distanced from ethical foundations, with little opportunity to question the morality and legality of practices and principles, and even less scope to determine the profession's future course. Social work's particular vulnerability to the impact of political ideologies, and to the social change that these create, is discussed later.

In other eras, we allowed children to be held in bondage, mercilessly exploited, deported, flogged, imprisoned and executed. Publicly, we now deplore both that past and cultures which refuse to share our new enlightenment, yet quite recently a former Conservative MP told me that he supports the harshest measures for children in care, including birching, and the general restoration of corporal and capital punishment. He is not alone either in believing that children are in care entirely through their own fault, and must be punished, or in privately owning attitudes which we assume to belong to harsher times.

In the eighteenth century, the Agrarian and Industrial Revolutions caused urban populations to mushroom, and urban crime rates quickly followed suit. Government of the day, composed predominantly of landowning gentry, responded with Draconian measures to eliminate the new 'criminal class', composed predominantly of the most impoverished and dispossessed. Subsequent to the 'Black Act' of 1723, some 250 capital offences entered the statute book, sparing neither child nor adult from the consequences of coveting the property of others. Little Peter McCloud was hanged in May 1772 for attempted housebreaking; five years later, a 14-year-old servant girl was sentenced to be burned alive for stealing a few pence from her master, and in 1831, hangman William Calcraft executed a 9-year-old boy in Chelmsford for setting fire to a house.

We built an empire abroad and dominated the world with intellectual and technical achievement, and thought nothing of putting children to death by hanging and burning, yet other less stable or powerful nations had already developed a greater regard for human rights. Among his many significant social and legal reforms, Emperor Joseph II of Austria (1741–1790), whose successor would see his empire bankrupted by the Napoleonic Wars, fought for abolition of the death penalty, while in Britain relentless technological progress completely outdistanced morality. The first tube trains took to the London rails in 1863, providing cheap and easy access to public executions, the last of which took place in 1868.

The poor child of history went down mines, up chimneys, into the workhouses, toiled day and night, and was flogged by his master. The rich child went to public school and was flogged by his tutors. Periodic surges of moral outrage have eroded some of the worst excesses of Georgian and Victorian values, but Britain only recently ratified the UN Convention on Children's Rights, with a number of reservations, and the UN continues to deplore our record and attitudes towards children.

The former Conservative government believed that a 'womb-to-tomb' welfare state encourages dependency and idleness, and like the present administration in the USA, it systematically reduced provision to the most needy and helpless, marginalizing the unemployed, the sick, the elderly, the mentally ill, the handicapped, convicted offenders, and problem children. New Labour's welfare policies seem to be travelling the same path. Without power of their own, the underprivileged look to others for protection, yet are perceived as non-productive and exploitative – a serious threat to social order and economic health in a society which historically measures individual worth by economic criteria. Paradoxically, they support a multi-million pound industry, creating enormous wealth for others.

Short of a return to the days of the Black Act, the poorest in our society are here to stay, and in the present moral and economic climate, it is only a matter of time before their disaffection *does* seriously challenge social stability.

Crime and punishment

Recent Home Office figures show a marked fall in notifiable offences among the 10 to 13 years age group since 1985, but offending children are still presented as a grave threat to social order, and become recipients of policies determined by unwarranted moral panic. We are unreasonably hostile towards the young, expecting them always to meet our expectations of yobbism, irresponsibility and criminality. Attitudes towards juveniles have hardened generally, and the underclass of juvenile offenders arouses a violent prejudice unleavened by any compassion. The murder of little James Bulger was tragic and terrible, and the detention of John Venables and Robert Thompson wholly appropriate, but since their sentencing in November 1993, the tariff has twice been increased – from 8 to 10 years by the Lord Chief Justice, and from 10 to 15 years by the then Home Secretary Michael Howard, apparently as a reaction to public pressure. The Court of Appeal ruled in July 1996 that Howard acted wrongly, and Lord Woolf, Master of the Rolls, stressed that proper punishment should not be subject to influences outside legal process which could amount to 'interference with the administration of justice'.

Class and crime are inextricably linked, as writer Jonathan Swift observed almost 200 years ago, comparing laws to cobwebs which trap small flies but allow the wasps and hornets to break through. The composer Beethoven made similar observations. The majority of our prison population comes from the lower social classes, like the majority of children in care, encouraging presumptions about the innate immorality of the lower classes which echo the notions of our Georgian forebears. The public school system can provide a safe haven for the rich delinquent, and although state-funded institutions for the poor like to boast an almost parallel ethos, they place little or no value on formal education, presuming their clientele to be intellectually as well as socially inferior.

Provisions for children in the private sector are probably little better, irrespective of fees which can exceed £50 000 per annum.

Our socialization processes expose children to various behavioural techniques, including the primitive, counter-productive exercise of control by inducing fear through the application of pain and humiliation. Believing we must cast out original sin, or simply reinforcing a bad habit, we subject children to criminal assaults which happily ignore issues of morality and logic, and which are no more a deterrent to antisocial activity than capital punishment is to murder.

The nature of social work

Social work sprang from the philanthropic ideal of giving practical assistance and support to the less fortunate, but as the work became organized and formalized into a profession, its nature underwent a radical change. As internal frames of reference developed, the existence of a body of expertise altered external expectations, leading to revision of what might be appropriate and useful activities for social workers. Rapid developments in the disciplines of psychology and sociology made their own impact, validating the new professionalism, but social work none the less remains particularly vulnerable to external influences, possibly because it lacks the common and defined purpose found in medicine – the model from which it borrows most – and thus, a solid professional identity.

Modern social work appears to bend to whatever social, penal and economic ideologies are dominant. Its purpose is unclear, it has no independent goals or standards, and its responses are reactive and crisis-driven. By its very nature as a public service profession, social work should be a socially interactive force, yet its weight falls only upon the client. It does not involve itself in defining minimum-welfare policies, or in lobbying government on disagreeable and inequitable social issues. From the client's point of view, social workers wield enormous statutory power, but never use that power to challenge the many injustices which bedevil our society. Apparently content to obey external hierarchies, the profession can show a blatant disregard for internal regulation or public accountability over the quality of its performance – when negligent service leads to tragedy, as in the case of Ricky Neave, managers and senior practitioners are rarely disciplined.

Social work does not enjoy a good reputation, even among those who have never had recourse to its services. Those who do may be left with the bitter memories related in a *Cover Story* programme on adoption (HTV, 24 July 1996), where some contributors equated social work with power and political correctness, arguing that prospective adopters must accept flawed frames of reference in order to succeed in the selection process. Social workers were seen as indoctrinated with political correctness, the acceptance of fashionable ideology being a prerequisite of their continuing employment.

Most people have little real understanding of what social workers do, but there persists a strong suspicion that they do more harm than good, or are at best ineffectual at great public expense. Media images are generally negative, concentrating on failure, but arguably there have been too many avoidable failures, from the tragedy of Jasmine Beckford onwards, and too little impetus towards professional accountability. The nature of social work and its dependence on psychological and sociological theory preclude for the most part quantifiable evidence of negligence or ineptitude. Negative interventional outcome is therefore easily attributable to the innate incorrigibility of the client, and less demonstrably so to iatrogenesis when, as in the medical model, the treatment makes the patient's condition worse. When quantifiable evidence does exist, as in the case of children abused in institutions, professional denial is the overriding response. Gwynedd County Council maintained that stance throughout the then largest police investigation of its kind in British history. In its midst, the then director of social services, Lucille Hughes, speaking on BBC Wales News, described the abuse allegations as 'wicked, stupid lies'. By definition, then, anyone voicing the allegations was a wicked, stupid liar.

My own career spanned almost two decades in institutions for the mentally ill, adult offenders and children, where each group apparently qualified for different forms of management, and interventions would be tailored to meet specific goals. In the Home Office adult offenders unit, the twin goals were containment and control, with rehabilitation very much a secondary consideration and a viable option only in limited circumstances. For the psychiatric patients, rehabilitation was ostensibly the preferred goal, but an analysis of the work done with this group clearly shows containment and control to be paramount, with recourse to medication and secure hospital facilities at times of patient breakdown. Rehabilitation only became an option when medical and social work personnel felt safe in regarding the patient as sufficiently 'reconditioned': by that yardstick, very few obtained permanent discharge, although most posed no real threat and, given the right aftercare, were capable of independence.

Many subtle factors conspire to determine the selection of people for admission to institutions, including the limits outside which behaviour becomes unacceptable to a social subgroup. Other factors determine continuing residence, including that of created dependency, but it remains beyond doubt that the main preoccupation of work with many client groups constitutes an unacknowledged social control, springing from our unwillingness or inability to tolerate what is not immediately comprehensible.

M's experiences show that a diagnosis of mental illness is easily made, and very hard to reverse. In her early forties, with a stable marriage, three teenage children and no pressing problems, she had a sudden and inexplicable breakdown, characterized by outlandish behaviour, and was admitted urgently to a psychiatric hospital. Hindsight suggests the onset of menopause as a possible precipitating factor. On the basis of presenting symptoms, she was treated with a battery of powerful drugs and sent home when the more bizarre episodes abated. However, she soon relapsed. Her medication was reviewed and changed, but she continued to deteriorate, mentally and now physically and, close to total collapse, she truly believed she was dying.

Her GP and psychiatrist concluded that she had a serious and incurable mental illness, probably pre-senile dementia (PSD), and they proposed early and permanent hospitalization. M and her family were devastated. Brought in as their social worker at the point of her breakdown, I regarded the pattern of her collapse as quite inconsistent with PSD, and began to look for other causes, including an idiosyncratic reaction to medication. Although the medical profession was not enthusiastic about inexpert interference, her GP agreed to investigate, and found that one of the drugs given in the early stages had caused a massive reaction, exacerbated by other chemicals in her system. Appropriate treatment enabled M to recover her equilibrium and well-being, but she was haunted by the metamorphosis – over which she had no control – from wife, mother and useful citizen to a serious and incurable problem requiring permanent incarceration.

Children come to the attention of authority when the socialization process appears to be deflected from its target norm by disruptive social or personal factors. Resocialization of such children proceeds from the assumption of fault in the child and its internalization mechanisms, even where problems clearly exist in the family, because once a child comes into care, it becomes a problem which requires a solution. At the other end of the spectrum, children who exhibit behavioural problems of mysterious origin may well have undiagnosed physiological problems, including *petit mal* epilepsy, old head injuries, or more obscure disorders. Even where medicine can offer treatment or stabilization, these children are perceived as a social problem, and in need of a psychological and social work solution.

Expectations of conformity appear to be at their most inflexible for children in care, and they tend to bear the brunt of randomly applied and ill-perceived psychological theory. Few children can comprehend what these expectations entail, and those who apply the theory have little understanding of their own. Even where residential social workers (RSWs) are professionally qualified, and most are not, their training is unlikely to explore in any depth the theoretical foundations of applied social work. Theories are generally presented as fact to be absorbed, and challenges to received wisdom are actively discouraged.

Analysis of the systems and practices in most children's homes shows staff engaged primarily in a form of social control founded on received moral judgements, and responding to imposed agendas, many of which are dictated by dwindling resources, financial cut-backs, increasing intolerance, and local factors. Even if it were encouraged, there is no opportunity to seek client feedback on the quality, impact and effectiveness of interventions, many of which are *ad hoc*, crisis driven, and oblivious to outcome.

Many of the young adult offenders with whom I previously worked had been through the childcare system. Some of these young men may have been born criminals, genetically pre-programmed, but others were creations of a failed system, grown into adults with no hand in their own making. At a later date, I was able to investigate pre-admission interventions with a large sample group resident in a Welsh Regional Plan resource which housed some 60 boys aged between 10 and 18 years who were judged too difficult or dangerous to be accommodated elsewhere. On average, I found 12 previous placements and/or interventions, but in some cases the figure climbed as high as 40 (Taylor, 1982)[5]. Few of the boys understood, except in the vaguest terms, why they were shunted from place to place like undelivered mail, or why earlier placements or interventions had failed. Most took the blame on their own shoulders, repeating what they were told by social workers, parents, police and probation officers. Their statements were borne out by the agency records that were available, but in most cases it was not possible to pinpoint any specific action or omission on the child's part. Some of these boys were non-offenders, some had only a negligible criminal history, and their current placement was therefore both inexplicable and probably unwarranted.

The most well-adjusted child can create turbulence in the calmest waters of family life at times, for childhood is a time of challenge and exploration. Some children, through no fault of their own, sink to the mud beneath, weighted down with slabs of prejudice which prevent them from ever rising to the surface again. J, admitted to care as a young baby, is a case in point. Although plagued by bouts of mental instability, her mother was able to care for J's older brother, and the implementation of well-planned support and monitoring should have enabled J's early return home. Alternatively, the professionals should have grasped the nettle at an early stage, and placed her for adoption. Instead, she went from one placement to another, each failing for unspecified reasons. Her mother kept in regular contact, vainly hoping to have the child returned, but at the age of 10 years, her previous placements by now too numerous to count, J was proposed for long-term admission to a specialist community home. The antecedents are complex, but she was allegedly so sexually precocious and uncontrolled that she constituted a danger to males and females of any age, and required 24-hourly supervision.

Assessment of her needs was bedevilled by the reputation she carried like a millstone, by her minor learning difficulties, and by the impact of her experiences, but staff waited in vain for the exhibitions of inappropriate sexuality. Eventually, she said that an adult male in a previous foster family had done 'naughty things' to her, which she had reported to her social worker at the time. At some point, there was a police investigation, but no prosecution ensued. J was moved to another foster home, taking her newly acquired reputation for mischief, to which all subsequent carers reacted, thereby reinforcing the damage. By the time she reached the community home, her reputation and self-image were irretrievably compromised. She later spoke of the physical, sexual and psychological abuses she had endured in several of the other placements for whose failure she had been blamed.

Clearly, at least one of J's transfers was provoked by her reporting abuse, and it is more than likely that many of the inexplicable and repeated movements of children from one care placement to another do not depend on the child's conduct, but on the risk of disclosure of abuse. In some cases, children who go to the extent of making allegations find themselves confined in secure placements far removed from their home territory, and even in locked psychiatric wards.

The growth of social work into a profession inevitably resulted in the adoption of a professional mystique, underpinned by a belief in élite insights and unassailable judgements, and informed by notions of superior social and intellectual status. All of these serve to validate the imposition of theories and practices, often based on false premises and wrong 'diagnoses', which are tantamount to an abuse of human rights. A huge rift already exists between the perceptions cherished by social workers about their role in society, and those held by the people on the receiving end of the service. The rift can only widen as social divisions and inequalities increase, and social workers expand their activities of policing civilians on behalf of the state, employing values and judgements which serve best the needs of a ruling minority. According to this scenario, the client who fails to co-operate, or who even rebels, is in so doing seen to confirm ownership of the anarchic proclivities requiring intervention in the first place. I suspect much of the profession's current malaise lies in the dichotomy between what social workers believe they would never do, and what they do most of the time – the irreconcilable conflict between professional perception and harsh reality.

Bad practice

Bad practice is not necessarily abuse, and abuse does not begin and end with overt physical or sexual assaults, but where one leads the other tends to follow, the consequence of carelessness and lack of respect for the rights of others. Bad practices arise from poor attitudes and the absence of financial and moral investment, and because they are endemic, they appear to be inescapable and inevitable. One of the most pernicious examples of bad childcare is the failure to maintain continuity of formal education. Many schools are quick to exclude children in care because of their presumed disruptive potential, and it is not unusual for children to go from school to school as they go from one placement to another, or even to be denied access to mainstream schooling for years on end. The consequences of little or no education for already disadvantaged children cannot be overstated, both in personal terms and in societal ones.

Another example of bad practice, from the child's perspective, is the indeterminacy of time in care. Many children, whether they are offenders or not, view committal to care as a sentence, but one without an end in sight, where all decisions about the future are dictated by remote authority. They generally have no idea when, under what circumstances, or even if they will ever return home, and even when conditions have been specified, social workers are prone to shifting the goalposts at whim. Children who take up offending, or who persist in re-offending, may only be trying to exchange a seeming eternity in care for a fixed term in custody.

The labelling of individuals as 'problem people' effaces their individuality in favour of category, and the perceived public mood may contribute elsewhere than in the Venables/Thompson sentences to the attitudes underlying institutional abuses. An article in *The Times* (6 February 1995) on government proposals for young offenders, headlined '"House of Pain" regimes for youth offenders', cited a groundswell of popular opinion against 'soft' – and by definition ineffectual – management. The first 'boot camp', based on the American model, opened on 22 July 1996 at Thorn Cross. Few senior British police officers appeared to have any faith in the system (*Sunday Times*, 28 July 1996), and what we know of the boot-camp regime suggests that it is inherently unethical, constituting the kind of practice that was so forcefully condemned by the UN Committee on the Rights of the Child. There is no hard evidence of any benefit to child or society in extremist reactionary policy. On the contrary, harnessing 'punishment' to 'treatment' encourages abuse and, at worst, replicates the appalling ethos of prison labour camps in the former Soviet Union.

The nature of abuse

He saw the blood and he gulped down savagery. Far from turning away, he fixed his eyes upon it. Without knowing what was happening,

he drank in madness . . . no longer the man who had come here but . . .
one of the crowd to which he had come.
(Aurelius Augustinus, AD354–430, *Alypius at the Gladiators' Fight*)

Child abuse, while of complex aetiology, is one band in the spectrum of
human behaviours – no more or less likely than other pathologies, and
not the exclusive preserve of the recognizable bad lot. Negligent and
apathetic management structures certainly aid the interests of abusers,
whether they are lone operators or part of a network, but policies thought
to be in the better interests of children, such as fostering, may also
contribute.

Informal fostering by extended families is as old as society. Fostering
as a formal childcare resource is a development of the last three decades,
and despite consistently high and unresearched failure rates, remains
ideologically preferable to institutional care, which it was expected in
the main to replace. Fostering is also, of course, much the cheaper
option. Residential resources have been systematically reduced, but the
expected pool of properly trained, equipped and supported foster families never materialized. In many areas, the sector is overcrowded, under-
resourced and poorly managed – factors which contribute to failure and
to the frustration and anxiety which can lead to foster-child abuse.
Another factor underlying failure lies in the dichotomy between social
worker and client perceptions – many children find an insupportable
emotional burden attached to a foster placement, where repudiation of
the natural family must take place in order to accommodate the goodwill
of the 'new' parents.

A more sinister risk may be posed by people who offer befriending to
foster children, and who as neighbours or acquaintances of the foster
family are unlikely to be vetted rigorously, if at all. The spotlight on
institutions as a magnet for abusers pushes the abusers into more shad-
owy areas, where diversified and disseminated control and supervision
are more accommodating to their stealthy infiltration. Their persistence
in seeking children to abuse is wholly predictable if paedophilia is the
compulsive sickness it is said to be. The Dunblane Inquiry clearly
showed Thomas Hamilton's attempts to infiltrate the Scout movement
when he was denied access to children elsewhere.

There are many misconceptions about child abuse, including the
commonly held notion that only sexual abuse is inherently damaging
and pathological. Physical abuse in some form or another is seen as
inevitable, and even naturally occurring, particularly where men and
boys interact. Yet some children in care have come to fear for their
lives, and are the victims of physical abuses that are clearly sadistic in
conception and execution, and handed out by power-crazed and brutal
individuals at their most rabid and uncontrolled, like their forerunners
in the Nazi concentration camps. Children go missing from care with

depressing regularity, and some of those who are never seen again may well be the victims of physical abuses which went one step too far and ended in murder.

Children uniquely experience abuse, and are uniquely affected, although the reported abuses are depressingly routine and repetitive. Possible variations on a theme of sex or cruelty tend to be self-limiting, as Alypius and his friends in the Coliseum audience discovered, with their appetite for excess becoming progressively more easily sated. When novelty deserted the presentation of death and depravity, the audience, now bored, voted with its feet.

Boredom may underlie ritual abuse, the still taboo subject which provokes such extreme scepticism and which, hedged about as it usually is with talk of Satanism, is often dismissed as the output of fevered imagination. Serving to confuse the issue of child abuse in all its guises, the dramas in Cleveland and the Orkney Islands left a very bad taste and a general impression of professional hysteria creating a mountain out of a molehill. None the less, and disregarding the over-zealous reliance on flawed diagnostic tools, there was at least a molehill of abused children in Cleveland, and we shall never know if our scepticism protected abusers in an isolated island community. Like a Coliseum audience, child abusers want thrills to offset boredom, and dressing up is one way of creating novelty and reinforcing a fantasy. Adopting the panoply and ritual of cultism is another, for child abuse – whether sexual or physical – involves obsessive and ritualistic behaviour patterns designed around a specific and predictable outcome, without which satisfaction is impossible.

The nature of institutions

Sed quis custodiet ipsos custodes? [But who guards the guards?]
(Juvenal, AD60–130)

The low status of children in the UK is reinforced by socialization techniques which draw heavily on violence and humiliation. It comes as no surprise, then, to find childcare institutions rife with their companion excesses.

In the artificially created environment of a foster home or children's home, the adult carers have defined roles and come armed with resources to meet defined needs. They are subject to specific expectations from the managing authority, which is in turn expected to serve the needs of society and statute. The institutional ethos is designed to endorse and reflect these external requirements, but institutions are societies in themselves, secluded and secret from the outside world. Some distortion of attitude is inevitable in such environments, and ethical boundaries will be more easily breached. The judgement of those within shifts constantly, coming to view what would clearly be seen elsewhere as bad practice or abuse as something peculiar to, and permissible within, its own setting. These twisted perspectives are by no means the exclusive property of the adults – children are quick to absorb the atmosphere around them, as are outsiders with whom they come into contact.

An overview of institutions where regimes are underpinned by hidden agendas of unethical practices and physical and sexual abuse, known of but unacknowledged by children and staff alike, shows patterns of behaviour that we still fail to recognize as danger signals. The children, forced to inhale foul air, probably unconsciously ape the activities of adults and create yet another hidden agenda within their own group, subjecting their peers to serious physical assaults only in part because staff encourage peer group control to make life easier. Some children also suffer peer sexual abuse. The founding premise of intensive intervention with misdirected youth relies on the fact that children are generally malleable and easily influenced. If denied access to counterbalancing values, children incarcerated with violence and depravity become violent and depraved. Indeed, their survival may depend upon it, and it is not surprising when, after this kind of long and painful apprenticeship, they spend adult life repeating what they have learned.

Staff appear disaffected, and some may express hatred for their work and contempt for their charges. Low morale is further fuelled by uncertainty, poor leadership and, crucially, by the hidden agendas operated by the abusers. Staff engage in avoidance and diversionary tactics, to minimize contact both with children and with the abusers, whom they see as exercising powers which are not open to challenge. Rather than face their own ineptitude and a long-standing and indissoluble dilemma, they spend time engaged in domestic or non-confrontational activity, stretching tasks to fill their shift, or shuffling papers behind locked doors. Perversely, the children come to be seen as the cause of all that ails the staff, and suffer as a consequence. They may be neglected, ill-fed and clothed, dirty and infested, or conversely, excessively regimented and thoroughly depersonalized. Generally, expressions of distress from children are either ignored or regarded as manipulative, while self-destructive behaviour such as solvent addiction, or even genuine suicide attempts, is viewed as an assault on the peace of mind of staff and on the controlling ethos. Little more than human warehouses, these institutions are dominated by a malaise that is generated by the conflict between fickle conscience and acquiescence – most people cannot tacitly condone serious wrongdoing beyond a certain point without a heavy toll on their own equilibrium.

Whether received by insiders or outsiders, allegations from children in care invariably provoke enormous suspicion, all statements other than admissions of wrongdoing being rendered suspect by the child's status. Physical injuries are 'explained' by reference to mishap, foolhardiness, enforced restraint and wilful self-infliction, at times so plausibly that investigators may come to believe that the child 'deserved' or 'encouraged' whatever took place. Utting found that children who absconded from abusive institutions were continually returned to the abusers' care, even if allegations had been made to police officers.

The psychology of denial affects all participants in the transaction of abuse, because abuse engenders terror, guilt, shame, rage, violence, isolation, sadness, deep self-hatred, destruction of self-esteem, survivor-guilt and disbelief in everyone it touches, either directly or indirectly, exposing the shared darkness of the human psyche. Given the wrong circumstances, the wrong leadership and the wrong freedoms, we are all capable of excesses of wickedness, but it is far more comforting to pretend that evil only exists on other shores and under other suns, rather than face the fact that it is alive and well in our own rainy backyard. Terry Waite has said that the most terrifying aspect of his period as a hostage was the uncertainty he faced day after day – moved blindfolded from place to place, he could not know whether he faced a simple change of cell, release, or a bullet in the brain. The psychology of terror relies on uncertainty and powerlessness, and there are horrible parallels between Waite's experiences and those of children in abusive environments. There are more gruesome parallels between the attitudes underlying abuse by European paedophiles of children in Third World countries, and those which regard boys in care as 'fresh meat' for the abuser's table. Like all flesh, such meat loses its flavour after a while, and finds its way into the swill-bin when new meat becomes available, for all abuse reduces its victims to a commodity.

Residential social work is traditionally a Cinderella service, badly paid and considered to be greatly inferior to field social work, which has always attracted the better qualified by its enhanced salaries and promotion prospects. Paradoxically, RSWs wield the greater power in their day-to-day contacts with clients, alongside an enhanced potential for good or ill. Without prejudging the conclusions of Sir Ronald Waterhouse, poor staff training, poor-quality recruits, poor pay scales, poor oversight, and ineffectual, naïve, corrupted or non-existent management will doubtless emerge as factors contributing to the disasters which befell children in North Wales.

The ethos of a children's home is determined by finance, politics, local needs, current ideology, sociology, psychology and penology, and it is usually left to inexperienced and poorly trained RSWs to implement these complex and often conflicting policies, and to create within their limitations an agenda for care in which the recalcitrant child is reformed, the damaged child is rehabilitated, and both are geared for return to open society. The intensity of these demands and the absence of enlightened guidance can disable even the most well-motivated RSW. Some collapse under the pressure, and pretending that the line of least resistance defines therapeutic freedom, let children run wild and into danger. Fred and Rosemary West targeted children's homes, knowing that little heed would be paid to missing inmates.

At the other extreme, convinced that without overt and implacable restraint children will automatically run amok, terrified RSWs worship at the altar of control, turning the home into a bloody battlefield, for control without a heart is a cruel thing. The siege mentality of institutionalization is the product of this fear, demolishing the boundaries between reasonable control and abuse. Many habitual practices, other than those concerned with the practicalities of group management, have evolved from the theoretical premise that without enforced obedience, anarchy rules. Self-determination and rational evaluations are impossible for RSWs enmeshed in the control machine, for they see themselves simultaneously fixed in the sights of out-of-control children and expecting a bullet in the neck from dissatisfied management.

Admission to care involves children in the loss of freedom, family, focus, purpose, privacy, independence, self-determination, identity and security. These are massive bereavements which cause grief and profound fear. What RSWs are encouraged to see as successful control gives no quarter to the antecedents of unrest and no opportunity to read the emotional atmosphere in which the children function. Interventions are crisis-driven and even panic-stricken, and punishment, the greatest weapon in the adult armoury, is fired indiscriminately at children who may be beside themselves with their own terrors, floundering and adrift in the uncharted waters of 'care', or simply opposing a genuine injustice – challenging behaviour is by no means proof of contumacy, and rebellion is sometimes a moral necessity. Human survival has depended on an ability to adapt constantly, and children will adapt to punishment. Then, apparently immune, and even wilfully provocative, they enter the downward spiral in which outright abuse becomes the last resort of inadequate adults overwhelmed by an eruption of anger, frustration and fear directed at the captives who caused their distress. Less dramatically, petty meanness and apathy govern the conduct of RSWs who have persuaded themselves and others that the children deserve what they get, and get only what they deserve. Overwrought and pathological behavioural patterns evolve stealthily in institutions, both careers and those being cared for reflecting each other until disentanglement of cause and effect is impossible, but such mutual reflections are an unsafe basis for judgements and decisions.

As isolated as their charges, and trying to keep abreast in their own uncharted waters, RSWs depend upon colleagues for support, guidance and protection in a hostile environment where few opportunities exist for evaluating day-to-day actions and reactions, or for making impartial judgements about whether these actions are moral, ethical, reasonable, constructive and legal. Analysis of practice, habits, routines and instructions is virtually unknown, the ethos of the institution being validated simply by its own existence. Despite being professionally qualified and widely experienced, I maintained practices that I now consider to be unreasonable and probably unethical, and certainly counter-productive in terms of child development, but which *appeared* to be necessary for the psychological and economic welfare of the institution. They sprang from the pervasive and chronic anxiety that total loss of control must follow upon ceding a little power to the children and, while they were trivial from an adult viewpoint, they were grossly detrimental to the children's quality of life, interfering with access to food, hot drinks, pocket money, clean clothes, soap, toothpaste, baths, outings and family contacts.

Within the staff group, the strongest personalities and not the most senior ones assume and exercise the greatest power, with others looking to them for instruction, assistance and permission in their own work. Those convicted of abuse in Leicestershire, Staffordshire and North Wales exercised their authority through a seductive yet menacing personality which exploited the inadequacies and goodwill of others and the frailties of the institutional structure. Received learning processes which are generated within and by the institution insidiously accommodate the changes which make abuse unremarked and unremarkable, almost casually redrawing the line between acceptable and aberrant, and writing up the new agenda for those whose own pathology is triumphant. Blind eyes, deaf ears and an almost infinite capacity for rationalization are common afflictions in abusive environments – even when people see and hear the evidence, they do not recognize what they see. When something happens and is condoned, and then happens again and again, they believe that there must be a valid reason, however unreasonable the occurrence – the learned response that anything can be seen as acceptable in its own context.

Denial is usually the first, and often the last, response to suspected malpractice on the part of colleagues in any profession, and social work is no exception. There is an enormous temptation to embrace any number of excuses, and to believe that the alleged wrongdoing is distortion, malice, exaggeration or blatant untruth. Vested interests contrive to prevent internal collapse of the institution, opportunistically settling old scores or repaying old debts in order to expel or compromise the threat. Common sense vanishes, and a consciousness peculiar to the environment comes to prevail, hardening resolve in the face of attack, eclipsing values, and wreaking untold damage upon the personalities that are colluding with each other to defend the indefensible.

The child

> The jury must bear in mind that the juvenile witnesses are not of good character.
>> (Crown Court judge summing up in child abuse trial in 1994)

> We seem to be incapable of doing anything about these vermin under the present system.
>> (Sir Gerard Vaughan, then Member for Reading, commenting on juvenile offenders in 1994)

As children rarely enter care of their own volition, but usually under duress, they are from the outset in conflict with the carers, for whom the control of potentially disruptive and dangerous children is the paramount consideration. Children isolated from the factors which previously moulded and sustained their sense of identity and self lose their power as individuals, as well as their status and even their humanity. Feelings of self-worth become so diminished that the child may appear to provoke treatment as a worthless, expendable object.

In abusive environments, the alliance of the child's own feelings of worthlessness and the sheer power of the abuser can be enough to inhibit disclosure. Where there are also threats of terrifying reprisal, children who are already familiar with the power wielded by the abuser and his colleagues perforce take them seriously, existing from day to day in an atmosphere of dread and hopelessness, and suffering profound and irreversible loss of trust in all adults. They may therefore deny abuse, appear to collude in suppressing allegations, or refuse to co-operate with investigations. Those who do speak out may display apathy and the emotionally flat responses which are misconstrued as evidence that victims were little affected by their experiences, or have recovered from them, feeding the misconception that child abuse is not intrinsically very damaging. Similar responses are found in prisoners of war, terrorist hostages and battered wives, and are characteristic of people forced to live with terror.

Undoubtedly, the disclosure and investigation of abuse cause untold stress, but counselling for the victim instead of prosecution of the alleged abuser is not the answer. Our adversarial system of justice is not kind to victims of institutional abuse, dragging up their past history to paint them as morally degenerate and, by extension, whitewashing the abusers as victims of criminal mischief, much as rape trials were once conducted. Prosecution of alleged child abuse had a high failure rate and a huge price tag, which no doubt influences decision-making by the Crown Prosecutions Service. In 1993, North Wales Police referred over 300 cases, of which less than 3 per cent proceeded, and those who had gathered up their courage to press charges found themselves abused yet again by the system.

Refusal to co-operate with a police investigation is viewed with great suspicion but, like rape victims, abused children harbour strong and long-lasting feelings of shame, convinced that at least some blame must attach to them. Young men who were sexually abused not uncommonly believe that disclosure will cause friends, family and sexual partners to label them as 'queer', while others, unable to live with themselves and their history, take their own lives. Many others, struggling to put some sort of life together, are haunted by guilt for their own survival, dogged by the unshakeable conviction that they bear some responsibility for what happened to their peers.

Admission to care opens a gulf between child and parents, enough in itself to inhibit confidences or demands, but on the rare occasions when children report abuse to their parents, and the parents inform the managing authority, the allegations are easily discredited – the child has too many obvious reasons for engineering removal from care, so the credibility of the authority and its officers prevails. Many children remain mute because they assume that their carers are invested with the right to do whatever their inclination might dictate, and that abuse, however horrific, must simply be endured.

Obstructing the whistleblower

> *Dans ce pays-ci il est bon de tuer de temps en temps un amiral pour encourager les autres* [In this country (Britain) it is thought well to kill an admiral from time to time to encourage the others].
>
> (Voltaire, 1694–1778, *Candide*)

Whether statutory, charitable or private, the organizations that manage children's homes are also institutions, and if potentially costly allegations of professional malpractice arise, the protection of the institutional body takes precedence. Individual components, whether an adult goaded to disclosure, or a child in need of protection, are sacrificed for the good of the whole, much as we remove a defective engine part or amputate a gangrenous limb.

In my experience, the identification and reporting of malpractice is thwarted by coercive and powerful mechanisms within local and central government, less formalized but none the less potent systems among practitioners themselves, the nature of children's placements, and the status and reputation of children in care. The credibility of these children is easily compromised. Where the risk of disclosure comes from an adult – a problem with few precedents in social work – history, according to Voltaire, points the way. In refusing to accept the unacceptable, I made myself unacceptable to employers and colleagues, some of whom shared my disquiet to the extent that they had earlier taken their own concerns to management. However, I was the only one to break out of the institutional edifice, to commit 'professional suicide', while others apparently relegated individual and collective ethics and sidestepped the mess I was creating on behalf of children who were generally regarded as intrinsically worthless.

From 1976 to 1980, I was deputy head of Gwynedd County Council's flagship assessment centre and, after professional training, I was head of a children's home from 1982 to 1987. From 1982 until its closure in 1984, I was also in charge of the intermediate treatment facility. Before 1981, oversight and line management depended on a small hierarchy involving a Homes Adviser, a Principal Officer and the Deputy Director.

From its inception in 1974, Gwynedd County Council, and certainly its social services department, were riven by old conflicts, historical clashes, and the political machinations of councillors and senior officers, to the inevitable detriment of services which were also under constant threat from financial cut-backs and imposed economies. The area previously administered by Gwynedd County Council is poor and underpopulated, with its half-starved underbelly hidden under a cloak of outstanding natural beauty. Local revenue is therefore low, and quality social services are very costly, especially where the community includes a high proportion of the frail and needy elderly. Financial support from the Welsh Office was probably never adequate, and while lack of funds and enforced cost-cutting do not constitute an excuse, they may partly explain the peculiar, probably irregular and certainly cheap oversight system which came to prevail after 1981 in the children's residential sector, and which in itself was crucial to the forces which took a stranglehold on that service. Total control was vested in one person, whose decisions were inviolate, and councillors and senior officers happily divested themselves of responsibility for residential childcare, either oblivious to or careless of the potential for corruption intrinsic to the arrangement – the maggot feeding on the apple core.

On behalf of central government, local authorities implement wideranging and powerful statutory tools, and must have in place regulatory mechanisms and safeguards. Internal reporting procedures usually pass responsibility to designated senior officers, and nationally agreed disciplinary procedures are designed to regulate staff suspected of criminal activity. Mechanisms and procedures only work where there is the will – without that will, as Utting shows, the best possible systems become impotent, and what should be effective security measures and safeguards are thoroughly undermined by complacency, incompetence and corruption.

Prompted by my discussions with a county councillor, the first police investigation in Gwynedd began in March 1986, and came to a halt some 6 months later, although much of the information about abuse obtained 6 years later by North Wales Police was probably available at this time. In October 1986, the police reported to Gwynedd's director of social services. She apparently made a conscious decision to ignore their advice, thus excluding the safety of children in care from the council's hierarchy of priorities. My own suspension occurred shortly afterwards, on the grounds that I had fabricated allegations of abuse and thus caused a breakdown in professional relationships. Dismissal was effected in November 1987, following a process of procedural and contractual breaches clearly designed for this one purpose, and over which even the then chief executive refused to exert authority. My fate, then, was not a knee-jerk response provoked by panic, but the calculated and determined excision of a problematic component of the institutional body. It also sent an unequivocal message to anyone else minded to follow my example. Professionally, I became as powerless as the children who unwittingly 'caused' my downfall yet, in the exception of nothing less than dismissal, I had moved psychologically beyond that point before its arrival.

I began lobbying the Welsh Office shortly after suspension, but without success, no doubt because my own position rendered all statements suspect, and because I was presented to agencies outside the council as the source and extent of abuse allegations – the parallels between my newly imposed status and that of children in care are striking. Dismissal released me from obligations to the council, and I decided to cast the net wider, taking my concerns again to the Secretary of State for Wales, and to the DSS Inspectorate in London, Margaret Thatcher, successive Health Ministers, the Home Office, the National Children's Bureau, where Peter Righton then held sway, and to any other organization which might be able to provoke a full investigation. Time and experience taught me to look for a way around the obstacles instead of trying to demolish them, but it was left to Harlech Television to take up the issue, and to produce a documentary which set out the facts. Without exception, other agencies and government departments, content to take the line of least resistance, felt no need – and certainly no moral obligation – to investigate independently and, like Alypius, were happy to become part of the crowd. Labelled a disruptive and deviant personality, just as children in care are labelled, and fool enough to stand apart from the crowd, I learned how quickly and easily it transforms itself into a pack.

Conclusion

> *Obsequium amicos veritas odium parit* [Deference begets friends, truth begets hatred].
>
> (Terence, CBC190–159, *Andria*)

Pressures from a multitude of sources influence decision-making at senior levels in local councils. The public, central government, insurers, unions, other agency professionals, and the councillors who constitute the local power base all have their own vested interests, which too easily outweigh all but the interests of expediency. Like police and probation officers, social workers face the risk of false allegations – hence the unwritten codes of silence, the rank-closing at times of crisis, and the covert structure built behind the public edifice. The recent history of institutional childcare tends to show that suppression of abuse allegations is the first and last response, and that one failure to address the issue with determination establishes a dangerous precedent and creates a conspiratorial environment into which successive administrations are sucked. In Gwynedd, the stances taken and the lines so publicly drawn since the first police investigation in 1986 caused untold damage, while the integrity of other government departments, agencies and individuals, who had the opportunity to act and did not do so, is permanently tarnished. During the 1991–1993 police investigation, the Welsh Office promised a public inquiry once any criminal prosecutions were over, but then reneged on that promise, and set Nicola Davies QC to undertake a paper exercise, barring her from taking witness evidence. We do not know what documents she saw, but she concluded that an inquiry would be of 'historic' interest only, and probably counter-productive. Ironically, the furore which then erupted over attempts to suppress a report commissioned by Clwyd County Council forced government into yet another U-turn[6].

My claim against Gwynedd County Council for unfair dismissal was settled out of court. Dismissal was withdrawn, and I received compensation and all legal expenses. *The Independent* (8 August 1994) discussed the issue of compensation for abuse victims, commenting on an absence of legal precedents, and on the insurers' perspectives, with Municipal Mutual (now Zurich Municipal) and the UK's major local council insurer, disputing liability. Potential claimants face a long, hard, uphill struggle before their cases are even likely to reach the stage of a court hearing, and many fall by the wayside, thwarted by delays which put their claim out of time, by dwindling Legal Aid funds, by lack of expertise in the legal profession, by a generally hostile climate, and by rulings in other cases which devolve upon their own. They may also be thwarted by collusive practices within the legal systems, for successful litigation will establish new precedents, elevate the moral rights of recipients of our childcare services, and emphasize the responsibilities of local councils and other service providers, creating an environment in which heavy financial penalties are the likely consequence of poor or negligent social service provision.

In the same edition, *The Independent*'s leader article, under the heading of 'Investigations that could go too far', suggested that a guilty minority of RSWs had damaged the profession's reputation, and that most RSWs faced the constant dilemma of restraining their charges from acts of violence in a climate of fear that was in part due to the 1989 Children's Act having tipped the balance of rights too far in favour of young people.

Thousands of children in care already live in a climate of fear, without an atmospheric change in sight, condemned by fallacies about their violent potential and intrinsic brutishness. Violence can occur in response to intolerable stress, overwhelming terror or, as the nineteenth-century mental health reformer Samuel Tuke concluded, in self-defence or as a reply to violence from others. Misconceptions envelop children like weeds, encouraging the growth of preconception, and the proliferation of confusion, polarization and neurosis – the 'Us and Them' syndrome with a vengeance.

We generally assume that children in state care are safe by virtue of their situation, and are loath to discard the assumption, despite considerable evidence to the contrary. 'Safe' does not only mean protected from the more outrageous kinds of abuse, but also protected from disadvantage and avoidably impaired social and personal development. Few children who enter care, even for a short period, ever recover educational, social, personal and family ground. Many graduate to prison, suffer one broken relationship after another, and breed illegitimate children who themselves enter the care system. Most live in near poverty, on the edge of disaster, uneducated and unemployable, haunted by their own inadequacy and a pernicious sense of helplessness, and the incidence of suicide, mental illness, prostitution and addiction among this group is considerably higher than average. A significant number of those who were abused in care themselves become abusers – three in Gwynedd are currently serving life sentences for murder. Arguably, their circumstances and prospects would be no better had they been left to their own devices, but that is not the point – care is designed to be advantageous, not ineffectual or positively harmful.

The moral values of our society are demonstrated in the quality of institutional environments, yet too many who are on the receiving end of those values learn only of their absence or distortion. Removed from disordered and dysfunctional home circumstances, children find themselves imprisoned with chaos and anarchy, apathy and evil, with despair their only realistic prospect.

Human rights are not a commodity or privilege, and we believe that we have moved beyond the dark days when the mad, the bad, the poor and the helpless were denied even a toe-hold on the ladder of humanity. Ian Brady, whose rights could be regarded as forfeit to his crimes, has petitioned the European Court for restoration of his right to humane treatment, while Myra Hindley, who continues to excite outrage, has the same right as any prisoner to a ruling on parole. Those in our society who are unable to protect themselves have the right to humane, invariable and enforceable standards of care and control, and it might now be necessary to particularize in statute the conditions under which the childcare ideal might come within reach. Whatever enactments arise, and however much we set standards and parameters of conduct to counteract the downside of human nature, in the final analysis the responsibility for their enforcement and promotion devolves upon us all. The social work profession, charged with the protection of children, must find itself a moral centre, allow its members the right to be responsible for their actions, and face the great dilemma of members policing each other as well as its clients, and of discharging that responsibility in an honourable manner.

Endnotes

1. The chapter opens with a quote from Beethoven, more noted for his music than for his social commentary. Beethoven was himself savagely abused by his father, who tried and failed to create a child prodigy to succeed Mozart. In later life, Beethoven engaged in a protracted and acrimonious legal battle to wrest custody of his nephew Karl from the allegedly immoral Johanna, widow of his brother Caspar Carl. The opening quote comes from Beethoven's petition to the Imperial Court of Appeal of Lower Austria. (MS dated 7 January 1820 in the Deutsche Staatsbibliothek, Berlin). For an interesting and pre-Freudian psychological report on Karl, prepared for one of the custody hearings, see the Appeal of Jacob Hotschevar, dated 11 December 1818, quoted in full in *Beethoven and his Nephew* by Editha and Richard Sterba (1957, Dobson, London).
2. The reorganization of local government in Wales in April 1996 created new unitary councils which replaced the two-tier system to which the former Gwynedd and Clwyd County Councils belonged. Liability for the former county councils has been inherited by the unitary councils. Bryn Estyn Community Home in Wrexham closed in 1985. In the former Gwynedd County Council area, only two community homes now remain, some having disappeared during cost-cutting and rationalization initiatives. Gwynedd's assessment centre, opened in 1975, closed two decades later after its regime collapsed. The building has now been demolished.
3. The report by Sir William Utting was published on 19 November 1997, and is available from HMSO.
4. The terms 'child' and 'children' refer to any minor. The term 'social worker' refers to generic or specialist workers in the field, and the

term 'RSW' refers to residential social workers or residential child care officers.

5. The analysis of pre-placement interventions on a sample group of boys resident in a Welsh Regional Plan resource can be found in an unpublished paper by Alison Taylor entitled 'Perceptions of Care'.

6. The document known as the 'Jillings Report' is an unpublished report commissioned by Clwyd County Council, which was completed early in 1996 by a panel chaired by John Jillings, former Director of Social Services for Derbyshire.

3

The experience of a watchdog group

Sue Amphlett

Parents Against INjustice (PAIN) is the national charity that specializes in providing advice and support to those who state that they have been mistakenly involved in investigations of alleged child abuse. I shall give a short background to PAIN and then address some of the concerns about, and pose possible solutions to, the poor practices of professionals and practitioners, as perceived and voiced by children, parents, family members and others, who become involved in enquiries or investigations of alleged child abuse or neglect. I can only address some of the practical outcomes experienced by families here, and I shall not be able to consider many other issues, including political agendas, resource implications, demographic considerations or the role of the media. I shall only be addressing the question of whistleblowing as it applies to our members. I wish to acknowledge the important work that is carried out on a daily basis by child care workers who are supporting children and families and enabling them to stay together. I also fully acknowledge that children abuse is a very serious social problem and that everything – within the limits of ethics, due process and accountability – must be done to deal with it effectively. It also needs to be recognized that parents who are wrongly accused of abuse or neglect or mistakenly thought to have abused or neglected a child do not stand in isolation. Their children will have been interviewed, examined (sometimes intimately), have had their names placed on a child protection register and, in some instances, have been removed from their homes. These children need 'protection from abuse', too. What follows from this is the necessity of a means of ensuring due process and support, so that both categories of children are protected.

Having said this, it is probable that some child care workers will find what I have to say harsh, and some may wish to believe that it is untrue. My role is to highlight what I know personally to be the inadequacies within the system.

Introduction

PAIN was set up in 1985 after a couple became involved with the child protection system when, over a period of months, their youngest child sustained a series of fractures and accidental scalds to her feet. Her own name and her older sister's name were placed on the Child Abuse Register, as it was called at the time. The youngest daughter was subsequently diagnosed as suffering from mild brittle bone disease. In the meantime the couple lived in constant fear that their children could be taken away from them at any moment. They felt isolated, marginalized and powerless throughout the investigative process, which included being questioned by the police. Their distress completely overwhelmed them, and 11 years later they are still coping with the deleterious effects experienced by their children and themselves. They reasoned that if they, as articulate and literate people, felt so powerless within the process then the effect upon others less fortunate than themselves was likely to be at least as traumatic, if not more so.

Accordingly, they set up the PAIN organization, which during a 10-year period has become a national charity with a unique brief. Its policies are determined by a board of trustees and it employs four full-time workers and one part-time worker. It has three main strands to its work. The first is to provide a telephone and face-to-face advisory and support service for those involved in the enquiry or investigative system of alleged abuse. The second objective is to collate the information gathered from these cases in order to influence procedure, practice, policy and law at local and national levels. The third objective is to educate and inform the media and the public about the investigative process of alleged child abuse and child protection procedures. During its development the brief of the organization changed from that of solely supporting parents and children to include all those who work or are involved with children, e.g. residential social workers, teachers, health visitors, nannies, childminders, nursery staff, school bus drivers and school caretakers. Any of these people can find – and indeed have found – themselves involved in concerns that have been raised about their involvement with a child; 10 per cent of our cases arise from this source. PAIN advises and supports approximately 900 new families or professional workers annually, and supports a further 2500 cases every year who are currently involved with some level of the administrative or legal investigative process.

Who is the whistleblower?

Many people assume that whistleblowing is about one professional or practitioner sounding the alarm bell about his or her organization or the practice of another professional or practitioner. It could be argued, however, that whistleblowing is not only about one worker's concern about another, but that it is also about how the government, its agencies and its managers and workers can be *made accountable* to the individuals on the receiving end of its services or actions. At another level such bodies must also be accountable to society as a whole.

The public is often unaware of any problems within such bodies unless, for example, these are brought to its attention by the media, for one reason or another. It is often only when the joint experiences of those on the receiving end of services or actions are highlighted that we, the public, even recognize that there might be a problem that could affect us all. Many individual experiences of maladministration, negligence or poor practice are not publicly identified, and the few cases which do come to light then appear to be isolated instances.

Long before PAIN was established there will, without doubt, have been thousands of instances when individuals were dissatisfied about the treatment that they received at the hands of a social services department or another child care agency. Some will have attempted to blow the whistle. A very small number will have been successful, either by suing for negligence or by taking a case to the ombudsman, to a judicial review or to the European Court of Human Rights. Most will have found themselves overpowered by the whole process and its damaging effects, and they and their cases will have sunk into oblivion. Only in exceptional circumstances such as Cleveland, Rochdale, Orkney, Ayrshire and Bishop's Auckland – where families became aware of other families in similar circumstances and banded together – were they able to persuade the media that there were issues of national importance that needed to be identified, which then led to national inquiries and open court judgements.

Those who come to PAIN for help say, almost without exception, that 'somebody has to be held *responsible* for what has happened to us – not just for us – but also so that it doesn't happen to someone else'. These families struggle to gain accountability from workers. Accountability means binding one to give an account of one's action or justification of what one has done (or not done). Whistleblowing – which is the process of making one's concerns public – is important for families if they are to achieve their second aim, namely that of preventing the same thing from happening to anyone else. What they discover in their efforts to hold 'someone' accountable is that it is usually a fruitless, thankless, frustrating and time-consuming task. Furthermore, such action is often interpreted by workers as being unco-operative and indicative of the fact that they have something to hide. In some instances complaints are upheld and recommendations are made about improvements to procedure and practice. We are sometimes left wondering how often such changes are put into practice.

We have anecdotal evidence to show that the recommended improvements are often not implemented. The evidence arises from our work with three families, living within the same local authority, who came to us within a 5-year period. In the first instance we supported parents through a complaints procedure. They complained about:

- lack of proper consultation throughout the investigative process;
- a failure to provide them with written material about procedure, practice, process and law;
- a failure to involve them fully throughout child protection conferences;
- a failure to carry out a proper investigation of their case.

The local authority upheld their complaint and wrote them a letter thanking them for pointing out the failures within the system. They reassured them that these failures would not occur again. Three and five years later a second and third family made identical complaints. Their complaints were also upheld, with similar reassurances being given that things would change. Clearly nothing had changed in the intervening years. Is this example an isolated one? It is impossible to know.

What is known, however, is that many of the instances of bad practice that were identified by Lord Justice Butler Sloss at the time of the Cleveland Inquiry in 1987 have been similarly identified during the Rochdale, Orkney, Bishop's Auckland and Ayrshire débâcles.

Lord Justice Butler Sloss says of the Orkney report:

> The report reveals a depressing and disturbing resemblance, four years on, to many of the criticisms made in the Cleveland Report. It was even more depressing to realize that no one in authority appeared to have read the earlier report, but no one seemed to have read or observed the comments on the Cleveland Report in serious publications which have been circulated since 1988.
>
> (Children in Scotland/National Children's Bureau, 1993, pp. 53–4)

Professor Stewart Asquith, speaking on the same occasion, said:

> There must inevitably be a sense of *déjà-vu* with regard to training in that many of the statements and proposals made by Lord Clyde in his report echo forcibly those made in the Cleveland Report. Lord Justice Butler Sloss, in expressing disappointment at the way in which lessons from Cleveland had not been taken on board, must surely have been speaking for many others.
>
> (Children in Scotland/National Children's Bureau, 1993, p. 98)

The poor practices identified in the above reports are no different to those described by hundreds of families across the country that PAIN hears from each and every year. PAIN uses the information gathered from these cases to illustrate such poor practices, thereby strengthening the argument for appropriate changes to be made at local and national levels. In effect we are acting as whistleblowers.

There is resistance to our claims about poor practice by some workers who either do not believe that such poor practice takes place, or cannot see the merit in such whistleblowing. This has been apparent in their attempts to trivialize our observations and recommendations. They have said, in general, 'Ah, but. . . . You (PAIN) only hear about the extreme cases. They are not representative of what really happens'. The above-mentioned reports, and our collaborative liaisons with local authorities and their workers, disprove that statement. Recently, however, there has been a sea change of professional opinion with regard to PAIN's view.

Daphne Statham, Director of the National Institute of Social Work (and one of the authors of Chapter 10) has stated:

> it is quite clear that while policy may have changed, thanks in large measure to the campaigning efforts of PAIN, practice has not. We still have to work out how to intervene in ways which are as constructive as possible for the family – whether or not abuse has happened. There are still lots of changes which need to take place in the system and having PAIN's voice come through and chart what has happened to the parents is extremely important.
>
> (cited in Siddall, 1996)

Brian Waller, chairperson of the Association of Directors of Social Services' Children and Families Committee stated:

> PAIN has prodded, poked and provoked Social Services Departments in an uncomfortable way. But, in the end, it was productive. PAIN made us think more carefully about the position of parents and that's a credit to them. Although at times it was seen as a thorn in the side of Social Services Departments we are now pleased that PAIN operated in the way it did.
>
> (cited in Siddall, 1996)

Phillip Noyes, Public Policy Director for the National Society for the Prevention of Cruelty to Children (NSPCC), said:

> PAIN responsibly filled a need which nobody else did and which local authorities can't by definition . . . its legacy will have been to convey that child protection systems are not just about service provision but also about justice.
>
> (cited in Siddall, 1996)

Rhonda Siddall said:

> The centrally driven new philosophy of partnership between families and Social Services Departments in child protection work owes a lot to

the campaigning and thinking of PAIN. ... Research evidence now shows that PAIN was right to press the points it did – as much as it did – in its formative years.

(Siddall, 1996)

The above statements about PAIN's influence were made only recently, in 1996. It is heart-warming to know that PAIN's view has percolated, if somewhat slowly, through to many quarters. Sadly, as this chapter shows, there are still many areas of practice that remain uninfluenced.

Accountability in inquiries or investigations

When a government or its agents undertake an intrusive action whilst carrying out their duties, it is incumbent upon them to establish proper checks and balances and to be accountable for their actions. Much of this chapter is based upon the government's failure in this regard.

The requirement to protect children from abuse or risk of abuse is not in question. Neither, would I imagine, is the requirement for a government body and its agents to be accountable for their actions, as stated above, particularly when such actions are of an intrusive nature with all the possible consequences to parents, children, siblings and other family members. The process used to identify and protect abused children is the 'child protection system'. Subsequent to the identification of a child who has been abused or is at serious risk of abuse, various actions are taken which may include registration and, sometimes, the removal of a child into care, or conversely the removal of an 'alleged' abuser from the home. Welfare and support services should then be provided in order to serve the best interests of the child in the future. A complicated and multi-agency process of investigation takes place in order to determine whether a child requires protection from abuse or risk of abuse. PAIN has drawn up its own definition of investigations of alleged abuse or neglect, since no such definition has been established at national level. It is as follows.

Investigation of alleged child abuse or neglect is the systematic process by which facts and opinions are collected, recorded and analysed ...

- by multi-agency child care professionals and practitioners
- from the child, his or her parents/family members, foster carers and other carers in his or her educational/social environment
- up to and including civil child care/criminal court proceedings
- inclusive of child protection conference and registration procedures or to the point at which a decision is made to take no further action

. . . in order to determine if a child is at risk or has been abused.

It is this process of investigation that many of our members are experiencing. The accountability of a local authority for the outcome of this process will, or should, continue long after this investigative process has taken place. I propose to examine, in relation to the above process, where the need for accountability arises and where it is not being properly addressed. I shall do so under the following five headings. A government body or its agencies responsible for the protection of children should account for their actions in relation to the:

1. determination of policies – taking into account research findings;
2. implementation of laws and procedures;
3. systems that it makes available to its clients for appeals and complaints;
4. evaluation and monitoring systems;
5. support and reparation services that it affords to its clients.

Determination of policies

I shall consider two main areas of concern: (1) a lack of strategic management at government level and (2) the inequalities of the legal aid system.

Lack of strategic management at government level

It is incumbent upon a government to develop effective management strategies, particularly when its agents are charged with carrying out interventionist procedures. Such strategic management must concern itself with developing policies which recognize that many families find the process of intervention to be traumatic, irrespective of the outcome.

If a child has been abused or is deemed to be at risk of significant harm, the Children Act 1989 and its accompanying regulations govern the subsequent actions to be taken and the various supports that are available to the child and his or her family. If, however, it is determined that the child does not require child protection action to be taken, little or no support is given to the families. Furthermore, most workers believe that such a determination is the end of the process. This is irrespective of the fact that court proceedings may have taken place, often with the child being in care during this time. For the family it is not the end of the process. It is usually the start of a whole new set of problems. Prosser (1992), in his evaluative report of 30 families who claimed to have been falsely accused, reported that:

> All families described the stress caused by continuous suspicion. They felt surrounded by 'Chinese whispers' and comments like 'there's no smoke without fire' were being made as they passed. Even many years on families found not guilty in court say they felt stigmatized and unable to 'prove' their innocence.
>
> (Prosser, 1992, p. 18)

We have also observed, perhaps surprisingly, that the amount of trauma experienced by children and families when a child has *not* been removed into care can be as great as when the child has been removed. This seems to be because, in instances involving the courts, the children and families feel that their voice has at least been heard and their views properly considered. In instances where there are no court proceedings, but where there was some level of investigation taking place, which may have included child protection conferences and registration, the families experienced a strong sense of injustice and felt that their civil liberties had been infringed. I have commented previously:

> Make no mistake, the investigative process is traumatic to most children, parents and family members no matter how well and empathetically it may be carried out. It engenders overwhelming feelings of loss of self-esteem and self-respect – which is particularly devastating to those who have little of either to begin with – it makes people feel insecure about their parenting abilities and their ability to protect and care for their children, for years afterwards.
>
> (Amphlett, 1994)

It is clear that children, parents and families who have been thus traumatized should be identified by the authorities, their needs should be recognized, and suitable support should be offered to them in their efforts to put their lives back together. This is not happening. Why are these families not receiving the support that they require? One reason is that the government does not collate national statistics about the incidence of investigations of alleged abuse, or of its outcomes. Until 1988 the only figures that were kept about the numbers of children on child abuse or child protection registers were those that were held by the NSPCC, who were responsible for holding the registers in nine local authorities. These areas accounted for approximately 9 per cent of the child population. Their figures were then extrapolated to describe what was happening in the rest of the country. Even if the 9 per cent of the child population could be said to be representative, this was clearly unacceptable. In 1988 the Department of Health instructed all local authorities throughout England and Wales to collate the numbers of children on their registers. These figures reflect those children who are deemed to be at risk or to have been abused, for whom there are unresolved child protection issues, and who are currently the subject of an inter-agency child protection plan. They are not an accurate or complete reflection of all abused children, because there are a number of children living at home who have been abused previously but who are no longer considered to be at risk, and who are therefore not registered. Conversely, based on our case-history experience, there are children on the register who have neither been abused nor are at risk of abuse, who have nevertheless been registered because workers have wrongly deemed them to be so. Finally, children who are abused will not be identified, and they are therefore not registered.

What is not collated is how many families have been investigated prior to the point of registration. PAIN has always maintained that there are more families being subjected to the process of investigation when, in reality, the child has not been abused, than there are families being investigated when the child does require protection or is at significant risk of abuse. However, the lack of national statistics allows many child care workers to continue with their assumptions that most of the families who are in the investigative system are there because abuse has occurred or because there is a significant risk of abuse.

This assumption justifies all manner of over-reactionary behaviour, including *not* believing children who say that they have not been abused. Of the cases handled by PAIN, 88 per cent arise not because the child has made an allegation, but rather because of what we call 'perceived' abuse. This is when someone else is concerned about possible abuse because of something they thought the child said, the way in which the child appeared to be behaving, because a third party says the child is being abused, or because signs and symptoms are present that may indicate abuse. In many of these instances the child says nothing at interview to cause alarm, and often states quite clearly that 'nothing has happened' and 'why are you asking me these questions?' At this point many workers believe that the child is lying or in denial. Concern about this issue has also been voiced by Lord Justice Butler Sloss:

> I wonder why it is that some of the most caring people interviewing children believe the child who says that something has happened, but are not prepared to believe the child who says that nothing has happened. Aren't they entitled to the same degree of listening whether it is yes or no? But there are all too many people now in the United Kingdom who only believe that which is said has happened and not that which has not.
> (Children in Scotland/National Children's Bureau, 1993, p. 56)

In 1995 the Department of Health (DoH) published *Child Protection – Messages from Research*, which incorporated some 20 pieces of research that focused on the investigative process and the child care and child protection system (Department of Health, 1995). One of these pieces of research, already published, has looked specifically at operating the child protection system within eight sample local authorities. It acknowledges that up until this point the government and its agencies had not considered the question of whether cases were 'founded' or 'unfounded': 'Before describing the way in which referred children were handled in the eight sample authorities we must confront the difficult problem of the "truth" or "falsity" of these reputed concerns. This issue has largely been left to parent self-help groups in this country' (Gibbons *et al.*, 1995, p. 47).

The DoH overview research report has estimated the numbers of families involved in the various stages of investigations or enquiries about suspected child abuse: 'Of the 11 million children, in England and Wales, some 160 000 investigations were taking place each year' (Department of Health, 1995, p. 28). Gibbons *et al.* state that 'about a quarter of families disappeared from the system at an (early) stage ... these families would normally know nothing about the allegation. ... After investigation another 50 per cent of the families referred left the system [prior to the initial child protection conference]' (Gibbons *et al.*, 1995, p. 80).

Hence 75 per cent of the investigations carried out did not lead to a child protection conference being held. Of the 25 per cent that did, a further 12 per cent did not lead to the child's name being placed on the child protection register. In effect, in 87 per cent of the investigations the children involved were not deemed to require and did not receive child protection action.

The researchers concluded:

> Some six out of every seven children who entered the child protection system were filtered out without needing to be placed on the child protection register. This represents an enormous burden of work for hard-pressed community services and also means that far too many families are left feeling 'unjustly' accused.
>
> (Gibbons *et al.*, 1995, p. 78)

Child Protection – Messages from Research merely classifies the 87 per cent of children who were weeded out of the system without child protection action being deemed necessary as 'unsubstantiated' (Department of Health, 1995, p. 26). This, in my view, is a far cry from having the case against one deemed 'unfounded'. It may be true, as is claimed by the researchers, that within the 87 per cent of cases there were some children whom workers felt sure had been abused, but there was insufficient evidence or information to demonstrate that this was the case. In other instances, it was impossible to show one way or another what had happened, thus leading to the use of the term 'unsubstantiated'. However, as we well know, there are instances – possibly many – where, for example, undiagnosed underlying medical conditions, wrongly diagnosed injuries or illnesses, inaccurate passing on or recording of information and malicious or false allegations lead to children and families becoming embroiled in the investigative process. They should be entitled to have their cases deemed 'unfounded' with clear exoneration of all concerned. Very rarely do local authorities make such acknowledgements – perhaps because of the fear of litigation or of being called to account in some other way – and certainly there is no right to the destruction of records, which is what most families want. I find the government's reluctance to address the issue of unfounded cases to be reprehensible in a so-called just and fair society, and to be an infringement of natural justice of one's right to protect one's reputation – yet another example of how difficult it is to make the government and child protection workers accountable for their actions.

The research has counted only the children involved, but in reality the total numbers of individuals involved will be considerably greater. They will include parents, step-parents, cohabitees, foster-carers, siblings, aunts, uncles and grandparents. In terms of human misery, then, there are many hundreds of thousands of people involved on an annual basis. We should remember, too, that the numbers of children on the register decreased considerably soon after the Children Act 1989 came into force, and were at their lowest level at the time when the research was carried out. Since that time the numbers on the register have risen to pre-Children Act levels. In reality, therefore, the number of investigations that have taken place in 1995 will be far greater than 160 000 annually, as predicted by the researchers. Using the mathematics described by the researchers, in the filter system of investigations previously described, it is probable that in 1995 alone approximately 200 000 children were involved in the investigative process. Adding a conservative estimate of five other family members similarly involved, the total number of people involved will have been approximately 1.2 million.

One reason why there is such a large investigative trawl is that many local authorities have not established effective gatekeeping policies. I have described gatekeeping in the following terms.

> The process by which child care teams should decide:
> - whether a case will or will not be investigated, i.e. whether it has reached the threshold criteria for intervention as required by the Children Act 1989;
> - how far into the process a case proceeds;
> - how its human and financial resources will be used;
> - evaluation of the use of resources by the collation of statistics.
> (Amphlett, 1992, pp. 25–32)

The Children Act 1989 defines the local authorities' duty to investigate as follows:

Where a local authority
- (a) are informed that a child who lives, or is found, in their area:
  - (i) is the subject of an emergency protection order; or
  - (ii) is in police protection; or
- (b) have reasonable cause to suspect that a child who lives or is found in their area is suffering or is likely to suffer significant harm.

(HMSO, 1989)

Many of our families report that they have been told by their social workers, 'we must investigate everything that comes to the department'. Clearly the threshold criteria for intervention are being applied at a much lower level than that required by the Children Act 1989. It is hardly surprising, therefore, that vast numbers of investigations are being carried out. This research validates PAIN's long held belief that an unnecessarily large investigative trawl is taking place in order to protect abused children.

Proposal: There must be a collation of national statistics of the incidence of enquiry or investigation of 'alleged' abuse cases with all its outcomes, including a proper determination of unfounded cases.

This will, I believe, do three things:

- It will show that there are too many child protection enquiries taking place, and also that better 'gatekeeping' policies are required and that the threshold criteria for investigations should be properly applied as required by the Children Act 1989.
- Carrying out fewer investigations will free up finite human and financial resources from this costly process. Such resources can then be used effectively for preventative and support work for those children who are in 'need'.
- It will alert the government, professionals and practitioners to the fact that many families require support and services during and subsequent to an intervention, and purely because of an intervention. Most importantly it will identify who they are, so that appropriate research can be carried out to identify what their needs are and what support and services they require.

Inequalities in the legal aid system

The Children Act 1989 Section 1(5) prohibits a court from making any order unless it is satisfied that the order will contribute positively to the child's welfare. Regrettably this principle – designed to improve the lot of the child – has inadvertently led to a greater number of families being disempowered by the investigative process. This is because many more investigations are taking place without legal intervention. Full legal aid becomes available to those with parental responsibility only at the point at which legal action is initiated by the local authority. Parents, children and families therefore often face this investigative process without the advice and support of a solicitor. Parents who need the advice of a solicitor have some options facing them, which I shall examine briefly.

The rules governing eligibility for legal aid are complicated and based on one's disposable income after deductions for tax, national insurance, provision for dependants, etc., and one's savings. People on income support automatically qualify. At the time of writing, those who have a disposable income of more than £6800 a year or who have savings of more than £6750 will not be eligible. People with disposable earnings or savings of less than these amounts will have to pay contributions towards legal aid costs.

It can be seen that the disqualifying or contribution levels are quite low and consequently many parents are not able to afford the services of a solicitor. Others, in order to avail themselves of the services of a solicitor, will use their savings or re-mortgage their properties. In addition to the services of a solicitor it may be necessary to pay for independent second medical and psychiatric opinions – a costly process. Families have told us of investigative processes that have cost them from £10 000 to £25 000, leaving them heavily in debt and sometimes bankrupt. The process may last for many months. I have previously commented:

> During this time interviews and examinations of children will take place as will interviews with parents, siblings and other family members; child protection conferences will have been held which may have resulted in registration; children may have been taken into care; alleged abusers will have been asked/told to leave their homes under so-called voluntary agreements; letters to social services departments, teachers, general practitioners and solicitors will have been written; reports will have been obtained and responded to; parents may have been attempting to obtain second medical and/or psychiatric opinions; the police may have been involved and interviews carried out, and the family may have been subjected to family assessments.
>
> (Amphlett, 1993)

During this time, parents and children will also need to know what are their rights. Parents will need to understand the term 'parental responsibility'. They will want to know whether they have a right to be with their children during examinations and interviews, and whether those questioning their children are properly trained and experienced so to do. They will want to know whether the correct specialist medical opinions have been sought or should be sought, what their rights are in relation to participation at conferences, whether interviews are being properly recorded, and whether they have right of access to them. They will also want to know whether they must comply with family assessments, whether to enter into voluntary agreements regarding the removal of the 'alleged' abuser, and so on.

Surely it cannot be right that a parent's ability to ensure that professionals, practitioners and child care workers are really acting in the best interests of their child is based upon whether or not that parent can afford to pay for legal advice. This is perhaps particularly evident when one remembers that in many instances the child has not, in fact, been abused, nor is he or she at risk of abuse. Furthermore, a family should not have to use its life-savings or put itself into debt – with the concomitant effects this has on the children – in order to protect itself against the misguided interventions of a government agency.

David Spicer, Assistant County Secretary to Nottingham County Council, has said:

> I feel that both the Cleveland Report and the Orkney Report really show the need for specialist child care and prosecution lawyers to be involved at the points where they really are going to be of most use to improve the quality of the work: that is, the beginning of the investigation and throughout the process.
>
> (Children in Scotland/National Children's Bureau, 1993, p. 62)

Proposal: Ideally legal aid should be made available to all parents and others with parental responsibility at the start of any investigative or enquiry process. The financial ramifications of this would clearly be prohibitive in view of the vast numbers of people subjected to the investigative process. Such a proposal is therefore unlikely to find favour. A second proposal is that funds should be made available to provide independent advice, advocacy and support for families undergoing the investigative process, at the start of the process and prior to legal action, if any is being taken, and throughout the process. Such independent advice could be provided by voluntary agencies. This service would engender a fair and equitable system for all children and families, irrespective of their means or capabilities or of the outcome of the investigation.

Implementation of laws and procedures

Under this heading I shall consider two main areas of concern: (1) the failure to empower families and (2) the guidance document on the inquiry or investigative process.

Failure to empower families

Probably the most effective way to disempower anyone is to keep them in the dark. Not only do you render them unable to *understand* what is happening, but you also prevent them from *contributing* to what is happening and, most effectively, you prevent them from *influencing* the outcome of what is happening.

A strikingly regular feature of distress displayed by most of the families that come to PAIN is their bewilderment and total lack of understanding about the process to which they are being subjected. In effect, they are living a nightmare in which their fears and terrors are exacerbated because very few of them receive any written information about what is, or should be, happening.

A government guidance document entitled *Working Together* (Department of Health and Social Security, 1988), which is still in force, places a requirement upon local authorities to tell parents the reason for their professional concern and to provide children, parents and families with comprehensive written and verbal information (Department of Health and Social Security, 1988, pp. 29–30). It demands that information be provided about procedure, practice, policy and law, about the process of child protection conferences and registration, the process of registration and complaints procedures, and about their right of ready access to Area Child Protection Committee guidelines (which govern the process at local levels.) Such information, it says, must be given at the start of the process. A later document, entitled *Working Together Under the Children Act* reiterates this guidance (Department of Health, 1991, pp. 8, 43, 44, 45). Our case-history statistics demonstrate that, 3 years after the Children Act 1989 was implemented, 85 per cent of our families do not receive written information about the process, 75 per cent receive nothing in writing about the child protection conference and registration processes, and 87 per cent receive nothing in writing about the complaints and representations procedure. Similarly, families are often told that their Area Child Protection Committee guidelines are confidential. One family was told that they could come into the social services department and read, it but that they were not allowed to photocopy it or to make any notes.

Working Together Under the Children Act, (Department of Health, 1991) reiterates an underpinning ethos of the Children Act 1989 – that working in partnership with children and families is essential. It is difficult to see how any real partnership can be achieved when families are so effectively disempowered by lack of information. Sadly, even in certain instances where local authorities have provided some written information, it has been so simplified and incomplete as to be rendered practically useless, and leaves many parents feeling patronized. Child protection processes are complicated and difficult to understand even for workers who receive training. For parents and families they are totally unknown and alien processes.

Working Together Under the Children Act (Department of Health, 1991) consolidates the previous guidance, *Working Together* (Department of Health and Social Security, 1988), and is issued under Section 7 of the Local Authority Social Services Act 1970, which requires local authorities in their social services functions to act under the general guidance of the Secretary of State. It does not have the full force of statute, but it should be complied with unless local circumstances indicate exceptional reasons which justify a variation. The onus is upon the family to challenge any variations. In my view, it is unreasonable to expect them to challenge their own local authority in order to determine, for example, why they have not been provided with written information. Furthermore, without prior knowledge of the existence of the Area Child Protection Committee guidelines or *Working Together*, they would not know that they should have been provided with the written information in the first place.

Proposal: We recommend that the sections of the Working Together *guidance, that refer to the duties upon local authorities to provide information – written or in any other suitable format – to children, parents and families, should be made statutory and enforceable.*

Guidance document on inquiry or investigative process

There is neither a code of practice nor a guidance document that details the way in which workers should carry out an inquiry or investigation into alleged abuse. This is despite the fact that local authority social workers have a statutory duty to investigate or to make enquiries (*The Children Act*, HMSO, 1989, s47). *Working Together* (Department of Health, 1991) does not give detailed guidance about the 'process' of making enquiries or carrying out investigations. It is, rather, more about the 'who' and 'how' of the multi-agency co-operation that is required in the protection of children, which is only one possible outcome of the investigative process.

A practice guide that details the proper and ethical manner in which enquiries or investigations should be carried out is long overdue. Parents, children, family members and others complain not so much about the fact that they were investigated, but rather about the way in which the investigation was carried out. Since currently there is no such guide, there is nothing tangible about which they can complain if they believe that bad practice has occurred.

The Department of Health informs us that they have no intention of producing such a guide. This is partly, we believe, because they want to move the emphasis away from the regulatory and controlling role of social services, and to draw attention to their caring and supportive role. This is particularly understandable in the light of the recent research which demonstrates that an unnecessary and massive investigative trawl is taking place (Department of Health, 1995). They want to persuade workers that a better way to proceed is by providing resources and services for families in the first instance and then – and only if absolutely necessary – to address child protection issues. In other words, the threshold criteria for intervention – because of possible child abuse concerns – should be applied as required by the Children Act 1989. There is resistance to this proposed practice by many Directors of Social Services, and perhaps understandably so. They feel that this will lead to an increased likelihood of children being left unprotected and possibly killed within the community, the responsibility for which will fall on their heads. We argue that, at present, a majority is being harmed during efforts to protect a minority. It should be no less acceptable to harm these children and their families than it is to leave children unprotected.

Whilst it will be better for workers to approach families with a view to offering services in a sympathetic way, there will still be a number of issues to resolve. First, at the point at which the concern arises that a child is in 'need' or may require protection, some level of information or evidence gathering will be necessary, whether it is called 'making an enquiry' or 'investigating'. Secondly, families have already told us that 'they (the workers) can call it what they like but to us it feels like being investigated,' because it is the process of gathering information that makes people feel that they are being investigated. So – call it what you will – this process has to be managed.

It is not sufficient to maintain that a guide, detailing the way in which investigations should be carried out, is not required on the grounds that all that is necessary is for workers to carry out the principles of good practice and to work in partnership with families. Herein lies the root of the problem. Social workers, in particular, are told that 'their client' is the 'child' and that 'their duty' is to 'act in the best interests of the child'. It is therefore not difficult to see why social workers receiving information that a child is being abused, or probably being abused, will find it difficult if not impossible sometimes to properly include children, parents and family members in the decision-making process, far less to consult properly with them about how the investigation will be carried out.

In recent years the European Court of Human Rights has found the UK government to be in breach of Articles 6 and 8 of the European Convention of Human Rights:

> Agencies need to be aware that the European Court of Human Rights, in finding the United Kingdom Government to be in breach of Articles Six and Eight of the European Convention of Human Rights in recent

child care cases, cited failure to involve the parents in decision-making as a factor in their judgements. . . . Parents should be informed or consulted at every stage of the investigation. . . . They should be invited, where practicable to attend part, or if appropriate the whole of case conferences.

(Department of Health and Social Security, 1988, p. 29)

These and many other examples demonstrate that good practice does not just happen because it is good practice. If it happens, this is because training, supervision and monitoring ensure that it happens, and these processes need to be governed by guidance.

Further resistance to such guidance comes from workers themselves who claim that it would restrict their professional judgement. I disagree. A guide would be concerned with the 'how' of a process and not primarily with its outcome – in other words, with 'how' the information or evidence is gathered and not primarily with the decisions that are made or the actions that are taken, although these may be indirectly affected. Furthermore, without a guide it is impossible for families to make workers accountable for their poor practice, for without it how will families know what is good practice?

As we have been unable to persuade the Department of Health to produce this guide, PAIN has initiated a two-stage project – now managed jointly with the National Institute for Social Work and the NSPCC – which involves a number of other national statutory and voluntary family and child care agencies on its steering committee. The first stage of the project has seen the publication of a book (Platt and Shemmings, 1996). This is the first time that the inquiry process has been considered in its own right and separately from the child protection process. The book reviewed the current position, and its various authors made recommendations intended to promote good practice. The Steering Committee brought together family members, professionals and practitioners in a series of meetings and workshops, the outcomes of which informed the authors' writing. In the second stage a practice guide for elected members, policy-makers, practice managers and front-line workers will be produced. Once again, the guide will draw on the experiences of families to underpin its practical recommendations and to draw the attention of its target audience to the needs of families during the investigative or inquiry process.

Systems for appeals and complaints

In this section I shall consider two areas of concern: (1) the failure to provide a multi-agency complaints system and (2) the failure to provide an independent arbitration and complaints body and family ombudsman.

A multi-agency complaints and appeals system

Most families tell us that they are not complaining about the fact that an investigation is being carried out, but rather about the way in which it is carried out. They recognize and accept that the apparent presenting problem or concern was at a level sufficient to warrant the concerns of workers. In general their complaints are about the following:

- the inadequate way in which the information or evidence has been sought, recorded and passed on;
- a failure to inform them properly and to include them in the various stages of the process;
- the misinformation that is held on records that influences decisions being made and actions being taken;
- their exclusion from conferences, either totally or in part;
- being denied the minutes of conferences, even when they have attended throughout;
- workers failing to listen to what they have to say;
- the selective use of information by workers to substantiate what they already believe;
- the view held by some workers, that parents are likely to be lying in any case.

How does a parent or a child make either an agency or an individual professional or practitioner responsible for their perceived failures? The answer is with extreme difficulty, if at all. The first problem is that the process of protection of children is a multi-agency function. Consequently, they have to deal with a number of child care agencies, not just one. They may have to take individual action through the separate complaints procedures of the police, the health authority, general practitioner committees, the education authority and/or the social services. The actions of any one, or all, of these authorities will nevertheless have overarching impacts upon the social service department whose staff are responsible for deciding what, if any, action should be taken, including legal proceedings. The process of handling one of these complaints, let alone a number of them, is frustrating, demoralizing and agonizingly drawn out. As one mother said to me recently, 'What is worse, is that you have to do it at a time when you're already mentally and physically exhausted'. Furthermore, no one body is responsible for managing the impact of one agency's action upon another. In addition, even if the complaint is upheld, it will not affect the decisions that have been made during the process because one is only entitled to make a complaint about maladministration of procedure, and not about the decisions that are reached. *Working Together* says of the Area Child Protection Committee (ACPC) – a multi-agency body:

Parents who wish to discuss or challenge a decision need to take it up in the first instance with the agency concerned. . . . It is not a matter for the inter-agency child protection conferences. Similarly, families who have a complaint about a particular agency service should take it up with the agency concerned. All agencies should ensure that they have clear procedures which will enable parents and children to pursue complaints. Local authorities are required by Section 26 of the Children Act to establish complaints procedures and parents should be provided with information about these procedures. Other agencies will have their own complaints procedures and complaints about a member or chair of conference should normally be made to the appropriate employing authority. ACPC procedures should cover the handling of complaints about a conference as such.

(Department of Health, 1991, pp. 44–5)

The same section also says that 'ACPCs could establish a special appeals procedure' or 'look to the procedure of the local authority as the lead agency.' Confusingly, it then goes on to say, in the same section, 'It is important however not to see the conference as in any sense a quasi-legal tribunal from which a right of appeal might be expected.'

Is there any other area in which a local authority can make a decision that is not open to challenge or appeal? Is it acceptable that this should be the case? I think not.

Proposal: There should be a multi-agency complaints system which has an overarching responsibility for addressing the complaints from each and every agency. The ACPCs should be responsible for establishing this complaints system. Decisions made by local authorities in respect of child protection conferences and registration should be able to be reviewed by means of an appeal system established under the auspices of the ACPC.

An independent arbitration and complaints process and family ombudsman

The process of complaints in relation to the law is governed by The Children Act 1989 (s26(3)). It relates to a child who is being looked after by them, or to a child who is in need. There is, however, no Complaints Procedure required under Part V of The Children Act – the part that deals with the emergency protection of children. Nor is there a statutory complaints procedure that deals with the non-legal phase of any investigation. Nevertheless, the local authority has the power in such circumstances to decide between two options. The parents may complain under The Children Act Complaints Procedure, in which an independent person, whose role it is to oversee the investigation of the complaint, is involved at the first stage. Alternatively, parents may only be allowed to pursue complaints under the Community Care Act, in which the independent person is not brought in until the second stage. The latter situation can clearly be disadvantageous, since what happens in the early stages of the investigation of the complaint is of prime importance.

The picture is confused even further when, as described above, some ACPCs have established their own complaints procedures as well as the complaints procedures established by each and every other individual child care agency, such as the police, and health and education authorities. Many of the families who have made complaints tell us that, in their view, their complaints were not properly addressed, nor were they properly investigated. From our experiences of reviewing the written complaints drawn up by parents and other family members, we believe that many of the complaints do not get past the first hurdle because they have not been couched in terms that are understood by workers, and because they do not refer to relevant guidance.

Complainants may go to other bodies or try to use other methods to make complaints, e.g. by complaining to the local government ombudsman or using judicial review to gain legal arbitration. However, they cannot complain to the ombudsman until they have exhausted all internal complaints procedures. By this stage it is usual for all but the most determined (and literate) to have fallen by the wayside.

When their complaints are not upheld, families say 'well they would say that, wouldn't they?' They argue that, in matters which are as fundamental as a family's right to privacy within their home life, any interference must not only be just and fair, it must be *seen* to be just and fair. They question whether such fairness can be guaranteed by the same agency or agencies that are responsible for the interference. They argue, too, that whilst there are bodies who are charged with guarding the best interests of the child, no one is charged with guarding the best interests of the family. Others have said that the efforts of various agencies to protect the best interests of the child have overridden the fundamental right of all parents to safeguard and protect their children themselves – sometimes from misguided and over-zealous professionals. There is also a feeling that some workers fail to see the importance of family life when they consider what are the best interests of a child. This feeling is endorsed to some extent by Lord Justice Butler Sloss, who said 'Would I be totally out of form to say that parents are human? Parents have rights, we ought to keep looking at the needs of children in the context of the family' (Children in Scotland/National Children's Bureau, 1993, p. 57).

They argue strongly for a person such as a family commissioner or ombudsman, who would work in conjunction with an independent arbitration and complaints body, and whose purpose would be to review complaints, provide arbitration and offer advocacy to assist family members – including children – in getting their complaints or concerns heard. This request is at variance with Recommendation 39 of the *Report of the National Commission of Inquiry into the Prevention of Child Abuse*, which stated that 'Commissioners for Children should be appointed for England, Scotland, Wales and Northern Ireland. In addition, in Recommendation 40 (ii) they state that 'the Minister with specific responsibility for children should be upgraded and entitled Minister of State and Minister for Children' (National Commission of Inquiry into the Prevention of Child Abuse, 1996, p. 127).

His or her functions would include reporting on the operation of UK legislation and developments relating to the implementation of the UN Convention on the Rights of the Child, chairing a ministerial committee for co-ordinating policies affecting children on which all relevant departments should be represented and presenting children's issues to the public and promoting the 'listening to children approach' (National Commission of Inquiry into the Prevention of Child Abuse, 1996, pp. 60, 61, 127).

Whilst we support the view in principle of supporting and promoting the welfare and well-being of children, we are concerned that the Commission has, or appears to have, ignored the fact that such provision is best made within their families. The Cleveland Inquiry Report repeatedly raised concerns (also found in other child death inquiry reports and research) that the child was viewed in isolation from his or her family. This led workers to draw the wrong conclusions about the best interests of children, such that they both inappropriately removed children from their families, with all the consequences of such action, and failed to remove others who subsequently died at the hands of their parents.

It is our view that children are best served within the provision of 'family', which receives little attention in this country, either in relation to its concept or with regard to legal or procedural support. A family commissioner or ombudsman would have a similar function to a children's commissioner, as proposed by the National Commission, but primarily in the wider context of the 'family' whilst also addressing specific concerns relating to children, parents and other family members.

There are a few families who, upon failing to get satisfaction through internal processes, will attempt to make agencies accountable for their actions by pursuing cases in the courts for negligence or malpractice. Many of these cases are pursued by families who are paying for this themselves. Frequently the cases are settled out of court and are conjoined with injunctions that prevent the parents or the children from publicizing their cases at any time in the future. The families usually accept the out-of-court payments because they have no more money to pursue their cases in court. It is understandable, therefore, that for most other families their only hope for a fair deal, as they see it, would be to have an independent arbitration and complaints body.

Proposal: There should be an independent arbitration and complaints body. Ideally this should be associated with a 'family commissioner or ombudsman' whose purpose would be to support and empower the integrity of family life in all its forms. Advocacy should be provided for those wishing to make complaints.

Evaluation and monitoring systems

In this section I shall consider two main issues: (1) the failure to identify the group and (2) worker accountability.

Failure to identify the group

In the discharge of their duties, the government and its agencies are required to monitor and evaluate their procedures and practices and their outcomes. We believe that our member group is not being included in such monitoring and evaluations. Why is this?

In the provision of community and child care services the collective term used for clients is 'users and carers'. The term 'users' relates to those who 'use' services, and the term 'carers' relates to those who not only 'use' services but also 'care' for those who 'use' services. These labels identify, among others, those with disabilities, mental health problems, special educational needs, drug abuse problems, AIDS sufferers, and the carers of those with these conditions. On examination it can be seen that these people are on the receiving end of the 'caring and supportive' role of government agencies. Our members, on the other hand, are on the receiving end of the 'regulatory and controlling' role of government agencies and, in particular, the regulatory and controlling role of social services in their statutory duty to protect children. Our members and others involved in the investigative process and child protection procedures are not readily identified by the terms 'users' and 'carers'. Certainly our families do not perceive themselves as 'users', but rather they perceive themselves as having something imposed upon them. Some people claim that our members are identified within the term 'users' and that this presents no problem. Contrary to this view, we have evidence to show that our member group is not being targeted in the early, and sometimes later, stages of audits that are being carried out at national levels.

I have recently been involved with two national working parties, one of which was managed under the auspices of the Department of Health and the Office of Public Management, and the other by the Department of Health and the National Institute for Social Work. The brief of the first working party was to audit 'users and carers' involvement in 'performance assessment' of social services departments. The second working party was to determine 'what service users and carers value and expect from social services staff'. At the time that I became involved, a considerable amount of steering work and consultation had already been carried out with various user and carer groups. The groups that had already been targeted did not include, in either project, parents or children involved in investigations of alleged abuse and child protection cases. Further to my involvement, the subsequent report produced by the Office of Public Management acknowledged:

> It is often difficult to identify who counts as a 'service user' or 'carer' and what is the best way for them to be involved. Some service users may be virtually invisible; others such as parents involved in child protection cases may be reluctant to make themselves known in public. It will be important to decide appropriate ways to consult and involve them.
>
> (Office of Public Management, 1994, p. 21)

Had such people been involved earlier in the process, I am sure that their influence on the final report would have been considerable. Consequently, I am not convinced that the term 'user' will, in itself, adequately identify those involved in investigations and child protection procedures.

Proposal: Our member group must be properly identified and included in monitoring and evaluation processes.

Worker accountability

Some of the complaints made by families relate to the practices of individual workers. These complaints are frequently centred around the way in which information is gathered, recorded and passed on. Parents tell us 'my social worker lied in court' or that he or she 'deliberately misled the court'. Usually, in our experience, these views arise not because the social worker really is lying, but because case histories have been inaccurately recorded and passed on. Social workers, in particular among all child care workers, receive little or no training in the collecting and recording of information. Our members say that social workers very rarely record case histories in writing when interviewing family members (unlike the police, for example). It will often be the case that they then visit a number of other families before returning to their desks to write up their notes. The probability of error occurring between hearing what has happened, as described by a family, and the subsequent recording of the information is high. *Working Together* states that 'Recording of such interviews (with parents and children) should be accurate and should differentiate between fact, hearsay and opinion. Accurate recording will play an important part in future planning and may need to be used in future court action' (Department of Health, 1991, p. 30).

Their records, then, are of prime importance when they draw up their reports, and the reports will be very influential in the decision-making and court processes. Social workers should be trained to record interviews properly, to validate the information they receive and to pass it on accurately.

The process of determining who is responsible for inaccurate and misleading information can be very difficult. Whilst there is the right of access to records, including social service records, there are particular problems in possible child abuse cases. These relate to information that is kept from those concerned, i.e. the parents or other family members, because it was received in confidence from third parties. Furthermore, workers are entitled not to release any information that they believe would be contrary to the best interests of the child should it be released (see Chapter 12 on freedom of information).

A second difficulty arises because social workers do not have a regulatory body to which they are accountable. There is therefore no official code of conduct which specifies the standards of practice and conduct that the public can expect, or to which an individual worker can be held accountable. Similarly, without such a regulatory body it is difficult to establish a standard level of competence across the country in relation to the practice social workers (see Chapter 10 on statutory regulation). The Central Council for Training and Education in Social Work (CCTESW) has also made recommendations to the government that social work training should be increased from 2 to 3 years and that an accreditation system should be established (see Chapter 9 on training).

Proposal: A General Social Services Council should be set up. There should be accreditation for social workers. A register should be set up of all social workers and social care staff. The initial training of social workers should be reviewed, as should their ongoing training and development.

Support and reparation services

Here I shall look at system abuse and make a final proposal. I shall consider the effects on children, parents and family members during and following the process of enquiry or investigation of alleged child abuse or neglect. There are many issues that could be considered within this section, including the 'perceived' right – as expressed by parents and children – that they are entitled to the destruction of records subsequent to an unfounded enquiry. It is only a 'perceived' right because records are not destroyed in most instances. Furthermore, many families experience extreme difficulty in merely obtaining an apology from social services departments. These difficulties contribute to the overall feelings of 'system abuse', as described below.

What is rarely recognized or understood by workers is that enormous damage is caused to children and families merely by the process of investigation or enquiry. We call this damage 'system abuse'. This phrase has been coined by us to describe the effects experienced by families, because families so often tell us that 'my child has been abused by the very system that set out to protect it. As a consequence so has my family'. The problems and feelings experienced by those involved include loss of self-esteem and self-respect, anger, resentment, fear, bitterness, anxiety, confusion, and lack of comprehension of what is happening and why it is happening, as well as sometimes the break-up of marriages and relationships, and financial and practical difficulties. Parents and grandparents have committed suicide, children and parents suffer long-term depression and anxiety, and children have problems establishing relationships with their peer groups, difficulties in coming to terms with puberty, and problems associated with coping with the disruption to their education caused by such a traumatic intrusion into their lives. I have already described this in the following terms:

> The damage to children is, at best, only containable and is usually, at worst, devastating. It spills over into puberty, the relationship with their parents and their siblings, their adult life, their subsequent contact with bureaucracies and all forms of their relationships. The effects on children who have been abused by the system are very similar to those experienced by children who have been abused by a human being. It is tragic and reprehensible that previously strong and stable families are often left weak and fragmented with children and parents alike suffering the consequences.
>
> (Amphlett, 1991)

Prosser writes of similar findings when evaluating the case studies of 30 families who claim to have been falsely accused:

> During our interviews many families referred to 'the system'. Initially it was considered that families were using the term to describe the 'faceless' quality of the various groups that formed the child protection agencies. When asked to explain the meaning of this term, many described feelings of powerlessness and impotence. Most families were able to articulate a clear set of impressions for which we use the umbrella term 'system abuse'. The nature of the evidence being used in proceedings and the processes by which it is acquired and used all seem to the parents to be part of a 'steam-roller' effect in which they are helpless and unheard victims.
>
> (Prosser, 1992)

He went on to describe the damage to family dynamics as follows:

> All data points to a new reserve and lack of trust in their lives.
> Fathers were distant from daughters and scared of any form of phys-
> ical closeness, lest it be misconstrued in some way, mothers avoided
> taking their children to the doctor or hospital because earlier visits
> had resulted in accusations of abuse; children felt unable to confide
> in parents or be close to them, perhaps because they felt parents had
> failed to protect them, perhaps because of what they had been told
> (or come to understand) of the accusations made against their
> parents; families attempted to heal themselves rather than seek help
> from supportive agencies; all families reported contempt (the term
> 'contempt' is used here to convey the overall feelings expressed;
> usually stronger, more aggressive terms were employed) for one or
> more of the agencies – social services, police, the medical
> profession.
>
> (Prosser, 1992)

Describing other effects on children following their experiences, he says,
'Two members of the Evaluation Unit experienced the sound of children
scampering around the house looking, so they told us later, for some-
where to hide. Strangers were equated with social workers and the threat
of removal by some children' (Prosser, 1992, pp. 18–20).

Platt, in posing the question 'Does it ever end?', states:

> Professional agencies working in child protection need to have a set
> task which is achievable, and which has a beginning, a middle, and an
> end. They must also understand that children and families cannot sim-
> ply move on, as professionals themselves do, to the next 'case'; they
> will live with their own 'case' for the rest of their lives. For some, the
> end of the enquiry marks a much-needed and welcome resolution of
> very serious family issues, or at least the beginning of such a resolu-
> tion. For others, to ask if the enquiry *ever* ends will meet with a
> resounding 'no'.
>
> (Platt and Shemmings, 1966, p. 263)

In the case described above the researchers were talking to the children and their parents a number of years after the child care workers had
walked out of their lives. No support had been offered to the family, and
the workers viewed the case as closed. Clearly it was not closed for the
children or their parents, and I suspect that it never will be.

*Proposal: Research should be undertaken into the effects, both short and
long term, upon children and families of the enquiry or investigative
process when abuse or neglect has not occurred. The type of reparation
and subsequent support that is required by children and families should
be identified and provided.*

Conclusions

There can be no greater need for justice and equity than within a system that allows the state to intervene in family life. In this chapter I have identified some of the areas where we feel that justice has yet to be done in the best interests of children and parents and their family life.

Our society will only be seen to be just in this regard when resources and services are made available to everyone to assist them in seeking fair adjudication of local authority decisions and proper redress of such decisions. Only then can child care agencies expect to be fully supported by the public and, in particular, by those children and families who are subsequently shown to have been unnecessarily involved in the system during their attempts to identify children who require protection.

References

Amphlett, S. (1991) (reprinted in 1994) *Working in partnership – coping with an investigation of alleged abuse or neglect.* Bishop's Stortford: Parents Against INjustice.

Amphlett, S. (1992) *System abuse and gatekeeping in partnership in child protection: the strategic management response.* Paper presented at Conference of the Office for Public Management and the National Institute for Social Work, London, 1992.

Amphlett, S. (1993) *Response to the Commission on Social Justice.* Bishop's Stortford: Parents Against INjustice.

Amphlett, S. (1994) *Secret suffering or false allegation? Recognising and appropriate reporting of alleged child abuse.* Bishop's Stortford: Parents Against INjustice.

Children in Scotland/The National Children's Bureau (1993) *Protecting children – Cleveland to Orkney – more lessons to learn?* Conference of Children in Scotland and The National Children's Bureau. Edinburgh: HMSO.

Department of Health (1991) *Working together under the Children Act. A guide to arrangements for inter-agency co-operation for the protection of children from abuse.* London: HMSO.

Department of Health (1995) *Child protection – messages from research.* London: HMSO.

Department of Health and Social Security (1988) *Working together: a guide to arrangements for inter-agency co-operation for the protection of children from abuse.* London: HMSO.

Gibbons, J., Conroy, S. and Bell, C. (1995) *Operating the child protection system.* London: HMSO.

HMSO (1989) *The Children Act.* London: HMSO.

National Commission of Inquiry into the Prevention of Child Abuse (1996) *Childhood Matters – Report of the National Commission of Inquiry into the Prevention of Child Abuse.* London: HMSO.

Office of Public Management (1994) *Joint reviews of social service departments. A framework for evaluating user and carer involvement.* London: Office of Public Management.

Platt, D. and Shemmings, D. (1996) *Making enquiries into alleged child abuse – partnership with families.* Chichester: John Wiley and Sons.

Prosser, J. (1992) *Child abuse investigations: the families' perspective. A case study of 30 families who claim to have been falsely accused, conducted by the Evaluation Unit, Westminster College, Oxford.* Bishop's Stortford: Parents Against Injustice.

Siddall, R. (1996) No pain, no gain. In section headed 'Parents: child abuse'. *Community Care* **15**, 16–17.

Note

Parents Against INjustice (PAIN) may be contacted at:
10 Water Lane, Bishop's Stortford, Herts CM23 2JZ, UK.

4

Blocked accountability: four stories

Geoffrey Hunt

Introduction

In this chapter I take just four of the cases which have been brought to the attention of Freedom to Care in the last few years and use them to illustrate ways in which organizational accountability in the social services and related areas works or fails to work. The point of this chapter is to bring to life the everyday working of the 'nervous and sensory system' of social services, in the way a doctor, or a specialist in neurology, might check on a patient's senses – ears, eyes, reflexes, balance, skin sensation and so on – to ascertain how far they are responsive to internal and external needs and demands.

The cases have been anonymized. I have not done this primarily out of a fear of defamation suits, but because I have to protect clients and employees and, furthermore, I want the reader to focus on the general issues of *accountability* and not on the personalities or particular workplace involved. These scenarios are not untypical. We are seeking an understanding of principle here, and our emphasis is on the procedural rather than substantive issues (although it would be wrong to think one could always make a clear distinction between the two).

How do we know that the stories presented here are not biased? After all, we do not get the management side of the story. The first point to make here is that, in a sense, they *are* biased. They are perceptions by employees of the situation they found themselves in, and are valuable as perceptions. Secondly, the record (memos, letters, etc.) shows what managerial and organizational responses there were in fact. Thirdly, managers and organizations have immense power and opportunity to make their case and very often without any voice being heard from 'the other side'. This book may be seen as making a small contribution to restoring the balance of audible voices.

To each case study I have appended a few questions that the reader might like to ponder.

The case of M

I had been working as an agency social worker in a Social Services Department's Children and Families Team when I was asked if I would like to transfer to another team. I declined but was subsequently informed that I was being moved. One of the cases I was then allocated was urgent, as the previous social worker had gone on extended sick leave and a court hearing was scheduled for 2 days hence. I later learned that this social worker had made a complaint against the Team Manager and refused to return to work unless she was moved to another team. On her return to work she was transferred on to the team that I had just left. Some time later another social worker confided in me that she had first been offered the place on the team I was now in, but she had declined as she knew what kind of reputation this manager had. The day I started work in the new team another social worker was gathering up his things to leave for another post and asked me, 'Did you jump, or were you pushed?'

My new Team Manager gave me a brief outline of a case I would be taking over. It concerned three children: child A, a girl aged 9 years; child B, a boy aged 6 years; and child C, a boy aged 5 years. The manager informed me that these children were to be placed to live on a permanent basis with their father. There had been a dispute between the children's parents over residence and contact. The couple had been separated for some 3 years and had subsequently divorced. The mother had remarried and had two more children with her new husband. The three subject children had lived with their mother and stepfather since the split and had Friday-to-Sunday weekend contact with the father. The mother had a Residence Order for the children and the father had contact. The father was living with his partner and had had two more children with her, and his partner's two children from her marriage also lived with them.

The family was not known to Social Services until 1 year previously when the father on weekend contact noted bruising to child C. He reported the injuries to Social Services, and after an investigation it was decided that the injury was caused by C's stepfather. The child's name was placed on the 'at-risk' register under the category of physical abuse. The stepfather denied causing the injury. The mother regarded the allegation as spurious and part of the 'mind games' she alleged that the father plays with her and the children. One year later, the father noticed bruising to child A. Child A informed the father that the mother had caused the injury. The father informed Social Services and took child A to the hospital where she was seen by a paediatrician whose opinion was that the injury was consistent with the explanation given.

The father then kept the three children. My manager informed the mother that if she tried to recover the children then emergency Protection

Orders would be sought by the Local Authority, and all three children would in any event be placed with the father.

The first thing I did was to visit the children. I interviewed each child alone. All three children's wishes and feelings were that they be allowed to return home to live with their mother. Child B, in particular, was very emotional and was desperate when he told me that he wanted to return home to live with his mother and stepfather. With the support of the local authority, the father's application for an Interim Residence Order was agreed. The court also gave directions for a Section 37 investigation to be filed into court no later than 2 months hence. I was to be the author of that report.

For the first week that the children were separated from their mother, they had no contact with her. Then the mother and stepfather were to have 1 hour's contact weekly in the Social Services office. Contact between mother, stepfather and the subjects' half-siblings was positive. There was a warm and loving relationship between all family members. In particular, during one contact session child B spontaneously looked up from his drawing and said to his stepfather 'I love you, Dad', to which his stepfather replied 'I love you, B'.

During one contact session I noted heavy bruising to child C, who informed me that the father's partner's children had caused the injuries. In the absence of my own manager I consulted another manager who advised me to record the injuries. Some of the bruising was fresh and some was fading – indicating that the bruising was ongoing and caused over a period of time. Later, this second manager sat down with me, read the file and generally discussed the case with me. During my investigation I became increasingly concerned that the children were unhappy and their emotional needs were not being met whilst living with their father.

The mother made an application to court to reverse the Interim Residence Order (IRO) to her favour. In the absence of my own manager I again consulted the second manager, who told me that if I thought it to be in the best interests of the children I could attend court and support the mother's application. This I did, but the hearing was adjourned. In the meantime my own manager returned and informed me that I could no longer support the mother. My manager and I attended court and my manager supported the father's application, as a consequence of which the IRO remained in the father's favour.

While waiting at court that day I mentioned to my manager that I had noted on file various references to allegations of sexual abuse. At this my manager reacted angrily and told me to drop the subject. He informed me that the children had been seen by an eminent child psychologist who had decided that they had been coached into making the allegations. In the file was the information that 8 months earlier the children had informed social workers that a friend of their father had sexually abused them. At this time the case was under another manager and, in line with child protection procedures, a planning meeting had been held between police and social workers. Later that day child A was interviewed by police but would not talk with them. A few days later a child psychologist interviewed child A. The child disclosed that on weekend contact a friend of her father forced her to kiss him. The psychologist expressed concern that child A may have been subjected to a certain amount of 'brainwashing', but no further explanation was given. The next day child B and child C were interviewed by the psychologist. No further details are recorded on file.

A later recording on file refers to the children implicating their father in the abuse, and concern was expressed as the psychologist had suggested early interviews with the father's partner's children and they had not yet taken place. The father lived in a different area and his partner's children were on Care Orders to this other local authority. Days later, a meeting took place, at which a psychologist, the children's mother and a social worker were present. Concerning child A's story about kissing, the psychologist did not think that the child had described anything remotely improper. Stories from child B and child C about touching were regarded as inconsistent. The psychologist felt that the children were not in danger of sexual abuse from either of the men.

There was also on file a letter from a Court Welfare Officer (CWO) who had seen the children in connection with residence and contact. During an exercise to ascertain the children's wishes and feelings, child B made reference to his father sexually abusing him. The CWO's findings were almost the same as mine, and his report concluded that it was in the children's best interest that they remain with their mother. However, also on file was an addendum report, dated only days prior to my taking over the case, in which the CWO suggested that if a change in the children's residence from mother to father were to take place then the children would, he expected, adjust within a short period of time.

As the weeks went by I became more concerned for the children's welfare. They were increasingly unhappy, but no matter what I told my manager he would not consider my concerns for them. Since last attending court my manager had started to bully me. He was always angry with me. He would call me into his office, shut the door and criticize me for trivial things. He constantly tried to pressure me into agreeing with him to place the children to live with the father. In fact, he made my life hell.

I was also concerned about the father's partner's ability to parent the children. She was a young woman who had difficulty transferring skills learned in one situation to another. Two of her four children were on Care Orders. A previous report referred to her as being unable to protect her children should she enter into an obstructive or abusive relationship.

While I was visiting the children's father I learned that he not only had care of his partner's children who were on Care Orders, but that he regularly cared for other children who were also in the care of the local authority. Still my manager was ignoring my concern about the children. After a difficult contact session, the mother telephoned me to tell me of her own concerns for her children, which included sexual abuse concerns. I relayed these concerns to my manager, but he waved his hand and ignored them. After this difficult contact session, another social worker overheard the father speaking to child B in a very interrogative manner. The next day the mother took the children from school. She telephoned me to inform me that the children were on holiday with her and that she would not be returning until the next court hearing.

My Team Manager was still insisting that the children, when found, would return to live with their father. I informed the senior manager of my concerns. She then decided that, when the children were found, they would be placed in care. The Local Authority then issued care proceedings and subsequently the children were placed in care. The Court also gave directions that I provide a statement to the proceedings. There was a discussion at the court hearing about who should conduct the children's psychological assessments. My manager kept repeating that the children must be sent back to see the same psychologist who had conducted the interviews regarding the sexual abuse allegations. I was then taken off the case.

The next day the children's foster carer made an urgent request for an interim maintenance payment. As no one else was available to take the payment, I agreed to do it. The foster carer asked me to write down what she had to tell me. While I was writing, child B came and placed himself between me and the foster carer. He said something affectionate to me, and I in return hugged him. Then he started to tell me in detail how his father had been sexually abusing him. The detail was such that a 6-year-old could not, in my opinion, have been coached in it. Child C also described to me different incidents of sexual abuse. Child A withdrew her allegations that her mother had caused the bruising. Child A also described to me a cruel psychological game which her father played with her.

I had not told anyone about my manager bullying me. I now told other team members. Two members informed me that they had also made a joint complaint against him with regard to his management style. When I went to see the senior manager to complain, another social worker accompanied me. The senior manager was not happy about this, and told me that as I was an agency worker she would rather deal with my complaint alone. Eventually I agreed and the other social worker left.

A few days later I became concerned because of the recent disclosures that my manager was not following child protection procedures. I again made a complaint to the senior manager, and this time I put it in writing. I cited the Social Services Department's child protection procedure which states that 'children are spoken to at the earliest opportunity whilst details are fresh in their minds'. I stated that in my opinion my manager was seeking to minimize the importance of these disclosures and was deliberately causing delay. The children's new social worker told me that the foster carer had informed her that child B was displaying sexualized behaviour. Instead of matters being processed within a few days, the memorandum video interviews (made for court purposes) did not take place until three and a half weeks later, and then the police were not involved. The same psychologist as before conducted the interviews.

When the children were interviewed I understand that they made no reference to sexual abuse. However, the children did refer to their father hitting their mother when, in their words, 'she hadn't done anything wrong'. The subject of domestic violence was also one which was ignored by my manager. The children's mother had alleged that the father had been violent towards her throughout their marriage, and was still violent towards her on occasions when the children were being picked up and dropped off for contact. I had confirmed with the police that such an incident had taken place recently. The previous social worker had told me that the eldest child had remembered seeing her father hitting her mother.

It had been a direction by the judge that I provide a statement to court. My manager knew what the nature of my statement was to be. At first he told me that it was not necessary that I write it. However, I was continually being asked for the statement by our legal department. I kept referring them to my manager and eventually he told me to write it. However, he would not proceed with the first statement which I wrote, without giving me a reason, even though he was being asked for the statement at court and was making excuses as to why it was not forthcoming. Then he told me to rewrite the statement using a different format. I did this, but still he would not proceed with the statement. Finally, after a great deal more pressure from our legal department, he wrote it himself. He used the basis of my statement, with changes and omissions which had the effect of favouring the children's father. The statement contained information I did not even know about.

While I was on the team, in the absence of my manager, I had dealt with a referral from a headteacher who was concerned about an older boy's behaviour. The teacher had received various complaints from parents and a complaint from a warden who looked after accommodation units for families. This boy had exposed himself to a very young child and asked her to perform a sexual act on him. I wrote up the concerns and showed this to another manager, who thought the concerns were of a serious nature and should be investigated. I put the write-up into my manager's mail-box. He then returned the write-up to me by dropping it on to my desk and saying that I should use the appropriate letterhead, but said nothing about the contents. Two months later I took a call from the same headteacher, who was extremely annoyed that no investigation or action had been taken.

A month after my contract with the local authority ended and I had ceased working for it, my former manager sent a 'progress report' to my agency. This report is very inaccurate and is seriously damaging to my professional credibility. I would raise a number of questions. First, it is against the local authority's policy for managers to send out disparaging references on a former employee without going through the Director of Social Services. Secondly, the report was not on letter-headed paper, although he was commenting on me as my former manager. Thirdly, how can a *progress* report be made on someone who had left a month before? It was bound to be seen as a reference. My agency then wrote to inform me that, in view of the comments which were 'of a very serious nature', it was impossible for them to offer me further assignments.

Four months after I left I was asked to attend the final court hearing, because I had provided a statement to the proceedings. While we were waiting at court the local authority's advocate read aloud from the care plan. The plan was that the children at the present time were to remain in care with the intention that they be rehabilitated to live with their father. Then the advocate again read aloud. She appeared genuinely surprised when she then read that if these children were to be rehabilitated to the father at the present time there would be 'grave concern'. I was later told that I would not be called to give evidence.

At one point I raised my concerns about the children with the children's solicitor. I then received a letter from the local authority's solicitor asking me to refrain from such contact. Although I understand the legal reasons given, I have to ask where a social worker can turn when their concerns involve a manager's practice. My official complaints against the Team Manager have not been acted upon. I believe, and there is evidence to suggest that, if the children return to live with their father, they will be at risk of sexual abuse.

Questions

- Is there sufficient space for professional social work judgement and decision?
- What would be the most accountable way of dealing with differences between a manager's and a social worker's judgement?
- How can a manager's judgement be laid open to fair challenge and scrutiny?
- Should not M have been given a chance to answer the allegations made by the manager in the 'progress report'?
- Consider M's claim that in the 'progress report' the manager alleged, without providing any corroboration, that M had 'misunderstood and misrepresented information'?

- What other issues of accountability to children, parents, social workers, managers and organizations does this scenario raise?
- Should not social services managers be made *individually* responsible for their acts and omissions, so that they cannot hide behind powerful organizational defences?

The case of P

I believe I suffered a nervous breakdown due to management's mishandling of a situation I was involved in as a social worker. As a result I was off sick on full pay for 6 months, on half pay for the following 6 months, and I received no pay at all in the last 6 months.

It all began in the spring of 1994 when I was asked by a Case Manager to compile a Comprehensive Risk Assessment Report with regard to a 5-year-old child being cared for by her mother, who suffered from mental health problems. While I was working with the family the mother was twice admitted to the mental health unit of the local hospital, and while she had been at home with her daughter I had deep concerns about the quality of care she was able to provide for my client – her daughter. My report was submitted to the Case Manager in July 1994, he told me that he found the report 'helpful' and he started to put my recommendations into place.

I did not continue working with this family as they were rehoused in another area, but I advised their new social worker to let my client's mother know that if she wished to query or discuss my report she could come to my workplace to do so. (I had been unable to share my report with her prior to passing it to the Case Manager, as she had been re-admitted to hospital and I was advised not to do so.)

In November 1994 my Team Manager told me that a complaint had come into the Department via the Commissioner for Carers and Users office with regard to the report I had written on this family. She advised me that I should not worry about it, as it was management's problem at the moment. I heard nothing further until just before Christmas 1996, when my Team Manager was going on leave. The Case Manager wanted to interview me since he had been asked by the Commissioner to meet with the mother to go through the report with her and to find out more about her complaint. My Team Manager did not feel that the Case Manager should interview a member of her staff prior to her (the Team Manager) understanding the content of the complaint so that she could interview me first. The Case Manager returned the report to the Commissioner mentioning this fact to him and saying that he would 'take no further action'. He made no proper minutes of his meeting with the complainant, but when he went through the report with her he wrote comments in the margins. That is all I ever saw in writing with regard to the mother's complaint, and I still do not know whether these were her actual complaints or the Case Manager's interpretation of them.

It was with this understanding of the situation that I was asked to meet with the complainant in the spring of 1997. By this time she had sought legal representation and I was advised that a solicitor would be with her. Because of my anxieties about the situation in which I now found myself, I requested from my acting Team Manager that I also be legally represented through the Department. However, she made light of the situation, saying that she felt my client's mother only wanted a solicitor for support on that occasion, and that she (the acting Team Manager) would be present to support me. I did not feel that a solicitor would have a merely supportive role, and I decided to write to the General Manager asking for him to agree to me also having a solicitor in the interests of the Department and myself. He ignored my request, but wrote to me saying 'I understand that you will feel anxious about this complaint but I hope it can be resolved by you and the Acting Team Manager meeting with the client'. In order to help me to understand the full situation he sent me all of the correspondence pertaining to the case to date.

This did nothing to assuage my anxieties, but rather it increased them. It was a collection of letters and memoranda sent between the Commissioner, the General Manager, my Team Manager and Acting Team Manager, the Case Manager and his line manager. I felt appalled that they had all been pushing this situation around for so long instead of getting to grips with it, and were now prepared to 'send me in'. I was particularly outraged by the Commissioner's response to the complainant when he referred in two of his letters to my report as 'suspect' and that 'in his view' the complainant had 'legitimate concerns about the accuracy of the report' without referring the matter to me first so that he could justify making comments of this nature. In fact this person has never met me, and had no knowledge of me until this complaint. I feel aggrieved.

I met with my client's mother on two occasions. In the event she did not have legal representation as she did not merit legal aid, but she brought a friend along with her instead. My Acting Team Manager came to support me, but I was surprised when I arrived at the meeting to find that the Commissioner had passed this case to his Assistant to deal with. I subsequently learned that this was one of the first complaints she had dealt with on her appointment to post. The meetings, I believe, were badly managed by the Assistant Commissioner, and I felt that my Acting Team Manager was unsupportive of me. She seemed to make light of the whole affair. In any case she would soon be leaving her post prior to my Team Manager returning.

At the first meeting I had pointed out that I had a case conference in the afternoon so would need to leave later in the morning in order to have a lunch break and prepare for the afternoon. It seemed that my request was not heeded and I had to remind the Acting Team Manager and the Assistant Commissioner that I needed to leave in time for the case conference.

I felt that the complainant really managed the meeting. She had been allowed to jump from one point to another with the report, to bring up matters other than those which the Case Manager had commented on, and sometimes the Assistant Commissioner and Acting Team Manager would pose their own questions and queries to me about my report in a manner that made me feel unsupported and isolated.

The result of these meetings was that they did not reach a satisfactory conclusion, and my client's mother by now wanted nothing other than the report destroyed. The Acting Team Manager suggested to me that she would seek legal advice about whether the report could be destroyed. By now I was very upset and tired of the business, and I said that I did not care what happened to my report. However, the principal solicitor of our Department wrote to the Acting Team Manager and emphasized that 'in my view the document could not be destroyed unless it is in its totality inaccurate, and this is clearly not the case here'. He justified his advice by citing legal reasons.

My Acting Team Manager and the General Manager above her decided not to follow the principal solicitor's advice and to destroy the report. A letter was sent to my client's mother explaining that the report 'has been destroyed in accordance with your wishes'. The Department apologized for having taken so long to resolve the matter, and wished her and her daughter every best wish for the future. I received a letter which, although it acknowledged the stress which had been caused to me, said that it hoped with good supervision I had learned any lessons which needed to be learnt. I wanted to reply that I did not think I was the only one with lessons to learn, but that there were many others in the Department, including some managers. I was dissuaded from doing this by my supervisor, a new member of staff, who then suggested that I should go on a course for report writing. I felt very demoralized.

It was now August 1995, and I managed to go on working until November 1995. I was still working with 'dangerous' families, and one particular piece of work was causing me a lot of anxiety, particularly in my by now frail state of mind and body. One weekend I could go on no longer. I knew I could not cope with another day at work, and I collapsed at home on a Sunday as I faced the prospect of work the next day. I have not been to work since, but as I grew stronger in the spring of 1996 I knew that I could not return to work until I had resolved this matter to my satisfaction. I wanted to do this because of the real concerns I had for the child who, I felt, could be living at risk as a result of the destruction of my report. I also wished to save the Department from any embarrassment they could suffer should anything untoward happen to this child as a result of her mother's mental health.

From March until July I corresponded with my Management Team to no avail, during which time I felt either insulted, intimidated, patronized or 'bribed' to take early retirement on ill-health grounds. I was beginning to feel that I had no other option but to disappear quietly when fortunately I was put in touch with Freedom to Care.

The response I received was like a light being shone into a very dark tunnel, and I could envisage the possibility of rescue for the very first time. Since then I have never really looked back, because in my deeper moments I have had someone to turn to for support and advice. Of course I was also very fortunate to have the love and support of my family throughout. A Freedom to Care case-worker took on my case and initially attended a meeting with my Team Manager in an effort to resolve my dispute. At this meeting we learned that there may still be a copy of my report in existence, and I was asked if I would be prepared to go through it with the Acting Team Manager. A meeting was set up when it was confirmed that a copy of my report still existed. However, the Acting Team Manager was unable to provide any evidence to satisfy me that my report was so inaccurate that it needed to be destroyed, and I was now also very angry that lies had been told to me and the complainant. Both of us had been told that all copies of the report had been destroyed.

Now I knew that a copy of my report still existed, and I still had not received a justifiable reason for destroying it, I felt that I had no alternative but to seek its return to the file. I wrote to the General Manager explaining my argument to him and requesting that my report be put back on file. My request was not granted, so I had no option but to seek a grievance hearing, which the Freedom to Care case-worker presented on my behalf in early 1997. The outcome of this hearing has been that my report is to go back on the file, and the family will be informed of this fact. I realize that in so doing the whole matter could be opened afresh by my client's mother, but I also feel that in this way any necessary action that needs to be taken to protect the child will now be taken, whereas after my report was destroyed the case had been closed.

I am now resting and recuperating from my ordeal in the hope that eventually I shall be able to return to work. These events spread over a time span of nearly 3 years, during which time valuable resources have been wasted.

Questions

- What rules of accountability should have been followed by the managers in dealing with the complaint lodged by the child's mother?
- What is the correct way of dealing with a report that contains claims with which a client or client's parent or guardian disagree?

- What aspects of the organization and management account for the breakdown in the proper and fair management of the complaint?
- How does the action of destroying P's report stand in relation to the *Access to Personal Files (Social Services) Regulations 1989* and the *Children Act Guidance and Regulations?*
- Was there unclarity about the organizational roles and responsibilities of the individuals involved and, if so, where?

The case of R

I was a qualified and experienced probation officer in Canada, with specialist training in work with violent offenders, sexual offenders, and offenders with identified mental health problems. During the last 3 years that I was employed in Canada I worked exclusively with this type of offender. This means that I have more training and direct experience in working in this field than the average probation officer. After I moved to the UK I requalified, taking an MA in Social Work with CQSW. I then started a PhD, doing research into risk assessment and professional discretionary judgement about sharing confidential information across agencies in community mental health.

While studying for the PhD I had two part-time jobs. One was as a local authority social worker carrying a caseload of child protection cases (key worker status), which meant that I received special training in child protection and became very familiar with common working practice around inter-agency liaison over sexual and violent offenders against children. My other job was working as a part-time relief worker at Hostel X, which is run by the Probation Service. It is the second job which led me to act as a 'whistleblower', and which gave rise to my concerns about poor public accountability.

Between May 1996 and September 1996 I was particularly concerned about the case management of one particular resident, whom I shall refer to as 'A'. The general feeling among staff at the hostel was that A was a dangerous person who was very likely to re-offend and could kill someone. He had broken rules of the hostel and his probation conditions several times during his stay. On two occasions his probation officer had given him 'final' written warnings, yet each time he had broken conditions again and no legal Breach of Probation had been initiated. On one occasion he had threatened staff and other residents with a hammer, and the police had to be called.

A had a very lengthy and continuous record which included convictions for more than one assault causing actual bodily harm, rape, and more than one offence of unlawful intercourse with an under-age female. Some of his offences were included in 'Schedule One'. Policy indicates that normal rules of confidentiality are relaxed whenever anyone has any 'Schedule One' convictions, and there is an expectation that all agencies which have any contact with the offender should be given certain basic information about these offences, so that they can be aware of the risks involved to children. It is the allocated probation officer's responsibility to ensure that this takes place, often by directly contacting the agencies to inform them, and by notifying the local Social Services office.

A was on probation for making threats to kill, and had also been identified as a 'potentially dangerous offender' – a Home Office procedure which also carries with it requirements for special supervision, monitoring of the offender's contacts, and relaxed rules of confidentiality and enhanced inter-agency communication. There was a copy of a detailed psychiatric report on file indicating that his long-standing 'personality disorder' was related to his offences but would not be amenable to treatment unless he himself was fully committed to it. Staff had serious concerns about A's alcohol abuse, his reluctance to fulfil his counselling condition, and his relationships with women and young teenagers while he was at the hostel, and these were issues which were clearly linked to his pattern of offences. At staff meetings people had expressed concern for their own safety, as well as that of other residents and of the general public. People felt that it was only a matter of time before A did something with which he would be charged.

My concern about the way in which the case was being managed peaked in August 1996. During a shift at the hostel, A told me that the day before he had been strangling his girlfriend. He said she had been at the point of passing out when he realized what he was doing and stopped. He also told me that she lived in a second-stage hostel (Hostel Y) for homeless women. When discussing this incident, A showed no insight or concern about what had happened; he said that he thought the 'heat' had made him do it. This incident showed he was at very high risk of re-offending violently in the near future, either by assaulting this girlfriend or someone else. In addition, I was concerned because the resident had an overnight pass approved to go and stay with the girlfriend. Proper procedures for checking about this (before agreeing a pass) had not been followed by the probation officer, who had in fact never spoken with the girlfriend.

I informed the appropriate people and asked the Acting Hostel Manager (in the absence of the usual Manager who was on holiday) to 'blanket ban' this man because this new information showed that he was a danger to staff, other residents and the public. There is a procedure which allows this, even for current residents who have not re-offended, and the Home Office's *National Standards* for supervision of hostels also allow it. Had the resident been 'blanket banned', this would also have given the probation officer fresh grounds formally to 'breach' his probation order, a legal procedure requiring a return to court where A's full response to probation would be considered, and where the court could consider anew whether to sentence him to prison. In this case, probation had been given as a clear alternative to custody, so there was a distinct possibility that A would receive a custodial sentence if the court learned that he was not fulfilling probation conditions.

The Acting Manager and Probation Officer agreed between themselves not to 'blanket ban' the resident. Instead they decided that the incident needed to be discussed with the offender, and I was told that he 'may not have really meant it' and may have been joking when he told me what happened. When I heard this I wrote a 5-page memo asking for this decision to be changed. I described all of the problems and incidents that had occurred during the months he had been at the hostel, relating all of them to identified risk factors involved with his current offence and past pattern of criminal behaviour. I predicted that he would re-offend violently within a very short time if action was not taken very soon, by way of a Breach of Probation, to prevent this.

In addition, 24 hours after informing the probation officer that the girl-friend lived in a women's hostel, I rang the hostel to check whether the probation officer had liaised with staff there about the nature of A's record (something which is expected under the Area Child Protection Committee's Guidelines for Inter-agency Co-operation, and which is in accordance with the Department of Health *Working Together* Guide-lines). Hostel Y staff were not aware until my telephone call either that A was resident at another hostel, or of the nature of his record. This caused them considerable concern since they often have young women residents who have fled violence, and since they also often have children and under-age teenagers visiting the premises. They also told me that the girlfriend had children who regularly visited her there. I documented this telephone conversation in another memo.

The result of these memos was that I was formally disciplined and warned. I was summoned to a meeting with the Assistant Chief Probation Officer (ACPO). Interestingly, correct disciplinary procedures were not followed during this meeting (e.g. I was told that I was not allowed representation). None the less, I was given a formal written warning for failing to follow correct procedures because I sent the griev-ance memo to the Chief Probation Officer, rather than the ACPO (despite the fact that at no point either before, during, or after the disciplinary meeting was I given any copy of the correct grievance procedure). I was also given a formal warning for breaching confidentiality, despite the fact that I had spoken within a network of professionals on a 'need to know' basis, and had only given out information which they had a right to know under the relevant inter-agency agreements. I was also instructed to leave risk management to managers in future.

The probation officer who had failed to follow National Standards (by giving A more than one 'final' warning instead of 'breaching' his probation order, and by failing to carry out proper checks before permitting an overnight pass) and who failed to follow both Child Protection and Potentially Dangerous Offender policies (by failing to liaise with the other hostel), was not disciplined. The resident remained at the hostel. Approximately 1 month later he re-offended, as I had predicted in my earlier memo, by strangling his girlfriend to the point where she passed out. Believing he had killed her, A turned himself in to the police. Fortunately, ambulance staff were able to revive her. A was charged with this offence and remanded in custody (he was later convicted). However, this is an offence which might never have been committed had the probation service dealt differently with A's probation supervision.

I continued to work for Hostel X. In addition to working there, I also did some relief work for Hostel Z. This was also a probation hostel, but one run independently by a voluntary association (i.e. not the probation service). I was very concerned about standards at Hostel Z. On a couple of occasions while I was working there fights broke out between residents on hostel premises, yet the residents involved were not removed from the hostel. Staff were afraid to express opinions, because several of them were being bullied by the Manager. I witnessed this bullying on a few occasions. In March I resigned, sending a letter to the Management Committee explaining my reasons.

For the next 2 months I exchanged letters with this Hostel. The Management Committee referred my 'complaint' to the Manager I had written about, and instructed me to follow their grievance procedure (which requires an initial response from the person being 'complained about'). I explained that I was not in 'grievance' about any decision she had made about me, but simply informing them why I was resigning. None the less, because I did want them to treat what I was saying seriously, I did my best to follow the hostel's grievance procedure. However, it soon became abundantly clear that the management of Hostel Z was simply using this as a tactic to avoid accountability. Twice, when I formally invoked subsections of the grievance procedure to move the discussion to the next stage (i.e. up to the committee level), my letters were not responded to, or I was told to discuss it with the Manager. Eventually, in June, the Manager of Hostel Z wrote to the ACPO (the same person who had disciplined me the previous summer) complaining about my 'complaint', and saying that I had repeatedly been told to follow the grievance procedure but had refused to do this. She said that she knew I continued to work for the probation service at Hostel X and she believed this meant I was not fit to continue working there.

Around the same time that this was happening a resident at Hostel X wrote a letter of complaint about me. He said that I was 'giving us verbal abuse and treating us like scum'. This was investigated by the Manager of Hostel X, who discussed the complaint with other staff, as well as myself, and also checked with other residents. He minuted this and gave me a copy of his decision, which was that he accepted I had not been verbally abusing residents or treating them inappropriately. It also emerged that this particular resident had a chip on his shoulder about taking directions from all female staff.

None the less, the ACPO began disciplinary procedures, basing this on the complaint from the Manager of Hostel Z, and the complaint from the resident. In July I was dismissed from Hostel X. In his letter of dismissal, the ACPO cited four reasons:

1. failure to recognize that my style could give rise to feelings of grievance from residents;
2. my view that, as a very experienced staff member, it is other staff who should change their practice, not me [a statement which I never made];
3. failure to accept reasonable instruction to adhere to Hostel Z's grievance procedure;
4. failure to recognize the significance of point 3, particularly following a similar episode last year at Hostel X when I disagreed with a manager's decision and was told to comply with proper procedures in future [i.e. referring to my complaint about how A's probation order had been supervised].

Two things strike me about the reasons given for my dismissal. First, I found it very strange to be disciplined for actions when the investigation about the resident's complaint showed that I did not do anything improper. Secondly, it appeared that one employer had decided to hold me accountable for something that had happened with a completely different employer.

I lodged a claim for unfair dismissal with an Industrial Tribunal. Initially, the probation service argued that I was not an employee since I did not have a written contract and did not work a regular schedule of shifts. They also argued that, despite the fact I had been continuously on their list of relief staff for over two and a half years, the gaps (sometimes of up to a month) between shifts I had worked meant that I did not have the requisite continuity of employment. There was an initial Tribunal Hearing in November 1996 to determine my contractual status. The decision went in my favour; the Tribunal ruled that I did have a contract of employment (even if it had not been formally written down), the nature of which covered the gaps between shifts. A second Tribunal Hearing was scheduled for April 1997. At the last moment the probation service conceded unfair dismissal and a £3100 settlement was reached.

The ACPO who disciplined me is still employed by the probation service and has not been held to account either for his unfair actions in relation to myself, or for the decision he made to uphold the decision not to breach resident A (who later re-offended as I predicted). Likewise, the

Manager of Hostel Z has not been called to answer for her part in the matter.

Questions

- How much scope is there, or should there be, for professionals to breach confidentiality in the public interest?
- Should risk management be left to managers?
- The probation officer who had failed to follow proper policy and procedure was not disciplined. Why not?
- Why was R apparently victimized? Was she too good for the job?
- At Hostel Z, staff were bullied and afraid. What could be done to change that situation?

The case of S

Around October 1996 I responded to an advertisement in one of the daily newspapers asking for anyone who had had connections with the social care services in area X in the 1970s and 1980s to get in touch with the Clerk to the X Child Abuse Inquiry. I had worked in X as a pre-qualification trainee child care worker from 1968 to 1970. From 1973 to 1975, following qualification as a social worker in 1972, I had also worked as a social worker for X Social Services Department. After long battles with that Department concerning their disregard of professional social work standards, and what I thought to be their appalling standards of service provision and practice, I resigned in 1975. I wrote to the X Child Abuse Inquiry and told them this, offering what limited information about my experiences there I could remember.

In time I received a letter from the Assistant Solicitor to the Inquiry asking me for a written statement with as much detail of people, places, dates and events as I could recall. I met this request whilst on leave in mid-December, and sent it to the Assistant Solicitor to the Inquiry about a week before Christmas. Allowing for the Christmas post I estimate it would have been received in the first week of the New Year.

On Sunday 12 January 1997 a local policeman called at the house and gave my wife a written message for me (the message was dated 11 January). He said to my wife, 'It's nothing to worry about'. The message asked me to telephone one of two specified Women Detective Constables of the X Constabulary on Monday between 8.30 and 9.00 a.m. As I was going to be travelling to a union meeting at that time, I telephoned the number given on the message later on the Sunday to try to arrange an alternative time. My assumption was that the message was in connection with my statement to the Inquiry, and the woman who answered the phone (who seemed to be a receptionist) confirmed from the extension number I had been given that the WDCs who wished to speak to me were from the X Constabulary Child Abuse Inquiry Team. I was told that it would be perfectly alright to phone on the Monday at a time that was convenient for me.

I phoned the X Constabulary on the Monday (13 January 1997) from the union office and spoke to one of the WDCs, who confirmed that she was a member of the Child Abuse Inquiry Team. She told me that they would be in my part of the country (a substantial distance from X) on Wednesday 15 January 1997, and asked if I could go to a local police station to speak to them. I said that would be fine, and arranged to meet them at 9.30 a.m. on that date. At the end of the telephone conversation she said I could have a solicitor with me if I wished. I said that this would not be necessary. It was only on reflection that I thought this slightly odd in relation to my rather innocuous statement to the Inquiry. At that time the mechanics of the processes had not dawned on me. I had not yet realized that the Tribunal Inquiry and the police enquiries were separate entities.

At the arranged time at a local police station I was greeted promptly and cordially by the WDCs. Visits to police stations and discussions with police officers are a reasonably common experience for me through professional activities, and I was approaching this visit as no different to many others. I went through to the rear of the police station with the WDCs and after they had had a brief word with the Custody Sergeant they led the way to an interview room. Once there, they asked me why I showed no surprise at being asked to talk to them, and I referred to my Inquiry statement.

I was then told that this interview was in connection with the police enquiries and, despite their enquiries having been in process since 1991, I was now being interviewed in connection with having been named as the perpetrator of an indecent assault whilst I was working at a residential home in X between 1968 and 1970. I was cautioned and was again invited to contact a solicitor. Knowing that I had nothing to answer for, I again said that a solicitor would not be necessary. They then conducted a taped interview. There was some exchange at the outset in which the WDCs expressed some surprise at this interview being conducted in relation to an alleged event that took place nearly 30 years ago.

After preliminary questions concerning what I could remember about the staff, children, conditions, activities, approaches and routines at the residential home, they read from a typed statement (what I hazily recall as a lengthy document) that a former boy at the home had made the allegation. He had said something like this: whilst I was on duty getting the boys up one morning, after finding he had wet his bed I had taken him into the shower, locked the door and had fondled his genitals saying something like 'do you really know what this is for?'. He said this was interrupted by another member of staff knocking at the door. I was told that the other member of staff, although named by my accuser, had not been found.

I said I had no memory for the boy and did not 'recognize' the events of the allegation. My use of the term 'recognize' was questioned. I told them that I was trying to think of possible actions or events which could have been misconstrued or misunderstood, but without success. I then told them that I had no knowledge of the allegations made. The WDCs went on to say that his statement included general information about me and my interests, some of which is accurate, and some inaccurate. They also said that he had stated I had later been sacked from the home, which is not true.

Throughout the interview, both WDCs were reasonable in their attitude and even friendly. One of them, the one reading from the statement, I noticed seemed to be nervous with a slight hand tremor as she was holding the statement. After the interview they said that they would be reporting to their Inspector but, because of the time lapse and the lack of corroborative evidence, 'I shouldn't lose any sleep over the matter'.

I told them that I worked with current child protection and sexual abuse cases and would immediately contact my employer to advise of the interview. They told me that I should not do this, that this was just an allegation and I should do nothing until a decision had been made about the interview. I told them that I would be telling my wife and family immediately, and said they could contact me freely at home if they wished to in the future. On returning to my office later that day I contacted my union and made an appointment to see a union representative on Monday 20 January 1997 for advice. I also contacted the union's advisory service and told them of the interview and allegation. I told my wife, and we told the whole of our immediate family over the next few days. We also told the parents of a teenage girl to whom I give music lessons.

On Thursday afternoon I was working away from the office, and on the Friday of that same week I had to go to another part of the country for a review there. When I arrived home on the Friday evening I found a hand-delivered letter from my senior manager. This letter said that she had been contacted by the X Constabulary informing her of the interview. I think this action, given the WDCs' instruction at the end of the interview, was unfair to me. The letter went on to say that she would like to see me on Tuesday 21 January for an informal interview, but with the Chief Personnel Officer present.

On 20 January I had a long discussion with my union representative and explained what was happening in detail. His immediate advice was that I must have someone with me at the management interview, and he telephoned my senior manager straight away. His attendance was agreed and, in order to accommodate everyone, the meeting was rearranged for 22 January.

The meeting was between the senior manager, the Chief Personnel Officer, my union representative and myself. I began by explaining that I had told the police after the interview that I would immediately advise my employer, but that the police had instructed me not to do this until I had received a decision about what action would be taken concerning the allegation. There seemed to be acceptance of my account and a consensus of puzzlement at the anomaly created by the police. The manager told the meeting that she had in fact received a telephone call from the police at mid-day on 15 January informing her of the interview earlier that day.

I gave the meeting a full account of the allegation as is set out above. I also said that I was very aware of the difficult position the Social Services Department could be in with one of their employees being questioned about child sexual abuse when he was working with child protection cases involving potential sexual abuse. I also said that I had no objections to the matter being known generally. However, the effects of possible negative publicity were acknowledged, and it was agreed that only those needing to know (including the Director of Social Services) would be told, although this would ultimately be my choice. It was agreed that I would continue to work normally with day-to-day supervision being relied upon to pick up any associated difficulties, and that my senior manager would discuss the matter with her line managers.

On 27 January, whilst at a union meeting, I was able to talk at length to my union representative and he subsequently wrote to my senior manager. Suspension was feared, but in fact no changes were made to my working arrangements or practice. I must say here that, from my point of view, my managers have dealt with the issue sensitively and have been supportive to me through a difficult time both personally and professionally. Meanwhile I withdrew voluntarily from my involvement in union activities until the matter was resolved.

There were no further developments until, returning home from a week's holiday on 22 February, I found a letter from the X Constabulary saying that the 'file detailing the allegations' had been submitted to the Crown Prosecution Service (CPS) and 'based on the evidence contained in that file, that no further action will be taken against you'.

I received a telephone call at work on 26 March from one of my union's solicitors – the result of an application by me for legal advice some weeks back. I was told he would be representing my 'criminal case'. He said that he would be writing to me but gave me direct advice over the phone not to answer any further questions from the police without his presence, and not to respond to questions from the X Inquiry. He acknowledged my update on the CPS decision, the availability now of the CPS papers to the legal section of my employing authority (although I have been told I have no right to see that file), and the fact that I could be called as a witness to the Child Abuse Inquiry. He talked of the latter possibly 'incriminating' me and the CPS re-opening the case as a result. I received a subsequent letter repeating the advice not to answer police questions, but saying nothing about contact with the Child Abuse Inquiry.

On 29 March 1997 I wrote a long letter to the Chair of Freedom to Care. My first thought, when I received the CPS decision, was that I should make sure that the Inquiry, if they did not already know, had knowledge of the allegation and the actions of the X Constabulary. What made me hesitate was my uneasiness about what had happened when I voluntarily contacted the Inquiry and it had received my statement, as well as the verbal advice from my union solicitor. As a result of subsequent discussions with the Chair of Freedom to Care and another member, I decided that my initial conviction of trying to ensure that the Child Abuse Inquiry was aware of the police investigation and the related issues was more important than other considerations, and that it was the only ethically responsible course. On 3 May I wrote a letter to the Assistant Solicitor to the Inquiry, on Freedom to Care letterhead, appending my letter to the Chair of Freedom to Care. That letter went by registered post with copies to appropriate individuals, including my local MP.

The far-reaching power of this false accusation is enormous. It is personally devastating because one of my proudest achievements is professional integrity. I fear it puts paid to any future appointments for which I may wish to apply. For instance, I had been short-listed for membership of an important Commission in their last round of appointments. I believe there is no chance of that now. I can no longer participate in and contribute to professional social work promotion and development, and I have to spend a great deal of my waking life chasing thoughts around my head trying to make some sense of what has happened to me.

In trying to wring out an explanation there are two whistleblowing events which may or may not be connected. The first is my own, rooted in the source of the origins of my interest in the issues surrounding whistleblowing itself – the frequent battles with social services management in X in the mid-1970s. Then follows my expression of those concerns to the X Child Abuse Inquiry as a response to their appeal for people to contact them. Close on the heels of this comes a 'whistleblower' accusing me of a serious offence. Is this really coincidence?

My statement to the Child Abuse Inquiry contained nothing startling, but it does mention Freemasonry. The statement could be more revealing about improper policies and practices of the local authority if there were further exploration and access to contemporary documentation. One question that flashes across my mind is whether it is beyond the realm of possibility that someone with something to hide should make a move to discredit a potential Inquiry witness.

Assuming that my accuser was indeed a resident of the X home at some time when I was a student there, I need answers to some important questions and I believe I have a right to the answers. Who is my accuser? Did he in fact make a clear and unprompted accusation at all? What does he do now? How old was he 29 years ago? Why was he at the residential home? What is the date of the events that are the subject of the allegation? Is my accuser a Freemason? When was the allegation made? What was the context of the making of the allegation? To whom was the allegation made? What were the circumstances of the making of the allegation? Is there a financial incentive to the making of such allegations?

Was the allegation made by him as an individual, or as part of a group of people? Was there encouragement from others to make this allegation? Did he make a single allegation or a number of allegations involving more than one person? How did the police locate me? What are the arrangements for administering the Child Abuse Tribunal Inquiry mail? What archive records still exist contemporary to the allegation?

Questions

- S's application for legal representation from his union contained a clause to the effect that, if he went against legal advice, he would forfeit union representation. Is this not in direct conflict with the principles of accountability, and a first-line barrier to responsible whistleblowing?
- What could have been done to achieve greater clarity and openness in the situation in which S found himself as an 'accused'?
- Although it is not clear what was happening in S's scenario, what can be done in general to prevent or inhibit organizations from making diversionary counter-allegations?
- How can relations of accountability be improved between police and social services in child abuse enquiries?

5

Swimming against the tide: a social worker's experience of a secure hospital

Susan Machin

> *Every now and then, one of the tall waves thundering in*
> *from the open ocean carries within it a dark sinister presence.*
> (*Trials of Life*, Richard Attenborough)

During March 1992, whilst I was employed as a senior social worker at Ashworth Hospital, I gave evidence to a public inquiry investigating allegations of patient abuse. Ashworth Hospital, along with Broadmoor Hospital and Rampton Hospital, is an institution that provides maximum secure facilities for mentally disordered offenders and other people who are deemed to pose an immediate and dangerous threat to others in the community. The hospitals are managed on behalf of the Secretary of State for Health by the Special Hospital Service Authority (SHSA) which was formed in October 1989. The SHSA took over responsibilities previously exercised jointly by the Department of Health and the Home Office.

The public perception of special hospitals is that they are solely for housing offenders in conditions of high security, particularly the high-profile or well-known people who are regularly reported in the press. This is not the case; some 20 per cent of Ashworth patients have committed no offence. Another feature of special hospitals is the length of stay involved, which at Ashworth is an average of around 7 years, although some patients are detained all their lives. For this reason, there have always been and continue to be reservations about the human rights implications of special hospitals. Even the application of the label 'special hospital' to what is actually a psychiatric prison smacks of the euphemisms adopted by totalitarian regimes the world over. However, whatever their other defects, most prisons are associated with the idea that a sentence has a determined length, and that release will ultimately almost always occur. At Ashworth it is possible for a patient to be detained by the state for life for an offence that would never attract such a severe penalty if dealt with through the penal system.

Some patients who have been detained long term at Ashworth were originally admitted when in their teens or even younger (at the age of 11 years in a particular case. of which I am aware). It is not surprising in these circumstances that organizations such as MIND have long campaigned for all special hospitals to be closed. There must be doubts about whether some patients at Ashworth need to be, or should be, detained under the repressive conditions inherent in a high-security establishment. This view is supported by a comment in a recent report on Ashworth by the NHS Health Advisory Service, which states that there are '30%–50% of patients currently in special hospitals but assessed as no longer requiring care in a high security environment' (NHS Health Advisory Service, 1995). The same report incidentally notes that a lack of suitable low- or medium-security psychiatric facilities has led to an increasing number of admissions to special hospitals in recent years.

The Inquiry

The public inquiry was instigated by the minister, William Waldegrave, in the light of a damning 'Cutting Edge' television programme shown on Channel Four in March 1991. This programme exposed evidence of horrific abuse of patients at Ashworth Hospital, and testimony was taken from former patients, relatives of patients and lawyers involved in their cases.

Prior to the Inquiry the government-appointed chairman, Sir Louis Blom-Cooper QC, wrote to all members of staff and patients in confidence asking for any comments that they might wish to making regarding care at Ashworth. 'Well over 1800 letters were distributed in total' (Blom-Cooper, 1992, p. 82). Only 30 members of staff responded, although 1365 staff were employed at the time. Only 21 responses contained any criticism. I was the only social worker to offer criticism, supported by evidence, and consequently was invited to give oral evidence to the Inquiry itself. My complaints focused on the denial of basic human and civil rights, which manifested itself in abuse of power between management and staff and consequently between those parties and the patients. Sexism, racism and homophobia were rife, and it is my belief that, at the time of writing (late 1996), little has changed since then.

I was aware of the background to special hospitals when I applied to work at Ashworth, and I resolved that, whatever the pressures, if I came across any instances of abuse of patients' rights I would take action. For this reason, I was one of only five Ashworth staff who gave evidence to the public inquiry about the patient abuse and inhumane treatment that had occurred there. Following the completion of our evidence, the solicitor who was acting for the SHSA stated to the chair of the Inquiry:

> Sir, could I respond on behalf of management? As far as I am con-
> cerned, those who have come today have proved their value and they
> are precisely the type of staff with the type of character that we very
> much welcome and that we seek to encourage.
>
> (Irons, 1992)

Reading this statement, who would have believed that just 3 years later the very same solicitor would present the management case against me at the industrial tribunal? The question then has to be asked – how could such a state of affairs have come to pass?

Social work and social conditions

My social work practice was born within the radical model. My formal training confirmed my belief that traditional social work models need to be challenged in the light of human experience and emotion, and that workers need to get alongside their clients in order to foster empowerment and counteract the effects of their disabling conditions of life. My efforts to understand the context of the social and economic conditions in which my clients existed did not distance me from feelings of warmth and compassion, or from painful emotions born from understanding the effects of poverty and deprivation.

At the time when I qualified as a social worker I was working within an institution – a medium-sized home for adolescents in the South of England. Consequently, the works of Erving Goffman had a poignancy that had a deep and lasting effect on my very being, and consistently influenced my relationship with clients. Goffman wrote:

> It seems characteristic of every establishment, and especially of total
> institutions, that some forms of deference will be specific to it, with
> inmates as givers and staff as recipients. For this to occur, those
> who are to receive spontaneous expressions of regard must be the
> very ones to teach the forms and to enforce them. It follows that in
> total institutions one crucial difference from civil life is that defer-
> ence is placed on a formal footing, with specific demands being
> made and specific negative sanctions accorded for infractions; not
> only will acts be required, but also the outward show of inward feel-
> ings. Expressed attitudes such as insolence will be explicitly
> penalised.
>
> (Goffman, 1961)

This analysis had been manifest in my experience as a nurse and residential social worker. At Ashworth the same explicit ethos was present – a direct contradiction of everything that I valued in terms of respect and dignity of the individual and the recognition of human difference as a value in understanding the importance of justice and equality within society as a whole.

It is a recognized fact that many of us in social work and related professions strived with conviction during the 1980s to de-institutionalize service delivery. Much of the thinking behind current 'care in the community' legislation was underpinned by the concept of *normalization* (Means and Smith, 1994). The effect of going to work in a special hospital during 1991 was shocking in terms of feeling that one was stepping back in time, accentuated by a profound horror of witnessing the worst institutional features described in Goffman's work.

When I was offered the post at Ashworth, a director on the management team, who was also my line manager, told me that he hoped that I would not have 'scales on my eyes'. Whilst the job I had applied for was attractive in terms of an employment package, the reality on the wards was grim in terms of the social work task. The incongruity of the whole situation hit me from the first day, and was never to be resolved for the duration of my time within the institution.

My welcome at the hospital was friendly – I have to say exceptionally friendly – but, rather like a closed gentlemen's club welcoming a new entrant, there was an assumption that such a greeting combined with an induction that was little more than initiation would seal a common acceptance of the status quo. The client group was perceived as unique, composed of individuals who were condemned and despised by society as a whole, and only the existing staff within the prevailing culture could 'cope' and from time to time return some to the community at large.

With hindsight, I suppose that I never passed the informal initiation rights. Once I caught a real glimpse of the lives of the patient I then recognized, as I described in my submission to the public inquiry, that:

> A patient first coming to Ashworth Hospital will feel a sense of isolation not only because of the implications of maximum security but also the knowledge that this detention is the last resort, often following a sequence of other placements. For the patient at this time no one moves on from a special hospital – it is the end of the road. Certainly the destructive strategies that powerless people have resorted to in the past to alter their situation are not successful in a special hospital setting. When an individual enters a total institution they do so without the benefit of written rules and regulations which are enshrined and understood by everyone else, both staff and inmates alike. A feeling of compliance and dependency is engendered.
>
> (Machin, 1992)

Ashworth is a large hospital formed from two former institutions – Park Lane Hospital, which was built partly as an overflow for Broadmoor Hospital, and the much older Moss Side Hospital. The resultant hospital, located on a huge site with more than 600 patients, was aptly described by the Chief Executive to the SHSA at the same public inquiry as:

> rather like a garden that had been left uncultivated with no plan, no order, some outstanding features, some things flourished, but in the confused setting, without proper care, without proper planning, the undergrowth blotted out the main features and while individuals tried conscientiously to do their individual best ... in management terms (there) was a vacuum.
>
> (Kaye, 1992)

It was right to recognize that some individuals tried to do their best, as it was equally correct to recognize that in some parts of the hospital excellent standards of care prevailed. Nevertheless, my experience identified a closed institution with its own traditions, with an undercurrent of sexism, racism and homophobia and no formal or informal balancing or redressing processes. Within the totality of the institution there existed autonomous wards with their own subculture devoid of adequate monitoring or managerial lead. Here it was possible for patient abuse to flourish largely unnoticed.

In these circumstances it would be quite wrong to apportion unconditional blame to, for example, the nursing staff, or to scapegoat the union to which the majority belonged, namely the Prison Officers Association. It was correct and more useful to attempt to understand the workings of the institution as a whole. Whilst the Committee of Inquiry undertook that task and produced a report that was worthy of praise, the aftermath (at the time of writing) has not produced a fundamental change, although there have been some improvements. Perhaps we now have an institution that is more positively rooted in the welfare model, but still impregnated with stigma and stereotyping.

My role as social worker at Ashworth

In my professional role I profoundly believed that patients should firstly be treated with respect and dignity, and secondly be afforded both human rights and the civil rights to which they were entitled. My rationale for ensuring that rights were afforded was the legal process which was available, and I became increasingly anxious in my awareness of the lack of legal expertise within the hospital, and the prevailing view that inmates were somehow not entitled to exercise their full legal rights because of the nature of their detention. For example, a psychologist or psychiatrist may persuade a patient not to pursue their right to review of their detention in case it interferes with their therapeutic treatment.

It was difficult to garner support for the position I took. The recognized trade union to which the social workers belonged at the time was a traditional civil service union with no history of representing social workers. Since my dismissal, the remaining social workers have become members of the union Unison. However, even with trade union support it will also be difficult to form a real consensus between social workers within a total institution such as a 'special hospital' – they also reflect wider society, and many would deal with ethical conflicts surrounding the treatment of mentally disordered offenders by aligning themselves with the medical model and not being prepared to challenge the power of the clinical professionals. It could be said that some professional social workers seek to enhance their professionalism by operating as therapists first (becoming clinicians) and advocates second.

Recognized professional practice and ethical codes such as those devised by the British Association of Social Workers (BASW) seemed to hold little validity within the institution, and a small, disparate social work team without a strong social work manager could do little to alter this balance of power, which was overwhelmingly in favour of not only the medical model, but also a medical model which sometimes denied civil rights.

My own involvement was fraught almost from the beginning. I worked on a ward where basic abuses of human rights occurred. To give an impression of the position I was in, I shall cite one example. On this particular ward, the majority of patients were classified, within the meaning of the Mental Health Act, as suffering from 'mental impairment'. Most had been incarcerated for many years and had had little contact with women. This ward was an all-male ward that was staffed by an all-male nursing staff, and the previous social worker had been a man. Contact with females was limited to infrequent contact with a female psychologist and a female psychiatrist. Whilst the hospital housed both male and female patients, day-to-day contact was not allowed. In fact, any contact raised the ethical issues surrounding the male psychiatrically disordered offender as very often being the perpetrator of a sexual offence, and the female offender as being a victim.

Understandably, institutionalized sexual activity flourished. The response of the patient care team (including nursing staff, psychiatrists, psychologists and social workers) was to create two sets of toilet facilities, one for the 'normal' patients and one for the homosexuals. The team even managed to persuade Mental Health Act Commissioners of the validity of the plan, which was to protect the more vulnerable patients from predatory homosexuals.

A generous spirit would perhaps accept that some individuals acceded to these proposals with a sincere belief that the vulnerable would feel more 'safe'. The most worrying feature of the whole exercise was the lack of any significant analysis or understanding of how oppressive regimes benefit from such unnecessarily rigid rules. It also appeared that no debate had taken place concerning homophobic attitudes either in the crudest sense or in the challenging of assumptions arising from medical and forensic models, e.g. that the behaviour of patients engaging in sexual acts was at best a manifestation of their illness, or at worst deviancy.

As far as I was concerned, this situation was my first test of my commitment to basic social work principles. In reality, the day-to-day results of such a policy were quite clear for all to see. The segregation of patients (for toilet purposes) was determined by nursing staff and, by a general rule of thumb, allocation to the 'homosexual toilet' resulted from having been 'caught in the act' by a member of staff. Allocation was used as a punishment, and the cleaning of the toilets by patients reinforced the segregation and at times was used as a punishment in cruel ways.

It was very difficult for caring nurses to challenge the status quo, and new entrants were very quickly persuaded that there was no alternative to managing patients by the use of strictly enforced rules. I was convinced that social workers had a duty to challenge such attitudes and that, if necessary, essential changes would have to be pursued vigorously. In the context of institutionalized attitudes I saw no role for consensus in such matters. I was not prepared to agree to such policies in order to comply with the majority view on patient care teams. I was bewildered that colleagues had not readily seen the potential for attitudes to develop in a direction that was frighteningly similar to those underlying the torture and cruelty that are universally condemned.

One question that arises concerns what exactly the role of *social workers* is in special hospitals. I fear that it is a question that still needs to be addressed if the recent findings of the Social Services Inspectorate and a more recent report from the National Health Advisory Service are to be taken seriously (Social Services Inspectorate, 1993). Both reports identify social workers as isolated within the institutions. From my own experience I know just how easy it is to slip into an institutionalized consensus and become party to practices that would be quite unacceptable in other settings. This isolation is exacerbated by the employment position of social workers at Ashworth. Unlike all other hospital-based social workers, their contract is with the Health Authority. Furthermore, following recent changes at Ashworth, social workers are now directly accountable to and managed by non-social work professionals.

I initially held the view that social work practice and honourable intentions would engender support from one's employer irrespective of their organizational status, i.e. social service department or health authority. Unhappily, I was proved wrong. I believed that the statements made to the Public Inquiry on behalf of the Special Hospital Service Authority, and that people who had spoken on behalf of patients would be supported, but again I was disappointed. I must make it clear that at the time of the public inquiry I did not see myself as a 'whistleblower', but as a worker responding honestly and with some commitment to patients' rights in a public arena. Indeed, until the time of my dismissal, I did not knowingly breach my duty of fidelity to my former employer, but used the systems and structures available to work in the best interests of my client group.

Staff placed loyalty to each other in a paramount position, to the extent of protecting staff who had abused patients. This was supported by a very macho culture in which toughness had to be displayed. Any sign of compassion or real care for patients was seen as weakness. My view is that the overriding value should have been respect for an individual's dignity, irrespective of whether they were staff or patients.

Internal accountability

Prior to the Inquiry, a myth had historically developed that then became enshrined within the thinking of the staff. This myth reinforced the view that the people who came to Ashworth as inmates were intrinsically bad and that, whilst some therapeutic intervention is possible, the over-whelming priority was to control and punish. This thinking, in turn, gave way to the development of a management model which somehow emu-lated a military model with hierarchical command.

Because of the 'dangerous nature' of the work, decision-making tended to be delegated upwards and not challenged. Theoretical debate was discouraged, and the decisions of management were not seen to be open to challenge. Complaints and grievances were simply not dealt with, and on one occasion when I pursued a legitimate grievance by fol-lowing an agreed procedure, the grievance was not heard but an informal compromise was reached which involved the whole social work depart-ment and caused further discord.

Some of these attitudes were rooted in the isolation which is a feature of Ashworth. As one of only three special hospitals it has no common links with any nearby establishments, whether hospitals or prisons. Added to this, its overall management in the past has been the responsi-bility of bodies such as the Special Hospital Services Authority (SHSA), which is based 200 miles away in London. Even while it was in existence there was relatively little contact between the SHSA and Ashworth in terms of the day-to-day management of the establishment. Now that Ashworth is run by a Hospital Trust which has sole responsibility for Ashworth, the scope of significant outside influence or intervention in its management is effectively nil.

Added to this external isolation of Ashworth is the nature of the estab-lishment itself. It is spread over a large site and consists of individual wards, many of which are in a secure campus. Management is based in a building outside the security boundary, and in the absence of systems such as full-time video surveillance it is unable to be sure of what is happening on most of the site. This inability to know what is happening is compounded by the fact that, while managers work normal hours for office-based staff on the usual Monday-to-Friday pattern, this is not the case for the largest group of employees, namely the nurses. Because of the need to staff the wards continuously for 24 hours a day 7 days a week, there are periods when the managerial presence on site is minimal or non-existent. There is therefore a significant divergence of experience from the nurses, who have to cope with a difficult and demanding job at times of the day and on days of the week when none of the senior management are present on site.

After the Inquiry Report

I was unprepared for the dynamics that followed the publication of the Inquiry Report, a report which confirmed that:

> A vivid picture emerged ... of life in a brutalising, stagnant, closed institution. The all-pervading nature of an oppressive sub-culture at Ashworth Hospital which persistently undermines the therapeutic approach and places constraints on those who do not conform to it, was made clear.
>
> (Lawrence, 1992)

Whilst much of the blame was, quite rightly, placed at management's door, the response of the establishment was to place the whole focus on *management* as a solution, and to establish a managerial autonomy that was capable of alienating itself from real human need, in terms of both staff and patients.

An endemic danger for managerial structures in bureaucracies, however modern and forward-thinking the leader may choose to be, is that they are allied to career-based systems of appointment and promotion. The implication of this is that a career is seen as a series of stages, each involving more authority, responsibility and remuneration. A consequence is that any challenge to an individual manager's competence, or to that of management as a whole, may be seen not only in terms of a possible threat to their current employment, but also as a source of potential damage to their future career prospects. This clearly makes it difficult, if not impossible, for individual members of staff, whether within the management structure or outside it, to question or criticize management's decisions, styles and strategies. Any challenge to management decisions may result in an over-reaction by that manager in order to protect his or her own interests rather than the interests of the individuals whom the organization is intended to serve. The combination of this form of managerial behaviour and a closed institution can, in the absence of any other controls, become a recipe for further abuses of human rights.

Instead of a great tidal wave of fundamental progress that might have been envisaged at this time, my own experience was one of desperately swimming against the tide, which became stronger than it had ever been before.

Certainly there was a positive side to the changes – work became more challenging and satisfying at ward level. Many staff, once they had come to terms with the shocking findings contained in the Inquiry Report, felt that they at last had permission to be progressive. More importantly, they did not have to feel ashamed of showing kindness and compassion to patients. I began to develop working relationships with nurses that would have been unthinkable prior to the inquiry. A bond which began to grow between many of us resulted from a growing awareness that the same management which had remained silent before and during the Inquiry were now becoming proactive in working towards a cultural change, with a determination to weed out the cancer of unprofessional practice. However, they were doing this without being able properly to identify the culprits. The institution remained closed with the additional 'terror' of unwarranted reprisals against many staff.

My own attempts to support some of these staff alongside my own professional practice, which remained constant, created feelings of insecurity that I had never hitherto experienced in my working life. A series of incidents appeared to undermine my credibility. In isolation they might appear trivial, and my own colleagues would dismiss them, perhaps feeling that I was developing a 'paranoia' in the wake of the stresses of the public Inquiry that followed just a week after I was physically attacked at the hospital.

This attack was certainly a symptom of the *malaise* at the hospital at the time. It took place just one week before I was due to give evidence to the public Inquiry, and after the papers I had prepared for that Inquiry had been circulated. I was seriously assaulted by a patient with whom I had been working, an incident which resulted in considerable physical injury. It took place in a side room on the ward in which the patient was an inmate, at a time when I should have been closely observed by nurses. Other patients on the ward reported that the patient in question had been 'wound up', prior to my visit to the ward, by some nursing staff. This attack was a sexual assault. Whatever the cause or consequences, I did proceed to give evidence to the Inquiry and declined to seek prosecution through the judicial system against my attacker, in the firm belief that he was just as much a victim of the system as I was. It is understandable and all too common to look to the pathology of the individual when it is too difficult to deal with the reality of the situation.

My worst fears were confirmed when I was summoned by management on 4 August 1993 and suspended pending an investigation arising from allegations of gross misconduct. Three allegations were listed, but two were later set aside. Ultimately I was sacked because 'on the balance of probabilities you did supply a patient with a catalogue of listening devices' (Letter confirming dismissal of Susan Machin from Ashworth Hospital, 8 February 1994, signed by Director of Personnel on behalf of the General Manager, 1994). I have always strenuously denied the charge and won my case at the subsequent Industrial Tribunal. As a result of the Tribunal proceedings it became known to me that the person who made the original complaints against me 'admits to keeping a "diary" of her dealings with me soon after the publication of the Inquiry Report' (Ashworth Hospital Management Memorandum, 2 August 1993; submitted to Leeds Industrial Tribunal and included in bundle of evidence on 12 January 1995, Case No. 23686/94). It is interesting to note when this diary was started. It is even more interesting to note that the same management memorandum stated that the complainant 'does not want to get involved' and had asked, 'could we "hold" the statement until people have been approached about corroborating it?'. The statement referred to was described in the memorandum as 'Appendix 1'. It clearly existed in either a handwritten or typed form, as the memorandum has page and paragraph references to it. Yet I have never seen this statement, and a request for its disclosure at the Industrial Tribunal was met with a management response claiming that it had never existed. Moreover, I was never given any opportunity to answer or comment on the allegations made against me in this statement before I was suspended.

As I have already said, I do not consider myself to be a 'whistle-blower', but this is a pattern of events which I am sure will be familiar to many other conscientious employees who speak up. It was even more unbelievable that it should happen to me because, in the Inquiry Report, which was approved by Parliament, I was given a specific, written 'guarantee of non-victimization'. In the event, this guarantee proved totally worthless. I believe that my dismissal was motivated in part because, after the Inquiry, I continued to challenge bad practice and ill treatment. Some of the long-term managers at Ashworth were not to know to what extent following the inquiry past abuses might be investigated – and in that situation, I strongly believe, I was perceived to be a standing threat.

I make these points in order to alert others to the consequences of proactive social work in the absence of strong managerial support. I now understand that some of the issues that were allegedly complained about would be examples of good social work practice in other settings, and that ultimately I was investigated, judged and punished without any professional social work input or advice. In other words, I was 'lynched' for being a whistleblower.

An example of this dichotomy is evidenced by the dynamic within a ward-based multidisciplinary team, of which I was a member, the team being headed by the psychiatrist working on that particular ward. One of the patients for whom I was responsible suffered from numerous epileptic seizures. These seizures often resulted in some confusion and, on one occasion, following a seizure during the night, the patient proceeded to dismantle his bed. The response of the team, including the ward manager and the psychologist, was to enforce a behaviour modification programme and insist that the patient pay for the damage to the bed. Of course, and understandably, the patient refused to do this. My advice to the team was that the patient could not be forced to pay, irrespective of any ethical or moral issues involved. Forcible deduction from his bank account would, in reality, be deduction from his invalidity benefit, which is unlawful without a court order. Such advice, which I also gave to the patient, was seen as undermining the therapeutic process and unhelpful to the team, even though my actions may have saved the hospital serious embarrassment in the future. Equally, advice to patients regarding applications to the Mental Health Review Tribunal and proactive support in the process was regarded as anti-therapeutic by some clinical staff. The individual who made complaints about me to management prior to my suspension made reference to such incidents, and obviously believed them to be deviant in nature.

There is no doubt in my mind that there was a dual objective. Apart from silencing me, the effect of my dismissal was that management had set an example to other staff. This kind of managerial action is a chilling prospect, for both staff and patients. I agree that the abuses of human rights that take place at Ashworth today might seem minor by comparison with abuses that have taken place in countries with oppressive regimes and during the Second World War, but the potential is there. I am reminded of this fact by a letter that I recently received from a patient. Irrespective of the proclaimed progress that has been made at Ashworth, he says that he still lives in complete despair and devoid of any treatment. The most poignant part of his letter was his address – his ward followed by his patient number.

The ability of that potential to result in serious harm to both staff and patients is magnified by the lack of parliamentary control. The SHSA is, at this time, a 'quango' and is deemed to be operationally independent by the Department of Health. There is a move to give Ashworth Hospital even more autonomy by setting it up as an NHS Trust. As has happened elsewhere in the NHS, the cult of managerialism will project a public relations image of a caring, effective and efficient way of providing for staff and patient needs. The actuality, as experienced by myself and others, is very different. It is an experience of a dominating and powerful clique who, at public expense and in the name of the state, will actively counter and eliminate progressive and enlightened opposition from any quarter. Even senior consultants have not been immune.

Unfair dismissal

Following a claim to an Industrial Tribunal for unfair dismissal, a decision was reached in my favour during May 1995, extended reasons for that decision being given the following month. This claim, and the subsequent decision, must be set against a background of current labour law in which a tribunal had to adjudicate on the basic facts as to whether an employer behaved within a reasonable band of responses to any employee facing allegations of 'gross misconduct', and whether any dismissing officer believed that action to have taken place following perusal of evidence arising from a thorough investigation. The burden of proof is a civil one and is taken on the balance of probabilities.

Given this scenario, it is perfectly possible for an employer to investigate allegations of improper practice, to arrive at an incorrect conclusion, and still to be found to have dismissed fairly if proper procedures have been followed. The decision in my case was that I had been unfairly dismissed, by a majority – which means that two members out of a tribunal panel of three found in my favour. To understand the merit of the decision requires direct reference to the written decision itself. This stated that 'The majority concludes that a reasonable employer, faced with the conflicting evidence with which this panel was faced, could not reach the conclusion it did on the balance of probabilities without perversity' (Tribunal Decision, 1995, p. 20). The minority member, who happened to be the chairman, could not join the majority members in this conclusion, although he had 'considerable doubt' about the way in which the investigation was carried out. The written decision goes on to say, 'He had considerable doubt as to whether Ms Machin had supplied the catalogue to the patient and felt profound unease at the way in which the allegations against Ms Machin were raised. However, he concluded that he could not find that the dismissal was unfair without substituting his own assessment of the evidence for that of the disciplinary panel' (Tribunal Decision, 1995, p. 21). Such substitution is not permissible according to current labour law.

However this decision is viewed, it was quite clear that the management at Ashworth Hospital did not emerge from this tribunal in a good light. Following the decision, they declined to agree damages and returned to the tribunal to claim that I had contributed to my own dismissal. On that occasion the tribunal found unanimously that this was not the case and awarded me maximum damages. They felt unable to order reinstatement on the basis that the trust between my former employer and myself had irretrievably broken down.

Conclusions

I spoke to a doctor in an ordinary NHS hospital recently who told me that management had just informed medical staff that, Hippocratic oath notwithstanding, their first duty was to the Trust and not to the patient. The issue behind NHS managerialism is not just the price that people like myself pay in terms of losing both a profession and a livelihood, but it is also the continuance of a fundamentally flawed and morally unacceptable way of running a public service.

It is bad enough that people such as myself and others have to swim against such a tide. It is worse that they sometimes drown in a sea of corruption, lies and deceit. One day, however, many more will take to the water.

Note

As from April 1996 the Special Hospital Service Authority was abandoned and all three special hospitals, including Ashworth, were redesignated as Health Authorities in their own right. They have the autonomy to develop their own business plans and to compete for work. The previous General Manager became the Chief Executive, and reports to a Board of executive and non-executive members headed by a Government-nominated chairman.

References

Blom-Cooper, L. (1992) *Report of the Committee of Inquiry into Complaints about Ashworth Hospital*. London: HMSO.

Goffman, E. (1961) *Asylums*. London: Peregrine.

Irons, A. (1992) *Transcript of Proceedings: Committee of Inquiry into Complaints about Ashworth Special Hospital*. Paper 42.7, p. 88.

Kaye, C. (1992) *Transcript of Proceedings: Committee of Inquiry into Complaints about Ashworth Special Hospital*. Paper 54.6, p. 5.

Lawrence, J. (1992) Staff brutality puts future of special hospitals in doubt. *The Times* 1 August, p. 5.

Machin, S. (1992) *Family involvement and visiting: submission to the Committee of Inquiry into Complaints about Ashworth Special Hospital*, p. 2.

Means, R. and Smith, R. (1994) *Community care, policy and practice*, London: Macmillan.

NHS Health Advisory Service (1995) *With care in mind secure – a review of the Special Hospitals Service Authority of the services provided by Ashworth Hospital.* London: Department of Health.

Social Services Inspectorate (1993) *Report of Inspection of Management and Provision of Social Work in Special Hospitals.* London: Social Services Inspectorate.

Tribunal Decision (1995) Reserved decision of the Industrial Tribunal. Case no. 23686/94, 21 June 1995.

6

Acquiescence in wrongdoing

Ron Thomson

> *The greatest evil is not done in those sordid 'dens of crime' that*
> *Dickens loved to paint . . . it is conceived and moved, seconded,*
> *carried and minuted . . . in clean, carpeted and well lighted offices,*
> *by quiet men with white collars and cut fingernails and smooth-*
> *shaven cheeks who do not need to raise their voices*
> *(The Screwtape Letters,* C S Lewis)

Introduction

During 1993–1994, one of the prevailing political slogans of the conservative government was 'back to basics', signifying a return to past
ethical and moral standards in society. This slogan had to be dropped
quickly when the media clearly showed that many of the politicians
promoting it were unable to live up to those standards. However, the
publicity led to the publication of the Nolan Committee report on standards in public life, and a code of guidance for all in public office.
Although we live in a time when public expectations of moral standards
from political and public leaders are at a low ebb, 'ethics' is now on the
cultural agenda.

It is recognized that problems with ethical standards in the workplace
extend well beyond the walls of Parliament. I believe that all of the
evidence indicates that the values of many people now working in the
caring and voluntary sector have changed for the worse, and as a consequence those who wish to act from the standpoint of professional ethics,
morality or justice are often being pushed aside.

In 1993 the Audit Commission reported that a survey carried out by
them showed that local authorities suffer around 54 000 detected
instances of fraud and corruption a year, involving losses totalling £25
million (Audit Commission, 1993). A follow-up report by them, published in December 1994, showed that detected fraud within the NHS
had been running at over £6 million during the previous 3 years (Audit

Commission, 1994, p. 10). This report also stated that the majority of the frauds could have been detected by colleagues and internal staff, yet one-third of the staff interviewed said that they would be unwilling to report fraud by colleagues. Of the Heads of Internal Audit teams whom they interviewed, over 20 per cent feared losing their jobs if they raised all of their concerns and criticisms with their managers and reported abuses and weaknesses in the system (Audit Commission, 1994).

If the very people who are employed to detect and prevent fraud and corruption are being pushed into a position of being afraid to report it, what does this say about the position of the rest of the staff? What does it say about the system in which everyone else in the organization is working?

What about charities – those organizations set up for the public good of the community by well-intentioned people with caring hearts? The annual report issued by the Charity Commissioners for 1995 showed that the number of charities found guilty of malpractice or maladministration had soared over the previous year, by one-third, to almost 400. A total of 45 charities had had their bank accounts frozen, 30 charities were ordered to restrict their activities, and nine trustees were removed (Charity Commission, 1995).

Three hundred people responded to a survey carried out in 1996 by the trade union Manufacturing Science Finance (MSF), about 50 per cent of them from charities and the rest from publicly funded housing associations. Nine out of ten said that they had wanted to raise an issue, but only 65 per cent had done so and, of those, over 80 per cent said that they believed they had suffered as a result (*The Guardian*, 1996).

Almost half (49 per cent) of 600 requests for legal help made to the charitable legal advice centre, Public Concern at Work, in their first year of operation were from employees concerned about corruption and financial malpractice by their employers (North, 1995). Freedom to Care, the corporate accountability campaign, has had a similar experience. The organization has publicized a large number of stories of conscientious employees who have experienced major problems including threats of violence, suspension, demotion, redundancy and dismissal after they have raised concerns about workplace standards (*The Whistle* – biannual publication of Freedom to Care, PO Box 125, West Molesey, Surrey KT8 1YE, UK).

Mike Probert Lewis, the Membership Services Manager of the Institute of Internal Auditors, is quoted as saying, 'Blowing the whistle is the short way to put yourself on the long term unemployment register' (Wills, 1995). In the same way, many conscientious employees have reported to Freedom to Care that once they had lost a job for 'blowing the whistle', new employers were unwilling to take them on in case their own practices were also criticized or exposed. This happened to me.

Fair references

I was offered a post as the Chief Executive of a charitable trust in the North West of England, only to have the job offer withdrawn before I had even started work. This happened immediately they discovered that I had been in dispute with my previous employer, a charity running a number of care homes for people with learning difficulties, over my allegations of bad practice. As the Trust were unwilling to tell me what they had been told by my previous employer, I was unable to confirm whether what they had been told was true or not. So, without being given a chance to defend myself – contradicting normal workplace disciplinary procedures – I was dismissed before I had even started work. By the time they had paid me compensation for breach of contract, two sets of legal fees, re-advertised the post, and so on, they had spent several additional thousands of pounds. I do not know whether they had something to hide in their practices which they were unwilling to have exposed to a conscientious Chief Executive. If they had really wanted such a Chief Executive, then they might at least have listened to my account of what had happened at my previous workplace.

Most whistleblowers find that nowadays it is virtually impossible to obtain fresh employment without a good reference from a previous employer. In my own case the reference by my previous employer had been given by someone who had not even worked alongside me at any time, a situation which – looking back – I suspect also occurred on a number of other occasions when I applied for jobs unsuccessfully. On this occasion it also happened on the telephone, which makes it difficult, if not impossible, to discover what has been said and hence to challenge the validity and accuracy of the reference.

The law since then has been clarified to give more protection to whistleblowers and others who may be given inaccurate references. In a recent House of Lords decision it was found that employers who provide a reference about an employee (or ex-employee) have a duty to exercise reasonable skill and care in the preparation of that reference (*The Guardian*, 1994). In one case, a woman who had the offer of a job withdrawn 3 days before she was due to start work successfully claimed that an inaccurate reference had destroyed her career prospects, and won £25 000 for lost earnings (*The Times*, 1996). However, in both of these court rulings it was necessary to be able to have access to the written reference in order to prove the case. Yet in many cases potential employers will resort to telephoning former employers and asking for verbal references over the phone in order to obtain quicker answers and information that would not normally be put in writing. There is little as yet that can be done to prevent this sort of situation from continuing to occur.

Expecting the impossible?

Is it acceptable for employers to expect employees to do something they consider to be unprofessional, bad practice, immoral or illegal? You may consider this a strange question to ask. Yet I am sure that such an expectation is quite common. Even the law is not, in practice, always clear on the issue.

The current legal system, and society in general, seem to have drifted towards placing the burden of proof on the victim rather than the victimizer. One often has the impression that the rape victim, the abused child, the neglected patient, and the relatives of corporate manslaughter victims have an unreasonable, even unbearable, burden placed upon them. The same applies to the conscientious citizen. When a person speaks out about abuses in their workplace, they are made to feel guilty, and have to prove beyond any reasonable expectation that they are not telling lies, that they are not being malicious, vengeful or envious, that they have not been paid to speak out, that they do not have an ulterior motive, or that they do not have a mental illness or personality disorder. Of course it is an important principle of justice that people accused of wrongdoing are presumed to be innocent until proven guilty, and I am not challenging that. I would argue, however, that equal rights and support should be given to the publicly spirited employee who speaks out.

When, as general manager of the above-mentioned care homes charity, I reported in writing to my board of directors that I had been threatened by a member of staff, they were unwilling to take any action against him. They were not even prepared to investigate the incident, since they did not ask me for the name of the person concerned.

On another occasion I reported that a person with severe learning difficulties (mental handicap) had been threatened with violence in front of witnesses by a member of the care support staff. A report came back to me saying that on 'thorough investigation' there was found to be no case to answer. However, I knew that the witness who had reported the incident to me had not even been interviewed during that 'investigation'.

Industrial tribunals in the past have often looked solely at aspects of employment law in isolation from the other pressures being placed on employees. They have often ignored issues such as the regulations adopted by professional bodies and the corresponding codes of practice and conduct. They have sometimes even ignored actions which employees have had to take (such as resignation) to protect themselves from potential prosecution in the courts. In my own industrial tribunal case my previous employer argued that I had brought the action for constructive dismissal *only* because they had made the other member of the senior management team redundant some 2 months after I had resigned. In their summary report the tribunal panel agreed that, because I had failed to submit the claim prior to that person being made redundant, the two issues were obviously connected. According to the tribunal regulations at the time of actual submission, because of holidays and the notice period, I still had nearly another 2 months in which to submit the claim. By waiting until I had taken full legal advice before submitting the claim I had effectively weakened my case. I no longer had any contact with any person connected with my previous employer, but I was still expected to anticipate what they would do some 2 months after I had walked out. However, when I took legal advice on this point I was told that there was nothing I could do about it. The law allows that period of time for people to obtain legal advice, but industrial tribunals are then apparently allowed to discriminate against those who try to do so.

There have also been a number of other cases of apparent injustice at tribunals arising where employees have taken the step of refusing to comply with instructions which they considered to be wrong or even illegal. However, many of these people were not supported by tribunal decisions because they had carried out those same instructions on previous occasions. It seems that if one carries out an employer's instruction once, then one is under pressure to keep following it because one knows one will have no legal support if one refuses to do so. This seems to be the case even if one only becomes aware of the fact that it is illegal, unethical or bad practice after one has complied the first time.

Too good for the job?

What happens when an employee goes on a training course which teaches new ideas or practices which prove to be unacceptable to the employer? I recall some years ago having to spend time counselling a person attending a 1-week training course I was involved in leading. The workshop was helping carers to look at how the image presented by the support services in which they worked affected the way in which clients are viewed by society generally. This person, a senior manager in a large social services department, had been affected by having to re-evaluate his whole career and professional work from an angle he had never seen before. He was worried about the problem he would now encounter back at his place of work, and how he could make the radical changes in working practices that he knew would not be widely supported by other senior managers and colleagues.

More recently I was talking to Bill (not his real name), a deputy manager in another social services department, about his experience of reporting physical abuse by his home manager to the department area manager. Bill had been sent by his department on a course on managing residential care. (This City and Guilds course is now widely recognized as the qualifying examination requirement for managers of residential care homes operating under the Registered Homes Act 1984.) Coming back with a number of fresh ideas on good practice, he was instructed not to introduce any of them, as his area manager 'did not agree' with them. The social services department had acknowledged that they had to retrain their staff in order to qualify for the new standards. However, they were not going to introduce the ideas that were being taught.

Bill had been previously trained as a nurse, and the course had confirmed to him the existence of a number of bad practices operating in his social services home. He had previously felt uneasy about many of them, but had begun to accept them as 'the norm' in social services departments. When he later started to report bad practice amongst colleagues, a number of allegations were then levelled at him by other colleagues and managers. These individuals had not previously made any complaints about Bill's work. The allegations began to surface only after he had started to press for the higher standards. At the time when I spoke with him he had been suspended for nearly a year despite having been cleared on appeal on all disciplinary charges made against him by his managers.

This type of reaction from work colleagues is not uncommon. It has been reported by a number of employees at support meetings organized for members of Freedom to Care. Colleagues are often worried about their own jobs and the risks of anyone raising concerns about practices and standards. In many cases we have heard reports of how the other staff have been actively encouraged – and sometimes even had pressure put on them – to make or support counter-complaints against the whistle-blower to undermine their case or integrity. It appears to be a case of attack being the best form of defence, belittling the complainant rather than attempting to look at the evidence concerning the matter being complained about. This type of defensiveness then discourages other potential complainants and whistleblowers from further rocking the boat. At a time of high unemployment it is perhaps not surprising that many workers will take the '30 pieces of silver', keeping their jobs irrespective of the betrayal of a work colleague with a justified complaint.

It is not just those people who go on professional training courses who become aware of their own errors of judgement in accepting 'the way things have always been done here'. Television, radio, newspapers and journals are now discussing more openly the subject of ethics and accountability. This awareness should be welcomed by all who are concerned about professional practices and want to see higher standards in the caring sector, particularly when dealing with vulnerable people. However, it brings with it new risks for a large number of people who have been forced or encouraged to rethink their positions. Where do they go for support? It can be difficult to blow the whistle, not just emotionally but also practically.

Markets and the voluntary sector

Public expenditure cuts and the market philosophy have not only had an impact on the public sector social services, but they have also thrown the voluntary sector provision into turmoil.

Certainly it would be true to say that many of the growing problems with accountability in the voluntary sector are independent of the introduction of market forces. These problems extend to the regulation of the sector. As the Charity Commission had previously stated that they 'were always willing to consider carefully any evidence of misconduct or mismanagement by Trustees or Officers of the Charity' (Charity Commission, 1997), I wrote to them about a number of actions taken or allowed by my former employers (the care homes charity I have already mentioned). I believed that these actions were illegal, and I stated that I believed that a member of the management committee was using his position as a charity trustee to line his own pocket. This was clearly in contravention of The Charities Act 1993 and the earlier 1960 Act based on the principle 'that a trustee must not have a personal interest in or place himself in a situation where his duty as a trustee conflicts with his personal interests' (Charity Commission, 1994).

I received a letter from the Commission saying that they had met with representatives of the charity concerned, and that they had found no evidence to support my suggestions and considered the case closed. They had previously refused to meet with me in order to hear the full details of my allegations. Their letter of reply showed that they had clearly been misled and given information which was irrelevant because it was about issues that I had not been raising. The Charity Commission regulates charities, and yet the public can have no confidence in its regulatory powers if it does not follow the basic principle of accountability of listening to both sides of a story. If you decide, like Nelson did, to put your telescope to your blind eye, then you will see nothing to cause you any concern.

It was not until the Commission was later reorganized and given additional powers to carry out more in-depth enquiries into allegations of malpractice or maladministration, especially where there is clear evidence of deliberate abuse, that we see the results. As a consequence, the Commission investigators, as stated earlier in this chapter, found that the conviction rate then soared by 34 per cent over the previous year. One wonders if this is again a case of 'too little, too late'. The recognition of the number of high-profile financial frauds in the City and the complexity of investigating them led to the establishment of specialized squads of lawyers and accountants. Even these specialists have been unable to obtain a significant number of convictions due to being unable to give juries sufficiently detailed explanations to enable them to understand the complexity of the movements of money between companies based in different countries, different laws and reporting regulations. One has only to look at the accounts of many charities today who have set up non-charitable trading subsidiaries and service companies to carry out work on their behalf, to see the similarity. A growing number of them are also having to tender against competition from other charities and the private sector to do work on behalf of the social services departments of local authorities and/or health trusts in order to survive. This competitiveness and complexity also creates problems of accountability and standards. Opportunities for wrongdoing abound, and the whistleblower may become ensnared in a web of colluding interests.

Dr Jill Mordaunt, Director of the Voluntary Sector Management Programme at the Open University, has been quoted as saying, 'With pressures increasing on voluntary sector organizations to compete on price for contracts, perhaps by skimping on staff training or cover, protecting whistleblowers from victimization might help defend vulnerable people from incompetence, corruption or abuse' (*The Guardian*, 1996).

According to Martin Sime, the Director of the Scottish Council for Voluntary Organizations, the situation is even worse, as there is no Scottish equivalent to the Charity Commissioners, and a number of recent scandals have rocked public confidence in charities. He also highlighted a point raised in a report by a special Government task force on the voluntary sector, which accused the Scottish legal regime of being weak and disjointed and called for a major review (*The Sunday Times*, 1994).

Market forces have, I believe, compounded the problems of the internal and public accountability of voluntary sector organizations. Voluntary organizations and charities have in recent years tended to become run more like businesses, each one seeking to grow to become the largest and most successful in the field, and competing with the others to get the largest share of the market. Each one tries to persuade the public that it is the most important in order to attract more business. These organizations try to lower costs through larger scale developments, and thus put themselves in a position to attract larger and larger sums of money in the form of grants and donations. This desire to grow has persuaded some of them that 'short cuts' are worth taking, irrespective of the final cost. Since it remains a basic truth that people would rather do business with honest voluntary organizations, some have to engage in secrecy and cover up, and may view questioning conscientious staff as a threat.

One of the market forces pushing this need to grow is the work of government quango organizations, such as the Housing Corporation, looking for 'value for public money'. Grants are being held up to housing associations as rewards in exchange for submitting the lowest tenders and highest numbers of beds offered, often irrespective of the quality of the housing management service, and this has led to publicly funded Housing Associations trying to outbid each other. It has been highlighted over many years that effective community care requires the development of small-scale housing provision, but at a recent meeting with a housing association I was told that they were not building any new schemes with over 40 places. When I pointed out the research showing that this was too large for a scheme to integrate people into the community, they told me of a similar scheme recently opened by another association with 400 bed spaces. Of course, building costs per bed space decrease as the size of the scheme increases, and in the same way economy of scale reduces the management running costs, but the needs of the individual tend to get lost to the same degree.

Over ten years ago I wrote an article which suggested, rather provocatively, that the voluntary housing sector appeared to be employing Rachman, the notoriously exploitative private landlord of the 1960s, as their housing management advisor (MIND, 1986). I had, as the Housing Officer for national MIND, become aware that a growing number of charities were introducing clauses into their residents' occupancy agreements which were taking away their residents' legal rights. For example, one charity set up to assist 'lonely single people' had a clause preventing residents from receiving any visitors in their rooms. The vast majority of agreements I was reading at that time tried to prevent residents from having any privacy, so that, for example, staff members were able to enter private bedrooms without prior permission being sought.

When the original founder members of these old established charities were working flat out as unpaid volunteers to establish these housing schemes for homeless and other vulnerable people, they were concerned with providing the residents with real homes. Later, as the career charity worker came in, those original purposes and ideals were 'professionalized' out, and instead rules and regulations were brought in for the residents to obey. The sector originally set up to support the more vulnerable clients by provision of housing was becoming more concerned with removing its clients' legal rights to satisfy rules imposed by the funding organizations such as the Housing Corporation. This had the side-effect of leaving the residents unable to defend themselves against unjust practices by staff.

It was another 2 years after my original article appeared before the National Federation of Housing Associations and the Campaign for Homeless and Rootless People (CHAR) were able jointly to publish guidelines designed to introduce some protection for residents in shared housing schemes (National Federation of Housing Associations, 1988). Even now, many voluntary housing organizations are ignoring those recommendations and eroding or denying their residents' rights in accommodation supposedly set up to help them to flourish.

So far we have only looked at the effects on employees, but other individuals, such as clients, relatives and concerned citizens, are also involved in caring voluntary organizations. The National Schizophrenia Fellowship (NSF) was founded in 1972 to provide support groups for relatives of people who were affected by schizophrenia. For many years the organization campaigned against closure of long-stay mental hospitals and the move towards provision of care in the community. The group, consisting mainly of relatives of people with schizophrenia, was concerned that if the hospitals were closed there would be fewer care resources to look after their family members.

With the growth of the contract culture in health provision, senior staff within the NSF saw an opportunity to change direction and to start to develop more of their own resources to ensure that the services they wanted were going to be available and run in the way they wanted them managed. This change was not entirely popular, and a number of the elected trustees of the charity spoke out against the policy changes, claiming that the changes in direction were partly a consequence of the personal ambitions and interests of some of the decision-makers.

For example, Rosemary Moore, a long-serving National Council of Management member and Charity Trustee of the NSF, pointed out that the organization had withdrawn a campaign against the closure of a Surrey long-term mental health hostel. This about turn occurred only after the charity had received a grant of £175 000 from Surrey Social Services Department towards the provision of an NSF short-term respite care scheme – a scheme serving a different need for a different client group (*Community Care*, 1994). In another article Moore pointed out that the NSF managers had issued a new policy document to the media which had not been seen or approved by the individuals elected by the membership. In her view, the document had also contradicted policy statements previously approved by the full Council of Trustees (National Schizophrenia Fellowship, 1994). Following a series of complaints to the press and the Charity Commissioners, the NSF National Executive took steps to remove Moore from the main Council of Management, despite the fact that she had the backing of her local NSF group and had been elected by the full membership (National Schizophrenia Fellowship, 1993).

The contract culture in community care, so heavily pushed by the Conservative government as a way of reforming local government and health authorities, has had a similar effect on the way in which a number of other charities work. Many local groups who were relying on grants to run their central office administration have now been told that they will not receive any grant from the local authority, but only a service contract to provide clearly defined service targets. The service contract usually spells out the right to cancel the contract if the local authority feels that the group is not meeting the set targets. These contracts are, by their very nature, difficult to define precisely, especially in terms of quality of care, but usually have the social services manager, as the person paying, as the final judge.

This limits the ability of campaigning charities to challenge the performance of social services managers in the provision of services to their client groups. You can imagine the response of a service manager reading in his local newspaper over breakfast, about a local MIND group criticizing the quality of care provided by a local social services day centre and then going into a meeting later that same day to review an application for that group to be given a fresh contract to run a similar service. He who pays the piper will call the tune, but at what cost to the disabled client groups who lose their voice and influence?

Silence is not golden

Strong pressure is undoubtedly being put on care staff to stand by and accept the things which they might once have regarded as being immoral, professionally unethical, or even illegal, but this is not an entirely new phenomenon. Over the years there have been numerous scandals reported about the treatment of some of the most vulnerable individuals in society – people who could not speak up for themselves because of fear of reprisal. Perhaps, however, the modern era of public sector 'whistleblowing' can be dated back to a statement made 30 years ago. A report published in 1967 about the ill-treatment and abuse of patients in Ely Hospital in Cardiff prompted the editor of the *Nursing Mirror* to comment in the editorial,

> More depressing even than the harrowing details of inept administration and resulting malpractice has been the message that emerged time and time again in reports such as these – that nurses who have attempted to put things right have suffered personal discredit as a result, and what is more, failed to alter the situation.
>
> (*Nursing Mirror*, 1967)

People have been willing to put themselves at risk by standing up for what they believe to be right. Yet some of the worst atrocities that have happened in the world have occurred because people have stood back and let them happen, even though they had the ability to speak out and stop them. We all know the result of the holocaust that took place in the early 1940s, when millions of Jewish people were exterminated in concentration camps across Europe.

We can all blame the Nazi Party, yet the party's leadership did not have the backing of the majority of the membership when they started their crusade. In 1928, a survey of the party members showed that 63 per cent were opposed to any harm being done to the Jews, 32 per cent were apathetic and only 5 per cent were in favour of harming the Jews. In 1942, the number of people opposed to harming the Jews had dropped to 26 per cent, the number of apathetic individuals had risen to 69 per cent, whilst the number in favour of harming the Jews had remained constant at 5 per cent. So with only one in 20 of the membership in favour of harming the Jewish people, Hitler and the other Nazi leadership felt able to carry out mass killings because they knew that the vast majority of people *would stay silent* (personal communication, 1996, D. Madden, Lecturer in Peace Studies at the Tantur Institute, based on original research conducted by the Hebrew University, Jerusalem). It was the apathy of the people that gave Hitler free rein to attempt to exterminate the Jews – not the support of the party members.

Of course, in raising concern about abuses of the elderly or other vulnerable groups of people in care homes today, we are not assuming that this can be put on a level with the holocaust. However, it is worth juxtaposing the two in order to understand that the effect of people staying silent when they know abuses or bad practices are taking place within their own workplace gives a permit to abusers to continue their wrongdoing and evil. We should also remember that the first people to be sent to the gas chambers in Nazi Germany were not the Jews but powerless Germans – the people who were resident in long-stay mental institutions. If we do not speak out against a system that abuses vulnerable people now, will we be allowed to speak out later when society turns against our own group? At what point shall we stand up and be counted? Will we still have the right to do so at that time?

Martin Luther King once said, 'we shall have to repent in this generation, not so much for the evil deeds of the wicked people, but for the appalling silence of the good people'. The action of those managers who try to stop people from speaking out about abuses – by using gagging clauses in employment contracts, making threats and bullying, dismissing conscientious staff, or making false accusations – is not the action of the good people referred to by Martin Luther King. Those managers are the modern equivalent of Pontius Pilate trying to wash the blood of Jesus off his hands in order to demonstrate his innocence in the affair when in fact he had the real power to stop it.

Conclusions

Society needs to show that it approves of the integrity and courage of professionals and all employees who speak out against authorities which seek to cover up abuses of all kinds. Protection needs to be given now to people who are being threatened by employers seeking to hide abuses and low standards, while we still have the right to freedom of speech.

We need to amend the employment laws that fail to protect employees, even if only to ensure that the human and civil values we seek to preserve are still there tomorrow. I do not know any person in the caring sector who took the risk of losing all that they had – their job, their career, their livelihood and their freedom – and spoke out to support the rights of others, without giving it a great deal of thought beforehand. It takes courage to challenge wrongdoing, but if we do not support those willing to do this today, will they still be here tomorrow?

References

Audit Commission (1993) *Protecting the public purse. Probity in the public sector: combating fraud and corruption in local government.* London: HMSO.

Audit Commission (1994) *Protecting the public purse. 2. Ensuring probity in the NHS.* London: HMSO.

Charity Commission (1994) *Decisions of the Charity Commissioners. Vol. 2.* London: HMSO.

Charity Commission (1995) *Report of the Charity Commission for England and Wales.* London: HMSO.

Charity Commission (1997) *Charity Commissioners Annual Report.* London: HMSO.

Community Care (1994) News report. 24 April 1994.

Department of Health and Social Security (1984) *Guidance notes on registration systems for residential care homes and registered homes tribunals.* London: Department of Health and Social Security.

The Guardian (1994) Law Report: House of Lords. Spring V Guardian Assurance plc. 16 July.

The Guardian (1996) Charity law: you know how to whistle. 26 June, p. 26.

MIND (1986) Housing matters. *Open Mind* **No. 24**, December issue.

National Federation of Housing Associations (1988) *Residents' rights in special needs housing. A Working Party Report.* London: National Federation of Housing Associations and the Campaign for Homeless and Rootless People.

National Schizophrenia Fellowship (1993) *Weybridge Branch Newsletter. July issue.* Weybridge: National Schizophrenia Fellowship.

National Schizophrenia Fellowship (1994) *Weybridge Branch Newsletter. September issue.* Weybridge: National Schizophrenia Fellowship.

North, S. J. (1995) Firms hear plea to open up. *Personnel Today*, 28 February.

Nursing Mirror (1967) Editorial. 16 June, p. 241.

The Sunday Times (1994) How Scots law opens the door to charity cheats. 4 September, p. 8.

The Times (1996) Brenton V Glamorgan University. In Law Reports section. 25 May.

Wills, J. (1995) Best behaviour. *Personnel Today*. 21 November.

Part Two

Developing the Profession

7

Social workers speak out

Geoffrey Hunt and Diana Campbell

Introduction

When misconduct finally hits the headlines, the following questions are on everyone's lips. How could this have happened? Why was it allowed to continue for so long? Why did no one report it sooner? Two surveys of social workers, one in 1993 and one in 1995, may go some way to providing answers to these questions.

The 1993 Survey

In September 1993, *Care Weekly* magazine (now closed) published the results of a survey into whistleblowing (*Care Weekly*, 1993). The 142 respondents (response rate 15.4 per cent) from across the UK were field social workers (29 per cent), residential social workers (50 per cent), some day/domiciliary workers (10 per cent) and a few others. It found that nearly four out of five of them had witnessed incidents of 'bad practice' such as neglect, failure to respond to needs, abuses (physical, verbal, mental and financial), falsifying of records and discrimination. However, a large proportion (about 17 per cent) of these witnesses to bad practice did not report it, mainly because of perceived poor managerial support and fear of isolation and victimization. The survey also showed unequivocally that the media was the last port of call for staff concerned about misconduct. No one wanted to go to the media. Staff wanted matters sorted out internally.

So why are organizations unable to prevent misconduct? The *Care Weekly* survey asked respondents what would discourage them from reporting misconduct, and 32 per cent cited poor management attitudes and said that they did not believe their managers would support them. A further 17.5 per cent feared that they would be victimized. A *Care Weekly* campaign on the issue, supported by a number of organizations, including Freedom to Care, generated a huge amount of interest among grass-roots staff, senior managers and MPs. Together with the University of East London, a conference was held which led to the idea for this book. Activity has continued to help whistleblowers find the confidence to report early any concerns that they may have about the standards of care in their workplace. Given this activity the University of East London was keen to see whether attitudes among staff are changing. Therefore, in late 1995 it undertook its own survey, which follows upon a related survey of whistleblowing health care professionals which it conducted in 1993 (Hunt and Shailer, 1995).

The 1995 Survey

In 1995, 2000 questionnaires were sent out and there were 357 responses (i.e. a response rate of 17.8 per cent). Over 50 per cent held some position of authority in their profession. To be more precise, of the total respondents, about one-third were team managers or leaders, just under one-third were field social workers/care managers (including those in senior posts), about 25 per cent were heads of a home, centre or school, and the rest were deputy heads, residential social workers, care workers, and a handful of education department social workers.

About 75 per cent of them were divided equally between field work and residential care, and the remaining 25 per cent were divided between day centre work, domiciliary work and work in development. Over one-third worked with the elderly, and nearly one-third worked with the learning disabled. (The precise breakdown for client groups, bearing in mind that some work in more than one category, was as follows: children/families, 75; elderly people, 124; adults, 42; people with mental health problems, 44; people with physical disabilities, 47; people with learning disabilities, 102; people with a multiple disability, 33; all client groups, 7.)

When asked which sector they worked in, 274 (77 per cent) said that they worked in the statutory (i.e. local authority) sector, 27 (7.5 per cent) in the private sector and 56 (15.5 per cent) in the not-for-profit sector. The overwhelming majority – in fact two-thirds – were experienced social workers, having over 10 years' service. The breakdown for length of service of the respondents was as follows: up to 2 years, 11; 3–5 years, 38; 6–10 years, 73; over 10 years, 235 (66 per cent).

Over 25 per cent of the respondents possessed university degrees. Formal qualifications were as follows (some fell into more than one category, of course): ASW, 27; CSS/CQSW/DipSW, 223; non-social work professional qualification such as RGN/RMN, 60; teaching qualification, 40; university degree, 95.

The survey included a good cross-section of demographic areas. In total, 64 respondents (18 per cent) said that they work in the inner city, 54 in the outer urban area, 56 in the suburban area and 181 (51 per cent) in the small town/rural areas of the UK (two respondents failed to answer).

(Note that in the following tables 'don't knows' include some answers which were spoiled or indistinctly marked, and that percentage values do not always add up to 100 per cent because of the method of rounding up fractions.)

The work environment

Two-thirds of the respondents identified a staff shortage in their work-place. They were about equally divided as to whether work was mainly frustrating or satisfying, but 50 per cent said that stress levels were destructive rather than creative. Over 50 per cent thought that there was insufficient administrative/logistical support, and they were equally divided as to whether they thought their salary was adequate. A total of 50 per cent thought that poor practitioners ('bad apples') significantly affected care, 40 per cent thought that managers do not understand staff difficulties, and 30 per cent thought that management's objectives are largely inconsistent with professional standards (see Table 7.1).

An open question asked, 'What do you think are the most important factors affecting everyday practice?'. Although the questionnaire had a separate section for issues of management, an overwhelming number of respondents in this section identified problems with management as the most important factor. The general drift of answers presents a distressing picture of contemporary social work. Questionnaire after questionnaire mentioned a lack of managerial support, a management out of touch with practice, too much form-filling, and poor team work and supervision. They said that there is little policy guidance, and little chance to reflect or develop practice since they were understaffed, overworked and too stressed to do anything but juggle with the latest crisis. Levels of sickness and absenteeism were high, there was far too much paperwork, and unqualified agency staff often made matters worse. Poor inter-agency co-operation and constant reorganization left staff feeling insecure and demoralized. A number of respondents mentioned a lack of honesty with staff and with clients, and poor respect for confidentiality. Respondents are, on the whole, certainly not describing a work environment consistent with corporate responsibility and ethics. Here are some of the answers in detail.

'All staff should be kept up to date and informed of what is going on – no secrets, no staff cliques. Regular staff meetings are very important.'

Table 7.1

Question: Please tick one of each of the following pairs of statements that most closely describes your place of work or how you feel about work. (Leave blank if you don't know.)

1	Shortage of staff	230	(66%)
	Sufficient staff	125	(35%)
	Don't know	2	
2	Mainly wrong skill-mix	43	(12%)
	Mainly right skill-mix	296	(83%)
	Don't know	18	
3	Mainly frustration at work	167	(47%)
	Mainly satisfaction in work	178	(50%)
	Don't know	12	
4	Destructive stress level	182	(51%)
	Creative stress level	133	(37%)
	Don't know	42	
5	Inadequate training	141	(40%)
	Adequate training	202	(57%)
	Don't know	12	
6	Lack of support for improving knowledge	132	(37%)
	Sufficient support for improving knowledge	207	(58%)
	Don't know	18	
7	Particularly difficult clients	196	(55%)
	Not particularly difficult clients	134	(38%)
	Don't know	27	
8	Managers do not understand staff difficulties	144	(40%)
	Managers do understand staff difficulties	193	(54%)
	Don't know	20	
9	Management's objectives are largely inconsistent with professional standards	107	(30%)
	Management's objectives are largely consistent with professional standards	227	(64%)
	Don't know	23	
10	Inadequate administrative/logistic support	194	(54%)
	Adequate administrative/logistic support	145	(41%)
	Don't know	18	
11	Inappropriate recruitment	101	(28%)
	Appropriate recruitment	230	(64%)
	Don't know	26	
12	Inadequate salaries	165	(46%)
	Adequate salaries	166	(46%)
	Don't know	26	
13	'Bad apples' significantly affect care	177	(50%)
	'Bad apples' do not significantly affect care	126	(35%)
	Don't know	54	(15%)

'At grass-roots level everyday practice is still generally very good – staff very service/client oriented. But increasingly senior managers become more concerned about running the SSD (Social Services Department) as a business and fulfilling political ideology which is at odds with the culture of welfare and social services. In too many cases our employers and managers do not support or care about the work we do. They are far more interested in their own ambition and right-wing political correctness'.

'The anomalous idiosyncrasies between each budget-holding district office. Autonomous decisions taken by maverick managers to cut budgets. Weakness or reluctance of area managers to discourage bad practice. The public thinking that services are needs led, while social services ignoring individual needs and choice. Problems with other agencies, particularly housing benefit claims. Social services financial services way behind with payments to carers for services provided. Huge differences between managerial policy statement in theory and the practice which actually happens'.

'High managerial expectations *vis-à-vis* lack of manpower resources. Oppressive case loads. Staff are abused by managers who do not seem to understand what is going on at operational level. Totally ineffective management'.

'Employers continue to treat social work staff as second class with appalling buildings to work in. There can also be varying levels of stress due to volume of work and additional pressures to provide statistical information on top of normal social work practice'.

'I believe social work has taken on the culture of managerialism – targets, budgets, accountability, value for money, throughput, etc. – at the expense of the values more traditionally held within the profession'.

'Level of work affects ability to plan and structure work, increases stress levels, affects confidence and has a domino effect on other cases. Management approval process and lack of resources beyond front-line staff propping things up – debilitates positive work'.

'Excessive bureaucracy and form-filling is oppressive to client and destructive to self-esteem and professionalism of workers. Confusion and poor communication in department as part of incessant change process. Confused procedures as a result. Shortage of resources and budget constraints. Dissonance between raised expectations of public and actual delivery'.

'Pressure of work which results in time only to deal with crises.

Assessment and speed of response taking precedence over long-term and preventive work'.

'Clients not informed of their rights. Difficulties in multi-agency co-operation, e.g. NHS and local authority have different agendas/ priorities'.

'The ability to work as a team and support one another through the highs and lows. Always maintaining an atmosphere of honesty with col-leagues – if I do something wrong I expect someone in my team to tell me'.

'Too much emphasis on pleasing the bosses. Shop-window care, but underneath there's poor practice'.

'A general lack of confidentiality in relation to both clients and staff matters'.

'Need a realization by staff that the home is the client's, and work to a Code of Practice'.

'Lack of understanding of basic care ethics from senior management – unprofessional attitude towards 'shop-floor' staff by senior management. Lack of support'.

'Budget considerations dictating policy rather than good practice – caus-ing tokenism in practice policies'.

'Need participation in determining future of the service and how it affects *me*'.

'The level of bureaucracy in social work hampers imaginative practice. The amount of back-watching by senior managers generates unrest and insecurity among field staff'.

'Need an understanding and sympathetic attitude from senior/middle managers. Managers should be truthful'.

'Distant, uninformed, business-oriented senior managers'.

'Management's objectives are inconsistent with professional standards'.

'Lack of planning for the future. Social services always tend to react to crisis rather than planning strategies to avoid future crisis. Planning and development is seen as low priority, and any undertaken tends to be done by high management ... who have little working knowledge to guide them'.

'Need an atmosphere where people can feel comfortable enough to share concerns about people they have a responsibility to help, and also for themselves. People should be able to put their heads above the parapets without getting their heads shot off'.

'Political interference – lack of resources. Management attitude of "You are on your own – do not bother us, but God help you if it goes wrong" '.

'Who is thinking about service users while "reorganization" is going on?'

'There's a siege mentality'.

'It seems that paper is more important than people. During the last audit, several cases were selected as examples of good practice. It concerns me that the audit concentrates on the process of assessment, i.e. completing the correct number of forms. The auditors did not focus on the outcome. The audit appeared not to be concerned with social work practice issues. People are left feeling that administrative work is more important to the Department'.

'So-called "business culture" influences. Over-emphasis on safeguarding rather than promoting children's welfare. Domination of the "blame culture", especially in child protection, leading to a "play safe" mentality'.

'Regional management (32 miles away) operates in a very controlling and autocratic manner. Genuine consultation does not happen. Clerical support is one typist for 19 staff. No computerized information system. No budget control'.

'Avalanche of pointless self-serving money-wasting paperwork. Increase in administrative tasks. Less time available for, and less value placed on, traditional social work. Funding problems. Low morale'. (From a social worker with over 10 years' experience.)

'Changes in top and middle management have resulted in changes to work practice – job security is not a concern to these managers, thus increased insecurity of staff creates stress. Top and middle managers do not see "people", only "budgets" and how to impose cuts – this directly affects *clients*, and experienced care workers, who are and will be lost to the care profession. PIII Residential Care is being destroyed'.

'Lack of higher management support and respect. A case where a member of staff has been suspended due to a client complaint is at present going on in the workplace. That poor staff member has received no support at all from higher management'.

Misconduct

The results in this section are rather disturbing. We allowed a number of people unconnected with social services to see Table 7.2, and they were all surprised at the high level of misconduct among professionals who are perceived as being 'front-line' helpers of distressed or vulnerable members of the public. One has to be careful in interpreting the data in the table. It does seem that some respondents may have included client misconduct against staff or staff misconduct against staff, although it is clear enough that the questions are meant to capture staff misconduct against clients, and the remarks added by respondents indicate that nearly everyone understood us to be talking about staff on client misconduct. Two respondents insisted on speaking of management misconduct towards staff, and made annotations in the margin to make this clear. Furthermore, we have to say that it is not always clear whether respondents are referring to incidents of misconduct by different members of staff or, at least in some cases, by the same person. One helpful respondent ticked nine of the misconduct categories and added, 'This all applies to one senior manager and her treatment of some staff, which was unsatisfactorily dealt with by top management'. One should also bear in mind that there is some evidence that people generally tend to under-report, rather than over-report, incidents of misconduct.

What Table 7.2 does suggest is the urgent need for more refined research on this issue, with cross-comparisons with the findings of regulatory bodies such as that for nurses, midwives and health visitors. The question of the incidence of misconduct is surely connected with the case now being made for a self-regulatory body for social/care workers (see Chapter 10). The relationship of the incidence of misconduct to high stress levels and low morale reported by social workers is also an important issue.

Two-fifths of respondents have witnessed verbal abuse of clients in the past 2 years, and one-third have personally reported this form of abuse. A surprising 25 per cent of the social workers questioned had personally reported to a superior the physical abuse of a client by other staff members in the last 2 years. Even more worrying (and this really needs to be researched in more detail), one in 12 respondents said that they had reported sexual abuse in the previous 2-year period. One-fifth had reported breach of confidentiality in the last 2 years, and well over 25 per cent had reported staff 'not responding to client' in the same period. It

Table 7.2

Question: Read the table below and then fill it in, a column at a time. In column A put a cross against misconduct that you have *witnessed at any time* during your career. In column B put a cross against misconduct that you have *witnessed in the past 2 years* of your work. In column C put a cross against misconduct which a client has *complained about to you*, but not witnessed by you, in the past 2 years. In column D put a cross against misconduct which you have taken any step to *report* to a superior in the past 2 years.

	A	B	C	D
1 Verbal abuse	131 (37%)	146 (41%)	119 (33%)	118 (33%)
2 Severe verbal abuse	118 (33%)	67 (19%)	41 (11%)	51 (14%)
3 Emotional abuse	144 (40%)	76 (21%)	54 (15%)	60 (17%)
4 Severe emotional abuse	57 (16%)	29 (8%)	16 (4%)	22 (6%)
5 Physical abuse	114 (32%)	48 (13%)	68 (19%)	84 (24%)
6 Severe physical abuse	28 (8%)	13 (3.5%)	16 (4%)	20 (5.5%)
7 Sexual abuse	28 (8%)	14 (4%)	28 (8%)	30 (8.5%)
8 Theft, fraud	92 (26%)	47 (13%)	58 (16%)	70 (20%)
9 Physical neglect	100 (28%)	59 (16.5%)	29 (8%)	50 (14%)
10 Not responding to client	192 (54%)	150 (42%)	105 (29%)	105 (29%)
11 Not consulting client	197 (55%)	163 (46%)	82 (23%)	90 (25%)
12 Lying to client	124 (35%)	61 (17%)	38 (11%)	42 (12%)
13 Falsifying or omitting record	88 (25%)	55 (15%)	13 (3.5%)	36 (10%)
14 Affront to privacy/dignity	195 (55%)	105 (29%)	59 (16.5%)	81 (23%)
15 Breach of confidentiality	158 (44%)	97 (27%)	43 (12%)	75 (21%)
16 Racism	101 (28%)	70 (20%)	23 (6%)	47 (13%)
17 Sexism	123 (34%)	83 (23%)	25 (7%)	43 (12%)

must be remembered that, to report an incident, staff did not need to have witnessed it. It could have been reported to them by someone else, e.g. a colleague, client or relative. One certainly needs to run a more refined survey to check on these figures, which admittedly are difficult for many to believe.

Respondents were asked to say, at the bottom of Table 7.2, what 'other' forms of misconduct they had encountered. A number mentioned 'ageism' and 'insensitivity to religious belief'. The vast majority had nothing to add, but here are some of the remarks of those who did.

'General talking about a client to another professional in a derogatory way, e.g. "He's an attention-seeker", and this being repeated to the client. This divides staff and is not good for clients and leads to mistrust – clients will stop attending/talking'.

'Enforcing a misinterpretation of the law or completely ignoring a legal duty by district manager – I did report it and advised client's carers of rights'.

'Segregation – ethnic minority clients are not admitted into white-dominated homes'.

'Emotional neglect. Preference given to non-confused client rather than confused client (e.g. allocation of single room)'.

Overbearing, false, patronizing attitudes to clients'.

'Institutional degradation of people'.

'Language – disregard for first choice, and omitting others from group conversation because they do not speak the same language'.

'Maladministration of medication. Use of illegal substances at work. Being drunk at work'.

'We have a very good working practice and policy and procedures'. (A head of home with over 10 years' experience who gives only one case of misconduct: 'Lying to client'.)

Raising concerns

Social workers were asked how they felt about raising concerns in the workplace (see Table 7.3), e.g. concerns about the kinds of misconduct listed in Table 7.2. About one-third of respondents thought that it had become more difficult in the previous 2 years to raise concerns, although nearly everyone agreed that although resources were scarce it was still important to raise concerns about misconduct. At the same time, 75 per cent thought that the law does not give adequate protection to whistle-blowers and needs changing. They were almost equally divided as to whether they would take a serious concern to the media as a last resort, with slightly more apparently being prepared to do so. Well over 25 per cent thought that constructive criticism is not generally appreciated by colleagues, but over twice as many thought the opposite, and the proportions were virtually the same regarding whether, when a concern is raised, colleagues are sufficiently co-operative and supportive. It is worrying that quite a large proportion of these social workers do not appear to trust their colleagues in whistleblowing situations.

The most common answer to the open question 'What do you think is the most important factor affecting your willingness or unwillingness to

Table 7.3

Question: Imagine you were thinking about raising a concern about misconduct (such as those listed in Table 7.2) *in your own workplace.* How easy/difficult would you expect this to be? Put a cross in one of the pair of boxes for each factor listed.

1   Constructive criticism is not generally appreciated
       by colleagues   105 (29%)
     Constructive criticism is generally appreciated
       by colleagues   240 (67%)
     Don't know   12

2   Colleagues insufficiently co-operative/supportive when
       concern is raised   83 (23%)
     Colleagues sufficiently co-operative/supportive when
       concern is raised   253 (71%)
     Don't know   21

3   Union not sufficiently supportive   118 (33%)
     Union sufficiently supportive   128 (36%)
     Don't know   111 (31%)

4   A national professional register (like that for nurses
       and midwives) would not help to improve skills   87 (24%)
     A national register would help to improve skills   216 (60.5%)
     Don't know   54 (15%)

5   A national professional register and code of conduct
       would not significantly help to improve conduct   65 (18%)
     A register would significantly help to improve conduct   238 (66%)
     Don't know   54 (15%)

6   I would not consider taking a serious concern to the
       media as a last resort because it is too risky for me   140 (39%)
     I would consider taking a serious concern to the
       media as a last resort even if it is risky for me   173 (48%)
     Don't know   44 (12%)

7   The law gives adequate protection to whistleblowers
       and does not need changing   29 (8%)
     The law does not give adequate protection to
       whistleblowers and needs changing   267 (75%)
     Don't know   61 (17%)

8   In the past 2 years it has not become any more difficult
       to raise concerns   211 (59%)
     In the past 2 years it has become more difficult
       to raise concerns   111 (31%)
     Don't know   35 (10%)

9   Resources are so scarce that there is no point in raising
       concerns about misconduct   15 (4%)
     Although resources are scarce, it is still important
       to raise concerns about misconduct   327 (92%)
     Don't know   13 (3.5%)

raise concerns in the workplace?' is support from management and the knowledge that one will not be victimized in any way. Many feared that they would be scapegoated or even lose their job, and a large number wondered how they could go on working with people once they had complained about them. There appeared to be more concern about lack of support from senior management than from middle management. Specific answers included the following.

'That others may turn against me – not understand my motives for doing so, think I am a goody-goody, try to get their own back, not talk to me, make life unpleasant, want me to leave'.

'I do not find it difficult to raise concerns as I feel protected by my role in the union. I am also used to negotiations/discussions with all senior managers. Have used the media in the past'.

'One chooses one's battle – but you could find a battle every day if you put your mind to it'.

'The huge difference between theory and practice and the collusiveness (*sic*) between managers to protect each other. Usually grievances have to be formalized (put in procedure) or nothing happens. I find that once a policy statement is issued managers believe that it automatically happens and then carry on, ignoring the reality'.

'. . . the hierarchy: most of them are not qualified social workers and don't like to talk the truth, they are biased, they use the procedure to suit themselves, and it takes too long to deal with the issues of importance. [The] innocent always pay the price. Directors of social services are too political and don't like criticisms because of publicity, don't listen to the grass roots'.

'Exhaustion! People are so busy and have little time, i.e. apathy rules. People seem to be only interested if it affects them, and to raise concerns can end up being a lonely crusade. Support, speed in dealing with problem, adequate systems to deal with them'.

'I do not have the tenacity or stamina required to follow the concerns through to the end'.

'Reaction of staff – splitting into for and against – becomes personalized. Proof is difficult – social work can be such an individualized job, workers skilled in hiding bad practice or transferring blame'.

'Job security. Informal peer group issues'.

'At the end of the day it's what I'm in this job for. If I failed to raise serious concerns about clients then I'm failing not only them, but also myself'.

'We have a responsibility to the people we offer a service to – if or when this is inappropriate then this is to be questioned and/or challenged'.

'I have in the past raised concerns and life was made difficult for me. Nothing I could prove victimization for, e.g. I was called to the office for a "talk" about incidents which had nothing to do with me, my request forms for training would go "missing" until it was too late to put them in'.

'Injustice and harm to clients/staff would make me raise concerns. I can't think of any factor that would prevent me raising concerns. Being sure of my facts and being able to evidence the concerns raised'.

'You, the innocent party, are made to feel more guilty than the person accused. Kangaroo courts are not good enough, encourage cover-ups'.

'Lack of power in getting rid of staff who are guilty of misconduct. County councils do not want bad publicity, so avoid confrontation. Fear of reprisals from senior management, being labelled a trouble-maker, thus affecting my career'.

'So very little confidentiality everyone would be told and then they become judge and jury'.

'On the only occasion I have had to make a complaint about serious misconduct both line manager and Human Resources asked for lengthy report and did nothing with it!'

'Within my own workplace the atmosphere is one of honesty and openness between staff team – raising concerns is seen as professional necessity. But the attitude of senior management – they'd rather not know, or this is the impression they give, when reporting concerns about external agencies'.

'Powerful unions and higher management both seem to see more need to support staff of lower grades than to support the clients abused – a lot of time is wasted and the result is usually that offending staff should be "counselled". It seems impossible to remove staff whose attitudes are such that they do not and will not understand when they are being abusive'.

'I would always raise concerns although I know others feel it affects their career prospects. Difficult to know *who* to raise concerns with – particularly in "incestuous" situations'.

'An appreciation of the limits on resources in social services to deal with problems in a general way leads me to favour localized initiatives in training and support. I would be more likely to raise issues in a staff meeting or supervision session than write to district manager'.

'The need to continue "working together" with those I have raised concerns about, knowing no one will have taken responsibility for resolving differences between us'.

'I am applying for a seconded place on DipSW. If I rock the boat I have no doubt that it will affect my future prospects. I have seen a colleague refused an interview for a post he was eminently suitable for'.

'I would always report serious concerns'.

Management

The social workers were asked a number of questions about their management (see Table 7.4). Over a third thought that top management was more likely to victimize than support a staff member raising a concern, but only half as many thought this of middle management. Nearly everyone thought that it was their business to raise strongly their concerns about scarce resources and poor management. They were about equally divided as to whether procedures for raising concerns were adequate or not, and well over 50 per cent thought that management puts the organization's public image before service standards. Two-thirds believed that whistleblowing is likely to bring about improvements in service standards in the long term, but over 50 per cent thought that there was inadequate access to independent means of investigation.

We looked to see whether there was any great disparity between attitudes in the different sectors – statutory, not-for-profit and private. Although the samples in the latter two sectors were small, they did voice more concerns about management standards, with almost 50 per cent mentioning poor management.

Conclusions

When one looks at comments about managers it is difficult to identify exactly what they are doing wrong, but there is evidently a communica-

Table 7.4

Question: Imagine you were thinking about raising a concern with management about misconduct *in your own workplace*. How easy/difficult would you expect this to be? Put a cross next to the factor that most closely describes how you feel.

1	Middle management is more likely to support than victimize staff member raising a concern	278 (78%)
	Middle management is more likely to victimize than support staff member raising a concern	62 (17%)
	Don't know	
2	Top management is more likely to support than victimize staff member raising a concern	188 (53%)
	Top management is more likely to victimize than support staff member raising a concern	129 (36%)
	Don't know	40 (11%)
3	It is not our business to raise strongly our concerns about scarce resources and poor management	20 (5.5%)
	It is our business to raise strongly our concerns about scarce resources and poor management	327 (92%)
	Don't know	10
4	Whistleblowing is unlikely to bring about improvements in service standards in the long term	82 (23%)
	Whistleblowing is likely to bring about improvements in service standards in the long term	239 (67%)
	Don't know	36 (10%)
5	Procedures for raising concern are inadequate	163 (46%)
	Procedures for raising concern are adequate	179 (50%)
	Don't know	15
6	Management puts the organization's public image before service standards	208 (58%)
	Management puts service standards before the organization's public image	98 (27%)
	Don't know	51 (14%)
7	There is inadequate access to independent investigation	196 (55%)
	There is adequate access to independent investigation	111 (31%)
	Don't know	50 (14%)

tion gulf, with staff not believing that their managers know, understand or have any real interest in what they do. This boils down to an inability to communicate and support staff. One could characterize this as a failure of corporate accountability to staff, and therefore to the public.

Victimization, mentioned by almost 25 per cent of respondents, is still one of the greatest deterrents to raising concerns. One respondent wrote that their family would always take priority. Other factors that staff raised about the working environment were lack of resources and under-staffing, leading to stress. Surprisingly few respondents commented on the effects of changes as a result of care in the community reforms.

The survey highlights some interesting conundrums about staff wit-nessing misconduct. It seems that a number of staff have witnessed an incident of questionable practice in the previous 2 years but failed to report it. For example, in all instances of misconduct covering sexism, racism, breach of confidentiality, affront to privacy/dignity, falsifying or omitting record, lying to client, not consulting client, verbal abuse and not responding to client, the number of witnessed incidents was consid-erably higher than the number of reported incidents.

However, as the misconduct in the eyes of the witness becomes worse, so the incidence of reporting rises. So, in the cases of physical neglect, severe verbal abuse, severe emotional abuse, the number of witnessed vs. reported incidents starts to even out. By the time staff are witnessing physical, sexual or financial abuse the number of reported incidents clearly outstrips the number of witnessed incidents.

The above cases seem to indicate that, when staff have witnessed misconduct which by anyone's standards is unacceptable, they are in no doubt about reporting it. In other words, most right-thinking members of society do not accept physical, sexual or financial abuse. Moreover, such incidents are so serious that they cannot easily be ignored, and there may also be physical evidence of wrongdoing. However, when one moves into other areas of misconduct, staff obviously find it more difficult to be sure of their ground. There may be a tendency for staff to forgive their colleagues and think, perhaps in the case of verbal abuse, that it is a one-off incident that is unlikely to occur again, or that it is due to high stress and is therefore understandable, or the client's behaviour invited it.

In the first survey (*Care Weekly*, 1993) over 50 per cent of the respon-dents said they would be prepared to give the perpetrator a second chance if they believed that the incident occurred as a result of ignorance or they were misguided, and would respond to training or supervision in the future. So what is it that really prevents people from reporting mis-conduct?

It is so easy for outsiders to criticize a profession of which they have little experience. The question that everyone should ask is, would they have the courage to challenge misconduct, whatever their field of expertise? We can all think of examples where the minor incident is allowed to slip by because we do not want to make a scene or create a fuss. As a society our ethical mores are what might be called 'flexible'. We are nearly all economical with the truth at times. For example, we do not rigorously uphold high moral values concerning company prop-erty, and we turn a blind eye to the many items 'pinched' from the workplace. To report that person would surely engender the wrath of colleagues – and that is the worst fear. People working in social work/care are no different.

A number of points are evident. There is a pervasive climate of fear of victimization among social work/care staff. Therefore those who do complain must be courageous, naïve or vengeful. There is absolutely no point in pretending that complaining is easy. Staff must go into it with their eyes wide open.

As an example of the naïve, a care assistant telephoned one of the authors one day. She worked in a 12-bed private care home for people with learning disabilities. She and three of her colleagues witnessed the abuse of clients. She had been at the home for 6 months when she reported the misconduct to social services and made a statement. Two months later she left the home. When she phoned us she was angry and hurt. She said:

> It is unbelievable what happened. It took two years for anything to happen. In court I was cross-examined for four and a half hours. I was humiliated. It was awful what happened. I cannot be surprised that people do not come forward. I cannot put into words what it was like. It was really criminal what they did to me.

This care assistant showed tremendous courage in reporting abuse, but sadly she was not prepared for the consequences of her actions. No one advised or supported her, and she had no allies in the professional sense. Surely this is one of the most vital roles that social services must undertake.

SSDs must make it a priority to support staff who have the courage to complain. If employers will not take such action, then it is little wonder that staff are reluctant to complain. The outcome of this complaint was that the home was closed down.

The profession desperately needs to develop a culture and a climate in which constructive criticism is positively welcomed, and in which each staff member believes he or she is responsible not only for his or her own actions, but for the service as a whole. So what would help managers and their staff? It is difficult to know whether managers involved in the caring business are simply particularly inept, or whether their situation is such that even the best managers would fail. What is perhaps now needed is a detailed survey to see how managers view their staff!

There is little doubt that staff would feel much more confident if some form of legal protection existed for whistleblowers. There is also widespread support for a general social services council. Although it all seems a dismal picture, it must be remembered that most managers are doing a good job and most staff are deeply committed to providing good-quality care for vulnerable people. Almost all respondents believe that it is important to tackle misconduct whatever the guise in which it presents. All that they need is a little more help.

References

Care Weekly (1993) Action for good practice. Supplement, 23 September, pp. 1, 13 et seq.

Hunt, G. and Shailer, B. (1995) The whistleblowers speak. In Hunt, G. (ed), *Whistleblowing in the Health Service*. London: Edward Arnold, 3–21.

8

Managerial procedure and professional practice in social work

Roland Powell

> *Human services are, without doubt, a sub-set of other service indus-*
> *tries, with which they share common attributes ... they also have dis-*
> *tinctiveness that must be considered not only when discussing them in*
> *a theoretical way, but also in developing practical approaches to man-*
> *agement, organisation structure and quality assurance. The essential*
> *nature of human services – the transformation of the consumer by the*
> *application of a service technology – means that mechanistic models*
> *of these latter issues will fail to account for the complexity and infinite*
> *diversity of human service delivery systems*
>
> (Dickens, 1996, p. 90)

The new managerialism and the genesis of whistleblowing

Social work's survival as it is presently understood as a knowledge-based professional practice is questionable in the rapidly changing environment of welfare and social care. The changes in the environment in which social work is practised are an essential background to the growth in whistleblowing by social workers. Central to these changes is the increasing power of managerial ideology, or managerialism. In a managerialist view, management is seen as being superior to other forms of organization such as professionalism. The imposition on social work of standardized procedures is one factor which leads to whistleblowing, as bad professional practice can continue so long as it remains within the procedures. The client of traditional social work has become the service user or consumer, reflecting significant changes to the relationship between social worker and client. This professional relationship has been reformed to be represented in the changing environment of social care as being similar to, or even the same as, the relationship of the customer or consumer in a commercial market relationship. The links between managerialism and consumerism as ideological power bases demanding free-market rights against a professional group in a public service have contributed to the growing need to protect professional freedom to make public their concerns. For many social workers it seems that there is a growing culture of fear created by the effect within social work organizations of a dominant, managerialist ideology (Mitchell, 1996, pp. 18–20). This chapter focuses on *collective whistleblowing*, but the fear of the new management is felt as much here as in individual accounts – so anonymity will have to be preserved here.

Organisations which represent social workers, namely the British Union of Social Work Employees (BUSWE), the British Association of Social Workers (BASW) and the public service union, UNISON, have all observed an increase in bullying by managers. Conflict about how the social work task is done – whether the task is led by professional knowledge or management directive – is an issue now recognized by those studying bullying at work (Adams and Crawford, 1992). The changes in the way social workers are being compelled to work and the links to managerialism and consumerism are indicated by Middleton, who believes that procedure has become a method through which a personal, caring, human profession is being 'mechanized' (Middleton, 1994).

Procedures as sources of power have created a situation in which it is increasingly difficult for social workers to be accountable for their professional practice legitimated by a professional knowledge base. Social workers find themselves in treble jeopardy from management, the media and their employers, because they are not permitted to be accountable to the people they work with as professionals, or to any regulatory professional body. The repeated proposals for a social work-regulating body and a universal training to degree level have not found favour with government, despite widespread support from every quarter (Thompson, 1995, p. 3; National Institute of Social Work, 1994).

Procedures can protect social workers, but even in this protective mode they can work against good social work practice. Procedures are, of course, necessary in any profession or organization. They provide some basic form of accountability, save time and give immediate guidance. However, procedures can be a management tool of considerable oppressive power. As the Clwyd child abuse case showed, procedures are not enough if professionals are not listened to and bad practice is tolerated or covered up (*Community Care*, 1996).

The strange death of liberal professionalism and the birth of *Sammy's Dad*

Minty has written:

Social work in Britain, as we find it today, is not practice led but policy and bureaucracy led. Social Services Departments sometimes appear to over-emphasize the legal/ administrative basis of the practitioner's authority at the expense of the professional basis. For our agencies it often seems more important that practitioners are 'in authority', i.e. that their behaviour is sanctioned by law and agency procedures, than that they themselves have 'authority' by virtue of their understanding, knowledge and skills.

(Minty, 1996, p. 53)

Questions have to be asked about the position of social workers, as the UK's largest group of caring professionals outside the National Health Service, and the recent phenomenon of whistleblowing. Why does social work have such a low public profile? Why, for a professional group largely accountable to democratically elected local authorities, is whistleblowing increasingly resorted to by social workers not only as individuals but as groups? The reasons why a social worker or social workers take the decision to whistleblow are as important as the act itself, and these have not been adequately explored. There are to date two basic grounds that lead social workers to whistleblow, namely professional grounds and ethical grounds.

Most whistleblowing has been by individuals, but there is a new collective form of whistleblowing or 'resistance'. The *Sammy's Dad* publication by social workers in Lancashire social services department (SSD) is, at first reading, a protest by social workers against an oppressive managerialism. This can also be read as a form of collective whistleblowing. *Sammy's Dad* sets out the repression of professionalism in one large SSD in these terms:

In summary, it is necessary to defend social work in Lancashire SSD because:

1. The structure of the reorganized SSD is detrimental to: (i) the individual's presentation of his/her need; (ii) the effective evaluation of need; and (iii) the appropriate meeting of need.

2. It is wasteful of public resources, frequently requiring the repetition of assessments by a succession of staff, and the generation of unnecessary paperwork and bureaucracy.

3. This produces an arid service environment, in which creative social work practice cannot flourish.

4. In order for senior management to justify the new structure and its accompanying management style, it has been necessary for the organization, covertly, to devalue professional competence and to redefine the relationship between the authority and its professional staff.

5. Management is not pursuing this strategy openly, nor is there any attempt to hold the type of consultative professional discussion to which hands-on staff are entitled and which any good

modern employer (especially in the highly competitive world of the private sector) would arrange.

6.   *Sammy's Dad* believes there is a case for an SSI [Social Services Inspectorate] inspection focusing on social work practice in Lancashire's SSD.

(Anon., 1996, *Sammy's Dad, No. 2*)

Professions have always changed to meet the needs of the people using their services, and often as a result of professionals' research. Changes in law and social policy decisions made by central government, such as the Community Care Act and the Children Act, have changed the role of many social workers at a stroke, forcing professional decision-making based on knowledge into a bureaucratic framework primarily constructed to manage resources and the relationship between the consumer and the organization. These changes leave little room for the case-work or the human relationship that are central to social work practice. Social work practitioners have consequently become more distanced professionally from their managers, even when those managers share the same professional training and socialization. It is against this background that collective whistleblowing at the organizational level has emerged.

Professionals have traditionally been able to call on a professional body of knowledge to legitimate their claims to power and to limit entry to the profession. Power for the professional has been the power to access a particular body of knowledge to speak with an authority that others outside the profession cannot claim. This source of power is central to any discussion of professional accountability, but a knowledge base can be 'proceduralized'. It has been argued by several authors that social work education has become proceduralized (Dominelli, 1996, p. 163). Meanwhile, medicine is now challenged by Government's and health managers' demands for 'evidence-based medicine' (*The Guardian*, 1996; see also Sackett and Scott Richardson, 1997, pp. 1–20).

What 'professional' now means is a problem, as new 'professional' bodies seem to appear which make no reference to any criteria other than their own. One of the latest players is the Institute of Community Care Managers, whose objectives seem to be to create a system of accreditation outside recognized professional qualifications for anyone who can meet a set of criteria that is managerial and bracketed off from practice and any recognizable professional knowledge base (Institute of Community Care Management, 1996). A direct relationship is being forged between the managers of caring services and those of profit-oriented commerce which bypasses professional knowledge, education and values. The creation of wealth in the market of commodities, buyers and sellers is very different from the caring wealth redistribution of social work and social services organizations. The kind of ideology underlying the Institute of Community Care Managers can be seen as legitimating management as a distinct activity separated from the professional practice which becomes subject to that management. It is the dominant position of a separate and 'technical' management which is one of the conditions that generates whistleblowing as an option for professionally trained social workers:

> The emphasis on managerial and market values, with the implied endorsement of self-interest and group interest as the key motivating factors (with their associated personnel policies) not only conflicts with the public service ethos that motivates many front-line staff, but is contradicted by the continued appeals of government to 'dedication' and the distinctive traditions of public service.
>
> (Hadley and Clough, 1996, p. 194)

Undermining the professional

Why consult a professionally trained person in the first place, if that person does not have knowledge, skill and resources that the client cannot gain or utilize by his or her own efforts? This lies at the heart of what people expect from a professional – not a person who fills in forms and simply processes a person and their needs as a procedure. The difference between a personal social service and the Benefits Agency (BA), for example, has been that a social worker would act in their client's best interest, while the BA employee would compare the circumstances of the client to the regulatory criteria and make a decision about which procedure should be followed. The two processes are clearly different. In the social work process the needs of the client are paramount, whereas in the BA process the law, management and procedures to control expenditure are paramount.

The principles of social work are central to the conflict between managers and professionals in social work because the values, policies and ethics that prevail decide to a great extent the fate of the client. No person wishes their needs, and whether they are deserving of help, to be defined by procedure alone. A major point of difference between the procedural forms of assessment of need for a service and the professional assessment provided by social workers is that the social worker should have discretionary use of a professional knowledge base to inform and guide the assessment process. This process will take account not only of resources but also of the needs of the individual and the wider community.

It is the professional element of *discretion* which is a problem for the new managerialism, which has more in common with the BA approach than that of professional social work. New legislation has eroded the professional discretion of social workers and imposed proceduralized assessments which minimize the ability of the social worker to account for his or her decisions by reference to professional wisdom, knowledge and skills. Professional practice is also limited by rigorous budgetary control, which is not only about how much can be spent but where existing resources can be spent, which limits options and opportunities for effective solutions to client problems. Taken together, this proceduralization creates a situation in which professional practice is seen to be eroded by replacing professional assessment as the means for deciding on the appropriate course of action in a particular person's or family's case with managed procedural methods of decision-making.

Increasingly, central government legislation sets up procedural frameworks which control the activities of professionally trained employees. One example of this strategy is the adoption of the term 'care manager', which is amorphous and designates a role which does not require any professional qualification (Department of Health, 1990). A second example is found in proposals setting out local authorities' duties to protect vulnerable adults made by the Law Commission, which contain no mention of social work but which propose significant powers to 'authorized officers' (Law Commission, 1995). Research on the abuse of vulnerable adults has been generated by social workers, and it has been SSDs which have led the way in practice to provide protection for vulnerable adults by supporting social workers. It is therfore ominous that the Law Commission has chosen to ignore the professional role and position of social workers, and set out a framework in which any local authority employee could be authorized to investigate an allegation of abuse and would be given wide-ranging powers, such as the powers to apply to a magistrate to:

- enter premises to interview the person concerned;
- apply to the court for an entry warrant;
- apply to the court for an assessment order;
- apply to the court for a 'temporary protection order'.

Despite the omission of social work from this major piece of proposed legislation, the new responsibilities will undoubtedly fall on social workers. The existing experience of the Mental Health Act, the Community Care Act and the Children Act suggests that, once again, social workers are being set up to fail. Legislation that imposes responsibility on social workers without providing resources has contributed to the erosion of professional decision-making and, perhaps even more seriously, has undermined public confidence in a profession that underpins a major public service.

Conflict between professional and managerial power bases throughout the last decade has been at its most visible in the NHS, where the principles and ideology of the market have been firmly ranged against professionals. Within social work the conflict has been different. Social work has not had a new set of managers imposed on it in the way that the NHS has. Managers at all levels in SSDs and voluntary social work agencies continue to be drawn from social work trained personnel, but this does not mean that these new managers can manage from a position where they are guided by social work's values and knowledge base. Managers must take on the role of management in an environment that pits management practice and ideology against professional social work practice and values. Management is now seen by many local authorities as the answer to their problems in providing the care management service that councillors need rather than the social work service that clients need (Stevenson, 1995). That a knowledge base is no longer necessary is illustrated by an advertisement for a director of social services, which makes the point that a professional qualification in social work is not necessary, but to be a driver of people is (*Advertisements*, 1996).

Procedure: uses and abuses

To understand the power that procedures presently have in social services organizations against good social work practice, it is necessary to understand how social workers use procedures, and how procedures can be used in the place of professional practice (see also Hunt, 1994, pp. 2–4). For example, anyone can be a care manager and complete the 'boxes' on a community care assessment form together with the simple arithmetic of the financial assessment forms. This form of procedural information-gathering is common to many workers in most organizations. A social work assessment is very different, takes much longer, and assesses a person's or family's needs across all areas of their lives. The messiness of people's lives reflected in a needs-led assessment does not provide useful management information, and meeting those needs would be expensive. Resource- or budget-led assessments are giving managers increased control over social work practice, which is being proceduralized to create a situation in which social workers only assess what employers want assessed. Social work therapeutic skills have withered as the 'purchaser-provider split' separates assessment from intervention that would meet need in a holistic way including, for example, the housing, emotional and social needs of a client.

Some procedures are benevolent and allow social workers to meet clients' needs by using them and in some cases creating them. In a national BASW survey of members (British Association of Social Workers, 1996) it can be seen that social workers are not anti-procedure (as Table 8.1 below shows). The very different attitudes of social workers are largely accounted for by the respondents' experiences across many different social work organizations. Of course, the tyranny of procedure is not universal, and many social work organizations are led by professional practice and research.

Table 8.1. Social workers should have strict procedures to follow in all decision-making on assessment and provision? (Froggett and Sapey, 1996)

Strongly disagree	4.7%
Disagree	34.5%
Neutral	17.8%
Agree	35.6%
Strongly agree	7.3%

(From British Association of Social Workers (1996).

Most of the changes to social work's environment have been presented as local government or welfare 'reform'. This reform is essentially political, as most social work is funded directly by local government, with major funding decisions being taken by central government. It can be argued that public services are no longer effectively administered in the interest of society and those people who are needy, but are managed by managers operating within an ideology that views management as being based on the limited model of the profit-oriented private company as the solution to virtually any problem. This is the 'universal Manager'. Management as practice and ideology was the bedrock of Conservative government 'reforms', creating the conditions in which social work is practised, yet it is rare for top-level managers or government to be called to account when things go wrong. Sue Amphlett, Director of Parents Against Injustice (see Chapter 3), commenting on the number of child abuse investigation procedures undertaken by SSDs, makes the point: 'Social workers have every right to be fearful because social services directors do not accept responsibility when a child dies – blame is laid on individual staff' (Amphlett, 1995, pp. 14–15).

The Pindown case was a failure of management, not a failure of professionals to recognize a rotten apple. Barbara Kahan, one of the authors of the report into the Pindown case, was clear in making a case for the concerns expressed by professionally trained workers to be taken more seriously than the needs of management: 'When people feel something is wrong they should not have to go through this agonized debate with themselves because they might lose their job or their promotion' (Kahan, 1991, p. 17).

Like Pindown, the Orkney situation was not primarily a failure of practice but a failure of procedure and management. During the Orkney Inquiry it was revealed that one of the social workers sent to assist local staff made it clear to the director of social work that she found the dawn raid unacceptable in terms of professional practice. The director's response was that it would go ahead anyway. The social worker took part with colleagues in this clumsy procedure because otherwise there would have been no adequate care for the children. In this example it was the professional commitment to care which caused a social worker to collude with bad practice (*Social Work Today*, 1991).

Models of management and accountability

The conditions which have given rise to whistleblowing by environmental, consumer and other public interest concerns are to be found within private industry. The structures of power found in largely unaccountable, powerful, private industrial corporations historically created the conditions for whistleblowing. The differences between the two types of organization are outlined in Table 8.2. Such differences are now perhaps less marked than in the past, so the same conditions for whistleblowing are becoming established in both public and private sector organizations. Public sector management is likely to be found to be inadequate in pure private sector management terms, but when judged against management tasks within the public sector, different conclusions are drawn. The attractive simplicity of profit-oriented managerialism does not answer the needs of social services managers whose environment has less well-defined policy directions than their private sector equivalents, i.e. greater constraints on their action caused by greater openness in decision-making, more direct and sustained contact from interest groups seeking to influence them, and more artificial time constraints on their actions.

These models are not mutually exclusive except in one important regard, which is that in professional and public service social work organizations a knowledge-based practice was in the past at least 'equal' to management. The main change has been an ideological one that has given management an ideological dominance within social work organizations. Research using 60 in-depth and anonymous interviews with social workers found that: 'This commercial approach was also seen as a threat to professional identity and in conflict with workers' professional values' (La Valle and Lyons, 1996, p. 11). This finding is not surprising given the major differences in operating environment and other factors between social work organizations and the private organizations whose ideologies and methods have had so much influence over the last decade.

Who has the power to empower?

T. Bamford, a former chair of BASW, saw what he termed the 'new consumerism' as a paradigm shift away from a producer orientation and

Table 8.2 Differential characteristics of public service and managerialist organizations

Public service social work organizations	Private profit- or product-oriented organizations
Parliamentary regulation, law, codes of conduct and local government policy define core tasks	Board of directors, shareholders, company business plans stressing profitability defining core tasks
National economic policy and management. Central government control of local government finance. Local government policy and spending priorities. Minimize free spend	Market-place signals, business lending rate, consumer confidence. Cost control. Maximize free spend
Comparative openness of local government with representatives politically and legally accountable for decision-making	Generally secretive; stress on decision-making success measured in bottom-line financial/market figures. Business confidentiality. Industrial espionage
Attentive public, wide stakeholder base. Influence of voluntary sector pressure groups	Narrow stakeholder focus on shareholders and management
Multiple values and aims: Public service ethics Public interest values Equity Professionalism Consumer participation Equality of opportunity	Relatively restricted values. Simple business aims. Business ethics are not codified. Outcomes measured in bottom-line cash terms
Primary resource base from public taxes	Resource base from profits, borrowing and share valuation
Extensive accountability at all levels. Managers have little power to manage as they are heavily constrained by legal procedures and political control. The management style of social services tends to be complex, a limited custodial role managing through budgetary and policy decision-making. Managers have little freedom to manage	Minimal accountability outside the organization. Main concern is to minimize corporate/organizational liability. The power of management is of prime importance so managers at all levels have freedom to manage
Responsiveness to political masters and short political time-scales. Rational responses constrained by political imperatives. Complex trade-offs	No national/local political responsibility; less artificial time-scales. Rational response to environment. Ability to lobby politicians, with limited accountability

Table 8.2 *continued*

Public service social work organizations	Private profit- or product-oriented organizations
Primary social values goals, e.g. child rights/protection. Equal rights for the disabled. Fair charges based on the ability to pay	Profit/market maximization aims
Performance indicators measurable by the effectiveness of services in increasing users' quality of life	Quantitative financial measures of performance. Product/market oriented R&D. Reduction of work-force rights to maximize production
Gatekeeping role to target expenditure. Major R&D role in innovative service development	Differential performance indicators applied throughout organization
Work-force highly unionized and professionalized. Professionals as managers – salaried	Managerial elite. Profit as main motivation. 'Fat Cats'

making new space for social work. Today this view looks wildly optimistic (Bamford, 1990). It can now be argued that it is social work practitioners who are disempowered and devalued by the very managers who have espoused 'empowerment'. Minty demonstrates with painful clarity that social work practice is held in low esteem in social work organizations (Minty, 1996, p. 52). An example of professional disempowerment is given in *Sammy's Dad*. It speaks of:

> a social worker who, concerned about the complexity of a child care assessment she was about to undertake, asked her manager for a colleague to accompany her and provide a second opinion. She was reduced to tears when told that she was incompetent to be making such a request!
>
> (Anon., 1996, p. 1).

The clients, or 'users', of social work are often the most powerless people in society, and it has been central to the ethics of social work to respect and value those people who are devalued by society. Virtually all groups of people who need and depend on social work services for the maintenance of their quality of life are represented by pressure groups of some sort. For example, MIND represents the interests of people with a mental health problem and also provides services. It is organizations such as MIND that have adopted some of the rhetoric of consumerism as a strategy to secure greater power for people who depend on social work and social services. In its most radical form this has created the concept of 'user-led services'. The outcome can be less services and, from a budgetary perspective, cheaper services. User-led services are also an opportunity to distance the purchaser from the provider, so users' organizations may be in the position of exercising budgetary control over their own members' needs. Parallel to the user demands for greater control over the services on which they depend there has also been a demand for user advocacy. Traditionally, social workers have advocated for clients to other organizations and professionals. In response to more rigorous gatekeeping, and partly in response to the increasing statutory powers given to social workers, user groups have demanded that they should represent users' points of view to social workers and, more importantly, to social workers' employers. This giving away of power to disadvantaged groups is supported by social workers and can be seen as a radical form of consumerism, but the rhetoric of consumerism is used in other ways to undermine professionals. In some user organizations managerialism is clothed in the dissembling rhetoric of consumerism, and in such organizations the conflict outlined here concerning who decides who gets empowered is as sharp as it is within SSDs.

Consumerism is a relatively new set of ideas which has found its political expression in the law through the creation of consumer rights such as the Consumer Credit Act 1974. More recently, the Citizens' Charter initiative and the watchdog bodies set up to regulate privatized monopolies have given new impetus to the idea of consumers having rights in a free market which, paradoxically, is seen as irresistibly powerful and self-organizing. The argument for 'empowerment' is an appeal to virtue, morality in a market-place that is conceptualized as asocial – a market of individuals in competition. The protection of consumers is at odds with the rhetoric of the free market, but the potential power of consumers in the market is considerable, as was demonstrated by Shell's immediate reaction to pressure from European consumers to halt the 'dumping' at sea of the Brent Spar oil rig. This particular exercise of consumer power was social, in the public interest. However, the individualist rhetoric of empowerment is about the empowerment of individuals so that the solution to what are plainly social problems is individualized, with the claim that all that is necessary is for individuals to 'take control of their lives'. This call to action on the part of the individual constructs individual power as sufficient to solve problems as diverse as unemployment, mental illness, child sexual abuse and poverty.

The value placed on the empowerment of the individual is analogous to the consumerist rhetoric found in the 'charters' proclaimed by central government and many quangos. What is in the charter can be quantified and measured, so if the proposed good can be measured it can be standardized, performance targets set and managed. Those elements of a service which are not employers' priorities and so not targeted or monitored are proceduralized away and demarketed, irrespective of client need. There is a link here between the moral imperative which demands that individuals 'take control of their lives', the demand that managers take control of their organization, and the belief that the performance manifested in taking control reflects the worth or value of an individual. The rhetoric of consumerist empowerment individualizes and isolates the person who in reality has needs in a real social world with real relationships with real people. It can be compared to the misapplication of psychodynamic theory by some social workers in the 1960s and early 1970s. This misconception by managerialist ideologues in the 1990s is perhaps another demonstration of the need for ever tighter budgetary control of the expensive realities of social life in an increasingly divided society.

Procedures and the law

In virtually all of the cases cited above the reaction to a failure of practice has been an inquiry, which has usually recommended changes in law and the tightening of procedure as the main response. Good or bad professional practice has not drawn the same attention as procedure and the application and interpretation of law. A survey of social services workers by the National Institute of Social Work (1994, 1995) found high levels of stress. In commenting on the findings, a director of social services identified 'new procedures' as a major source of stress. A UNISON representative identified 'the changing attitude of middle managers' as a major problem (*Community Care*, 1995a,b).

What *can* be managed is a continuing problem. The messiness of people's lives is not yet subject to a 'technical fix' and is difficult to 'manage', fraught as it is with the ethical and moral dilemmas that always emerge from human life. Drawing boundaries which can provide some degree of control seems to be an objective of the managerial creation of procedure as a source of power against social work and reality. Law, guidance, codes of practice and directives force change in practice, but this is not done directly. Managers can and do use law, guidance, codes of practice and directives to justify procedures and targeting. Professional judgement remains fairly safe from the judicial gaze, but procedure is altogether different. It is through procedure that government and the law gain access to the ability to disempower professional practice in social work. As some commentators have said, 'It is possible in the future that even if the courts do not become enmeshed in trying to define precisely some of the vague terms in community care legislation, they could still state what procedures might be associated with those terms' (Mandelstam and Schwer, 1995, p. 64).

Procedure as a management tool, rather than a professional one, is becoming a major obstacle to good practice in social work. It seems that procedural social work, which is really a contradiction in terms, is the preferred standard by which practice is to be assessed in law. Procedure ensures conformity, which is now demanded of social workers in some organizations, and speaking out from a professional knowledge base is a high-risk strategy. The model social work team leader:

> doesn't make waves and doesn't criticize the system and doesn't raise her head above the parapet. Someone, I suppose, who goes along with the drift of things. If they bring out a policy that is just unworkable, never say it is unworkable. Just accept it and work with it as you can.
>
> (Hadley and Clough, 1996, p. 143)

When social work has gone publicly wrong the inquiries that have followed have been legalistic, and it is perhaps no coincidence that the law is procedural and grounded in precedent. Procedure and precedent bring some certainty to the 'messiness' of people's lives. What the law does not understand is everyday social work practice with its built-in uncertainties, concerned as it is with relationships, emotions and differences in values and perceptions, but of course community care has moved social workers into an area where procedure abounds: 'The judges are more likely to uphold procedural than substantive expectation' (Mandelstam and Schwer, 1995, p. 80). This may be interpreted to mean that the social worker and his or her employer did not meet the client's expectations or needs, but if the local authority procedure was followed then the law is satisfied. Where social workers have chosen to whistleblow and have engaged the help of the workplace freedom-of-speech organization, Freedom to Care, the majority of cases have been where the social worker has been concerned with bad practice that has affected service users. This is social work in its traditional role of advocate for people who are relatively powerless. It is paradoxical that as procedure and regulation have increased, the need for social workers to resort to whistleblowing seems to be increasing. It is unfortunate that the law has so little to offer workers who are fettered by procedure, and even less to clients.

As most social workers are employed by local authority SSDs, and it is those SSDs which have increasingly been given the tasks of implementing new legislation which has the effect of 'proceduralizing' the delivery of services, the effect of new legislation has to be seen as pivotal to the undermining of professional practice. For example, the Department of Health in its recommendations to social services on the Care Programmes for people with a mental illness set 'Mental Health Policy, Strategy and Procedures' as the first standard on their list (Department of Health, 1995).

'Community care' is not simply a restructuring of the welfare safety net – it is a procedural *tour de force* 'accompanied by a formalisation of procedures and a flowering of forms' (Lewis, 1995, p. 33). The anonymous Assistant Director mentioned in Hadley and Clough's work effectively 'blows the whistle' on the procedural impact of community care:

> We've got 21 different financial assessment forms, because we've got so much charging and different ways of getting into charging and income. It's a checking and verification task that the benefits agency people used to do and it's an area subject to careful financial audit. So it is frustrating for qualified social workers to get bogged down into that. I think that the paperwork has increased. A system that's supposed to be less bureaucratic is actually more bureaucratic.
>
> (Hadley and Clough, 1996, p. 30)

The tensions and mismatches between professional practice which analyses each individual's needs and the reality of a managerially driven 'cost-shunting' exercise, in which managers compete to minimize free spend, is nowhere more starkly seen than in local authority social services like Lancashire that have implemented the 'purchaser-provider split' without any research or development. The experience of those working in such environments seems to be that it is 'more time-consuming, controlling and restrictive' than previous professionally delivered services (Hadley and Clough, 1996, p. 185). The contrast between the market and social work is described in Hadley and Clough's conclusion:

> In the personal social services, the transactions between users and workers are often equally unlike the simple exchanges of the market place. They typically involve discursive, face to face relations . . . often over a period of time. These are developmental relationships in which the establishment of trust and an appreciation by the provider of the unique circumstances of the individual consumer are essential to the ultimate effectiveness of the service being provided.
>
> (Hadley and Clough, 1996, p. 196)

The Children Act has had a major impact on social work practice, and as the Audit Commission has observed, this has in many ways had a negative impact on the very children and families that SSDs are intended by society to help (Audit Commission, 1994). The Children Act intends to set a balance between the discourses of law and social work, but intervening is the discourse of the consumer. Nowhere in the Act is this discourse recognized directly, but the effect of the notion of the 'service user' as 'consumer' runs through the Act and its associated publications. The *Memorandum of Good Practice* proceduralizes how children are dealt with in the interests of criminal prosecution, not those of the child (Bilton, 1994, p. 32). Howe makes a similar point about the proceduralization of child-care social work, where professional skill and knowledge are subsumed under procedures which meet the needs of more powerful professions and local authority employers (Howe, 1992). If the child is the 'consumer', their interests seem not to have been considered, while those of the police and the legal system appear to have achieved paramountcy. The ability of a local authority to suppress a child abuse inquiry report due to fears about insurance cover and legal liability to the abused children shows that the market has little concern for children as consumers (*Community Care*, 1996).

Beatrix Campbell has expressed very well the proceduralization of child care social work: 'the government's gaze has been fixed not on the phenomenon (child abuse) but on procedures and professional responses' (Campbell, 1995).

Demarketing professional social work

Many of the managers at all levels in social work have been practitioners, and it is to a large extent this professional past which legitimates the managers' apparent right to manage for social workers (Table 8.3). The complexity of the management task compared to that for managers in the profit-oriented private sector can be seen in Table 8.2, but there are other significant dilemmas for social services managers. Senior social services managers have to advise their political masters in local authorities from two directions – that of skilled professional and that of manager. This process of turning policy, law and practice into the delivery of services is more complex than that facing managers in the private domain. The most marked contrasts within Table 8.2 are that profit-oriented private domain managers work in conditions in which they must constantly seek to bring about change to secure their organization's place in a dynamic market. By contrast, social work aims to bring stability to people's lives and needs to practise from a stable organizational base.

Table 8.3 All social work managers should be experienced in social work practice?

Strongly disagree	0.0%
Agree	33.1%
Neutral	3.7%
Disagree	2.9%
Strongly agree	60.3%

From British Association of Social Workers (1996) Professional Social Work Survey.

Procedure is a powerful method which can be used to control groups of professionally trained employees. Procedure can be dissembled – disguised as consumerism, management, organizational or even professional accountability. Procedures that simplify professional practice can be clearly seen in the procedural approach to community care assessments. Organizations have attempted to standardize assessments through procedures which require social workers to complete paperwork which simplifies the assessment into a questionnaire. The effect of procedure on practice follows the same logic of simplification. Reducing clients' needs to the lowest level of complexity has the effect of simplifying the management task and reducing management dependence on professional competency. It would be difficult to see how this empowers consumers, and it is at a very basic level at odds with the consumerist rhetoric of individual choice. Writing in 1989, Ackroyd set out the way in which the conflict between management and social work practitioners was seen at that time:

> attempts by management to apply standardized performance measures, which are recurrent, are fraught with difficulties and give rise to effective resistance by practitioners.
>
> While suggesting that public sector services are not highly standardized or commodified, this does not, of course, mean that the social work client or the patient in hospital is not subject to routine treatment or standardized procedures. As with other kinds of goods and services, public services are subject to rationalization, standardization and routinization. But since the services are complicated, there are obvious limits to any such tendencies. The essential point remains that the delivery of a public service depends on a complicated process of evaluation as to eligibility of the client and appropriateness of services; hence, judgements are typically undertaken by public service workers themselves. Crucially it is their professional expertise that influences the appropriateness of certain courses of action within conditions of external constraint. Any rationalization and commodification that goes on must follow lines taken as being appropriate in terms of the professional standards of the worker concerned.
>
> (Ackroyd, 1989, p. 611)

Social workers do not have the degree of professional autonomy of the established professions, but SSDs are highly dependent on their professional judgement and expertise to fulfil their many responsibilities. Attempts to reduce professional power so that quantifiable outcomes can be applied are not frustrated by disempowered social workers, but by the complexity of the tasks facing both professionals and the organization. It is this dilemma of managing the organization and the profession which needs to be clarified if clients are to get the best possible service and the conditions for professional whistleblowing are to be reduced.

> The Directorate prefer to have staff who have been trained, that is
> schooled, rather than staff who have a professional education. There is
> an important difference. Schooling merely inculcates certain ideas
> which can then be applied as little rules, which leave no room for dis-
> cretion, in the same way as the Department's eligibility tests are
> applied to those seeking help.
>
> (Anon., 1996, p. 6)

One final symptom of proceduralization is that training has now
overtaken education in social work and in social services. The danger
of employers having the main power base in the decision-making
processes that have produced the Diploma in Social Work in its original version and the more anodyne revision implemented at the end of
1995 is one of the main routes through which professional practice is
being eroded and procedural decision-making introduced. Both
Dominelli (1996, p. 163), and Hadley and Clough (1996, p. 13) identify what they see as the new managerialism with the work of F. W.
Taylor, an early theorist of mechanistic, 'scientific management'.
Jones believes that real social work education must be 'demanded',
and that the current Diploma in Social Work is losing any credibility
(Jones, 1995). In some respects these academic critiques are a form of
whistleblowing shared by social workers who find their role as practice teachers undermined by the procedural competencies of the
Diploma in Social Work (Powell and Powell, 1995). Without the freedom to assert social work values, any notion of empowerment is simply dissembling rhetoric. The key value statement of BASW's
Guidance on Whistleblowing is the paramountcy of the service user
and carer. It is clear that managerialist procedures cannot replace such
values in social work practice (British Association of Social Workers,
1995).

Demarketing is a strategy to remove the apparent need for a service by
making it unavailable, and in some social work organizations as well as
in 'training' this process seems to be under way. If social work is to be
'demarketed', then it is the least powerful in society who will be the
losers (Mark and Brennan, 1995). They will slip through a safety net
woven from concepts of managerialism, empowerment and competition
for scarce resources allocated by procedure. Coulshed makes the point
that 'perhaps we (social workers) are only as competent and effective as
our systems allow us to be?' (Coulshed, 1991, p. 2).

If professional social work practice is to be guided by social work
values and knowledge, then the demarketing of social work as a professional practice should be brought into the open, and it is perhaps a new
collective form of whistleblowing, such as that in *Sammy's Dad* and in
Freedom to Care, that may be the way forward. Bad practice is not only
individual but organizational.

References

Ackroyd, S. (1989) Public sector services and their management. *Journal of Management Studies* **26**.

Adams, A. and Crawford, N. (1992) *Bullying at work*. London: Virago Press.

Advertisements (1996) Advert for a Director of Social Services, Sefton Council in *The Times*, Business Appointments, 25 July 1996. Advert in *The Guardian* Public Appointments section, 24 July 1996, p. 17.

Amphlett, S. (1995) Lives at stake. *Community Care* **20–26 July**, 14–15.

Anon. (1996) *Sammy's Dad*. Clandestine publication of some Lancashire social workers.

Audit Commission (1994) *Seen but not heard: co-ordinating community child health and social services for children in need*. London: HMSO.

Bamford, T. (1990) *The future of social work*. London: Macmillan.

Bilton, K. (1994) *Child protection practice and the memorandum of good practice on video-recorded interviews with children*. Discussion Paper. London: British Association of Social Workers.

British Association of Social Workers (1995) *Guidance on the free expression of staff concerns*. Birmingham: British Association of Social Workers.

British Association of Social Workers (1996) *Professional Social Work Survey 1996*. May/June 1996, unpublished results. Birmingham: British Association of Social Workers.

Campbell, B. (1995) A Question of Priorities. *Community Care* **24–30 August**, 18–19.

Community Care (1995a) Social work carries the highest level of stress. **29 June–5 July**, 9.

Community Care (1995b) Making waves. **4–10 May**, 22.

Community Care (1996) The North Wales Children's Homes Abuse Inquiries. 4–10 April, 3.

Coulshed, V. (1991) *Social work practice: an introduction*, 2nd edn., London: British Association of Social Workers.

Department of Health (1990) *Community care in the next decade and beyond*. London: HMSO and Department of Health.

Department of Health (1995) *Social services departments and the care programme approach. An inspection. Social Services Inspectorate*. London: Department of Health.

Dickens, P. (1996) Human services as service industries. *Service Industries Journal* **16**, 82–91.

Dominelli, L. (1996) Deprofessionalising social work: anti-oppressive practice, competencies and postmodernism. *British Journal of Social Work* **26**, 153–75.

Froggett, L. and Sapey, R. (1996) *Professional Social Work* **June**, 10–11.
The Guardian (1996) Lives in the balance. Society Section. 22 May, pp. 2–3.
Hadley, R. and Clough, R. (1996) *Care in chaos: frustration and challenge in community care*. London: Cassell.
Howe, D. (1992) Child abuse and the bureaucratization of social work. *Sociological Review* **40**, 120–45.
Hunt, G. (ed.) (1994) *Ethical issues in nursing*. London: Routledge.
Institute of Community Care Management (1996) *Information Sheet (2) and Chairman's Letter*. London: Institute of Community Care Management.
Jones, C. (1995) Demanding social work education: an agenda for the end of the century. *Issues in Social Work Education* **15**, 91–110.
Kahan, B. (1991) Social work and management. *Social Work Today* **17 October**, 17.
La Valle, I. and Lyons, K. (1996) The social worker speaks. *Practice* **8**, 5–14.
Law Commission (1995). *Mental incapacity*. Report No. 231. London: HMSO.
Lewis, J. (1995) Bedtime story. *Community Care* **13–19 April**, 32–3.
Mandelstam, M. and Schwer, B. (1995) *Community care practice and the law*. London: Jessica Kingsley.
Mark, A. and Brennan, R. (1995) Demarketing: managing demand in the UK National Health Service. *Public Money and Management* **15**, 17–21.
Middleton, L. (1994) The tyranny of procedure. *Professional Social Work* **December**, 6.
Minty, B. (1996) Social work's five deadly sins. *Social Work and Social Sciences Review* **6**, 48–63.
Mitchell, D. (1996) Fear rules. *Community Care* **14–20 March**, 18–19.
National Institute of Social Work (1994) *General Social Services Council Conference Report: The Way Forward*. London: National Institute of Social Work.
National Institute of Social Work (1995) *Working in the Social Services*. London: National Institute of Social Work.
Powell, R. and Powell, S. (1995) Practice makes perfect. *Professional Social Work* **September**, 4.
Sackett, D. L. and Scott Richardson, W. (1997) *Evidence-based medicine*. London: Churchill Livingstone.
Social Work Today (1991) Orkney Report (news item). 3 October, p. 3.
Stevenson, P. (1995) Care management: does social work have a future? *Issues in Social Work Education* **15**, 48–59.
Thompson, G. (1995) Epic struggle for standards still needs professional push. *Professional Social Work.* **February**, 3.

9

Whistleblowing and training for accountability

Mike Cox

Regulating social work education

Tucked away right at the end of the 1995 British Association of Social Workers' (BASW) Brighton conference, where (it is said) tactics guaranteed it a drastically limited debate, was a resolution: 'That this Annual General Meeting calls upon Council to commence negotiations to accredit appropriate degrees which are awarded by Universities within the United Kingdom, as such recognition is a legitimate activity of a professional association' (BASW Conference, 1995, Motion 22). That resolution was calling for a drastic change in the way that social work education, training and qualification are regulated today – calling for a reversion to academic and professional control.

Before the establishment of the Central Council for Training and Education in Social Work (CCETSW) in 1971, the content and style of social work education and training was set, monitored and regulated by professional associations such as the Association of Psychiatric Social Workers, training councils such as the central government's Central Training Council in Child Care, and the colleges themselves (CCETSW, 1987). Those bodies also awarded the qualifications. It was a professionally centred operation which ensured the installation and maintenance of high professional standards, and the observation of professional ethics was guaranteed a high place on their agendas. One important facet of that arrangement was a high degree of public, self and professional accountability through professional ethics.

The resolution, then, was asking for a small step in the direction of restoring professional influence and approval of study standards. Fortunately, there was enough floor and proxy support to force a poll (a detailed audit of the voting as opposed to a show of hands). The poll, in a gathering dominated by social work managers, was lost by one vote – a surprising indication of the depth of feeling and concern around what is seen, in the continuing general debate, to be an insidious and persistent dilution of professionalism and professional accountability in social work.

CCETSW, itself a child of the Council for Training in Social Work created by the Health Visiting and Social Work (Training) Act 1962, has regulated and shaped all social work education and training in the UK since its installation in 1972. Before 1962, there were varied arrangements – via undergraduate and postgraduate education (many universities, for example, offered a psychiatric social work option) and vocational training courses organized and regulated by individual professional bodies – for the qualification of local authority welfare services social workers, child care officers, psychiatric social workers, hospital social workers and almoners, probation officers, education welfare officers, residential social workers, child guidance social workers and a multiplicity of social work disciplines. At the time of the Seebohm reorganization of the various social work disciplines and organizations into generic local authority social services departments (except probation in England and Wales), CCETSW was established as the national regulatory and awarding body for social work training and qualification (Baraclough, 1995, p. 9).

However, CCETSW is – at the time of writing – a quango. As is readily recognized, it is susceptible to central government control of its policies. In 1993 there was Government insistence that CCETSW should bring forward a major revision of its Paper 30, which provides the rules and requirements for the current primary social work qualification, namely the Diploma in Social Work (DipSW). 'The timetable agreed with Government committed CCETSW to producing a "Firm Draft" of a revised "Statement of Requirements" and a "Firm Draft" of the Rules and Requirements for DipSW Programme Providers, by 31st October 1994' (CCETSW, 1994, para. 2). My own perceptions of what has turned out to be a continuing process are of much wheeling and dealing between the various parties consulted, CCETSW and Government – mainly covert and unpublished. There are some rare indications of the 'behind closed doors' pussyfooting which must have gone on, as in the Probation Consultative Group when looking at 'Evidence Indicators': 'These needed to be phrased in a way that is acceptable not only to probation interests but also for Ministers – if the DipSW is to stand any chance of proving acceptable' (Probation Consultative Group, 1994, para. 2).

Anecdotally, the impetus for Government pressure for the revision of Paper 30 arose out of ministerial disaffection with what was said to be an undue emphasis by Paper 30 on political correctness and a preoccupation with anti-discriminatory issues. The seemingly disproportionate emotions that the Paper aroused are typified by press comments made around that time: 'It has ... inspired Stalinist demands for political rectitude . . .'; 'Amid all the unfocused wittering of the document, one clear obsession is detectable: race'; 'This elevation of racism into disease or original sin is the real clue to the obsession' (Appleyard, 1993). Given the balance of evidence, even though that is overwhelmingly presumptive, I am convinced, not in the least because quangos are of that ilk, that CCETSW is open to and subject to party political influence and direction. That the direction of the Conservative government of the 1990s was the commercialization of social work is another matter, but it is one which holds other implications for accountability.

Whatever the rights and wrongs of rewriting the DipSW requirements may be, the result of the review is a dilution of the values of professional social work, with the functions of social work becoming increasingly ambiguous. A pertinent example is that the professional obligation to speak out against malpractice and adverse social welfare policies, which was reasonably clearly contained in the 1989/1991 Paper 30, now has no dedicated place in social work education as a result of the review (CCETSW, 1991, p. 8).

A tradition of speaking for and speaking out

Pre-1970 and the 'Seebohm' national reorganization (the creation of social services departments), there were separate statutory social work disciplines. Broadly, these included child care, welfare (elderly and physically impaired people), and mental welfare (mental health/psychiatry and learning disabilities). The Probation Service had been set up as early as 1907 by the Probation of Offenders Act. Psychiatric social workers practised in hospitals, clinics (especially child guidance clinics) and, gradually after the Second World War, in community care – a development of the American mental hygiene movement which started in the late nineteenth century to develop hospitals as places of treatment rather than as places of incarceration. That approach, with the introduction of new methods of treatment for mental illness, paid attention to the influence and involvement of the family of the person with mental health problems in the family home – itself an extension of child guidance practice which was a separate and important discipline in social work practice that was highly professional. Almoners – probably the earliest specific social work discipline and firmly hospital-centred – focused on means of alleviating the hardships arising out of physical illness and its treatment. Social workers employed by voluntary, independent and private organizations ran alongside the state sector and continue to do so (Osborn, 1995, p. 10).

There is much blurring of origins. Many separate elements of positive social work had been present in the everyday work of those administering local systems for the control and care of people experiencing hardship and poverty, since the Middle Ages:

> Public Authorities had had some statutory responsibilities for destitute children since a series of Acts of Parliament in the sixteenth century. This legislation was codified in the Elizabethan Poor Relief Act of 1601, which gave church wardens and parish overseers the power to levy rates and to set to work or bind as apprentices vagrant and pauper children.
>
> (Pugh, 1968, p. 3)

As Heimler points out, 'In the nineteenth century . . . some asylum superintendents even went out of their way to see that patients had jobs to go to on discharge and advertised in the Press for suitable employment' (Heimler, 1967, p. 8). In these annals there is certainly also an evolving tradition of advocacy – speaking out for those who were vulnerable – and an evolving tradition of ordinary public employees, and especially those involved in charitable work, speaking out for the reform of inhumane policies, conditions and activities. That tradition of advocacy was written into the developing codes of practice of the embryo profession of social work and the principles behind 'speaking for' and 'speaking out' became part of the foundation for the education of its developing kaleidoscope of professional practitioners.

In 1895, the then Charity Organisation Society, now the Family Welfare Association, appointed an 'Almoner' to the Royal Free Hospital, London, in response to a recommendation of the House of Lords Select Committee in 1892. The remit was to ration free (charity) treatment to those genuinely unable to pay, and to guard against misuses of this. That new service grew into an embryo profession, and in 1907 the Hospital Almoners' Council was set up to organize and monitor standards of training and recruitment. Academic training began in 1912 at the London School of Sociology, which was later to become the London School of Economics.

From there, the organization of education and training in the expanding social work disciplines became a function of the academic centres in partnership with professional bodies. By the late 1940s, there was also a growing interest from local and central government departments. The statutory mechanisms of change were as follows: repeal of the Poor Law on 5 July 1948; the Children Act 1948; the National Assistance Act 1948; the Younghusband report, 'Social Workers in the Local Authority Health and Welfare Services 1959'; the Health Visiting and Social Work (Training) Act 1962; and the Council for Training in Social Work (Baraclough, 1995).

Whistleblowing as an essential social work function

In the past 40 years or so there seems to have been an increasing tendency to discredit and suppress the individual social worker who simply cares enough – who has a commitment to professional social work ethics and social responsibilities, and who has the courage to express opposition to policies, strategies and practices that run contrary to professional values. The forces of suppression, which are sometimes extremely subtle and elusive, usually corporate, but frequently political, and often find support from sensationalist media, are undoubtedly successful. As well as CCETSW, in my opinion, academia has colluded with this. I think that speaking out has been discouraged by academia as a rather revolutionary tendency, disparaging it for students who enter training with a healthy natural expectation that social work should inform policy-makers and 'contribute to the formulation and implementation of policies for human welfare' (British Association of Social Workers, 1986, para. 10.i).

As recently as 1981, Martin Davies, Professor of Social Work at the University of East Anglia, and an influential force in social work training in the late 1970s and early 1980s, presented one view of social work as a 'radical model of practice, one which will align the worker against the state and the forces of oppression'. Already he is building a picture of an extreme corporate antagonist. He asks, 'Can a social worker employed by the state continually denounce the objectives of his own department, and can he freely engage in political confrontation with a view to undermining the foundations of social and economic power?' (Davies, 1981, p. 10). This radical social-work bogeyman who is constantly battling with the forces of authority and the establishment, with the sole aim of total rebellion, seems to be – in terms of cognitive psychology – the automatic assumption which enters the minds of today's social work managers when the social work practitioner dares to question or criticize organizational policies, attitudes and actions. It is an interesting juxtaposition with the proud reforming stances of the nineteenth-century practitioners and the installation of advocacy as one of the fundamentals of social work activity.

Whistleblowing and accountability, in the annals of social work training and education, are located around the tradition of advocacy. By contrast, today's curriculum seems to very delicately and cautiously reach out the tip of its toe into the steamy backwaters of confrontation with corporate policy, walking all around the boundaries afraid of being pulled into areas where Central Government dogma may be upset. There is, too, a widening gap between professional objectives and corporate objectives, which may be essentially influenced by government policies, because finance is conditional upon the observance of the latter.

The local authority social services career structure also reinforces that growing gap by limiting and even suppressing the role of the social work practitioner. It is not uncommon for a newly qualified practitioner, after 2 or 3 years of practice, to move into first-line management where the pressure is for loyalty to the organization above all else. This too often leads to a disregard of professional values where they conflict with departmental policies. Standing up for professional values where they are not in line with policy frequently threatens career progression and even job security. First-line managers today, having frequently lost national terms and conditions of employment in favour of corporately imposed local contracts of employment, are often the first to go during the swathes of redundancies which result from the apparent rolling programmes of reorganization that social services departments have undergone in recent years.

There seem to be feudal legacies here, too, perhaps perpetuated in the 'master-servant' structures that are still present in employment law. There is a residual flavour of eighteenth-century establishment attitudes affronted by the questioning of the ordinary man. The establishment attitude still exists in some quarters whereby the social worker questioning something that is thought to be dubious is brought up short with the question 'just who do you think you are to challenge your betters?'. I am reminded of Tom Paine's written retort to the government after their accusations that his 'Rights of Man' undermined their social and economic foundations: 'I am, Mr Dundas (the Home Secretary), not your obedient humble servant, but the contrary' (Pimlott, 1995, p. 32). This may personify the healthy adversarial professional stance, but it also challenges managerial authority. It leaves the practitioner in a dilemma as to whether accountability to professional ethics is viable, given the possible alternative of disciplinary action and even dismissal.

My contention is that the 'rebel social worker' setting out to wreck the political and social foundations of authority and the state is a negative image perpetuated by some authorities to prevent the free and open exchange of information. Institutions in the UK shy away from direct forms of public accountability and they give out clear but underlying messages that if one speaks out, one will almost certainly be typecast as a maverick or a troublemaker, and risk damage to personal credibility, as well job loss and blacklisting for employment elsewhere. Is my claim far-fetched? Or is it a reasonable proposition given the cultural context of the UK workplace, local authority power games, central government manipulation, and today's commercial and business ethos in the care services?

Some actual experiences of social work practitioners indicate in some quarters an openly stated management strategy consciously and deliberately designed to minimize and even eradicate practitioner involvement in agency policy development. My own experience nationally as an activist in BASW and as a contact worker for Freedom to Care is of a degree of reflection of that position throughout the UK. It is clear that there has always been a corporate tendency in this direction, usually covert, and ranging from reluctance to co-operate or listen to tactical repression and punishment of attempts to fulfil professional or public accountability by speaking out about – and sometimes against – dubious organizational policy or practices.

CCETSW were saying in 1987, for the then primary Certificate of Qualification in Social Work, that they promoted 'knowledge, skills and attitudes ... based on the traditional professional values which put the clients' needs first and stress the ethical responsibilities of the worker, including his obligation to continue learning and to develop practice'. Then immediately following, and with darker tones, 'Such professional values have been overshadowed in recent years by the questioning of professionalism and by the growth of powerful bureaucracies which tend to emphasize organizational needs' (CCETSW, 1987, p. 6, para. 1.9).

Managerial policy which runs counter to professional social work ethics and responsibilities cannot fail to give rise to confrontation if the practitioners are properly trained and committed professionals. One means of trying to minimize the potential for confrontation in the work-place from the managerial point of view might be to move towards a deprofessionalization of social work. In my view this is happening in the following ways:

- the increasing use of unqualified staff in local authority social services departments as 'community care practitioners';
- the increasing managerial insistence on social workers operating exclusively in a market-style climate as assessors and purchasers of services (where they have to try to use skills in which they are not trained and to discard skills in which they are trained);
- the mushrooming of private care services which almost exclusively use untrained, unqualified staff.

If we consider this in the context of a lattice of accountabilities in the caring services it is a gloomy picture indeed.

Accountabilities and their linkage

Accountability can be usefully viewed as having separate ownerships. In social work it is normally assumed that accountability is corporate or, in the isolated instance of the approved social worker, individual statutory accountability (but still interpreted by most organizations as a function of corporacy). An organization may be conceived as a lattice of account-abilities which are more or less linked. It is a similar concept to that of the 'quality chain' in total quality management, but with each sphere of responsibility ideally reciprocally meeting all of the others' requirements. The individual spheres of accountability in this context are:

A. Professional;
B. Employer;
C. Public;
D. Statutory;
E. Employee;
F. Self.

In social work (and in other disciplines) there are often separations and conflicts between the different spheres. There has been an unavoidable increase in conflict since the formal implementation of policies in the health care services which have hard business pivots, i.e. which turn primarily on fiscal values and sometimes direct financial gain. The spheres should overlap very closely if they are fully and positively functional (Fig. 9.1). The usual configuration for social services departments is a set of separate or nearly separate spheres (Fig. 9.2) in which the employee and statutory spheres (D and E) will be interlocked and interdependent, but all of the others are operating on their own or in conflict.

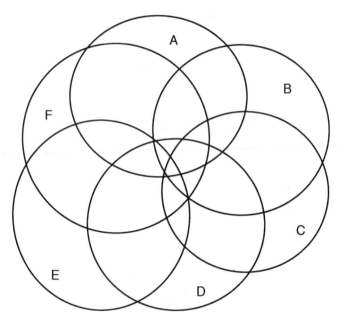

Fig. 9.1

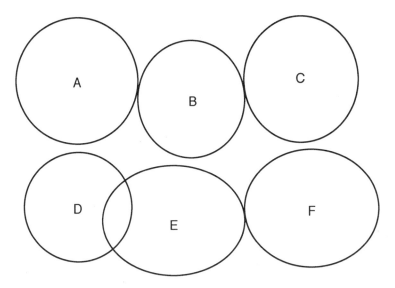

Fig. 9.2

Keeping this model in mind, I shall now give an outline of the various accountabilities and then look at how recent and current CCETSW curricula have paid attention to them.

Professional accountability

The most far-reaching contemporary issues cluster around the juxtaposition of employee and employer accountability, within the context of employee accountability to their profession. I shall give this most attention. Let us start by looking at a clear example from another profession, namely nursing.

The Royal College of Nursing's report entitled, *Whistleblow: Nurses Speak Out* states that 'Under the terms of their professional code of conduct nurses can be struck off the professional register for failing to report concerns about standards of care' (Royal College of Nursing, 1991, p. 4). The statutory regulatory body, which is the United Kingdom Central Council for Nursing, Midwifery and Health Visiting (UKCC), states in its Code of Professional Conduct:

> Each registered nurse, midwife and health visitor shall act, at all times, in such a manner as to:
> safeguard and promote the interests of individual patients and clients;
> serve the interests of society;

justify public trust and confidence; and
uphold and enhance the good standing and reputation of the professions.

> (United Kingdom Central Council for Nursing, Midwifery and
> Health Visiting, 1992).

Furthermore, the UKCC has recommended that this code and its other documents about ethics and standards 'should influence the design and content of contracts between commissioners and providers of health care'. It specifically suggests that the code be included in a clause in employment contracts and that 'a policy exists for registered practitioners to express to their employers' concerns regarding standards of care in the spirit of the Code of Conduct and Accountability for NHS Boards (produced by the Government Health Departments in the four countries)' (United Kingdom Central Council for Nursing, Midwifery and Health Visiting, 1995, section 6).

In social work, the position is nowhere near as clear. BASW, a professional association, does have a Professional Code of Ethics which it requires its members to observe. Part of that code says:

> The social worker's responsibility for relief and prevention of hardship and suffering is not always fully discharged by direct service to individuals, families and groups. The worker has the right and duty to bring to the attention of those in power, and of the general public, ways in which the activities of government, society or agencies create or contribute to hardship and suffering or militate against their relief.
>
> (British Association of Social Workers, 1986, para. 9)

This code was developed by the members of BASW between 1970 and 1975, with antecedents in and derivations from the pre-existing professional social work associations which had merged to become BASW, as well as from international social work sources. It has an excellent provenance but no statutory authority. It is not backed by any regulatory body, such as the UKCC for nursing and the General Medical Council (GMC) for doctors.

To compound the difficulties, BASW membership represents only a small proportion of those employed in social work in this country and the majority, not belonging to BASW, do not necessarily recognize professional principles. Yet another, as yet unevaluated, factor must be the managerial proportion of BASW membership and their contribution to the maintenance of professional values. A statutory regulator – a 'General Council' for social care – is badly needed (see Chapter 10), but the establishment of such a body was rejected at the Social Services Conference in October 1996 by Stephen Dorrell, the Health Secretary at that time (*Professional Social Work*, 1996).

The BASW code also specifies professional responsibilities to contribute to social planning and action and the body of professional knowledge – to 'contribute to the formulation and implementation of policies for human welfare', not to 'tolerate actions of colleagues or others which may be racist, sexist or otherwise discriminatory' and to 'work for the creation and maintenance in employing agencies of conditions which enable social workers to accept the obligations of this code'. It also states: 'There is a clear implication' in the latter principle 'that employers should recognize the whole code' (British Association of Social Workers, 1986).

CCETSW has, since the inception of the primary social work qualification, DipSW, included core professional values in the curriculum (CCETSW, 1991). There is also some recognition of a potentially adversarial relationship between employer and employee. However, it appears to me that all the CCETSW papers only skirt around the implications of the employee's professional responsibility (and accountability), which sometimes require speaking out against the employer's policy and practice.

Sir William Utting, Chair of the National Institute for Social Work, talking of the need for a regulatory body in 1994, declared:

> Social work demands from its practitioners standards which are manifestly professional. Yet almost anybody can practise as a social worker. Qualifications for appointment are largely for employers to determine. Employers can control and discipline social workers without regard to any wider responsibilities to the public, and some naturally put their own interests first.

In that same article he reaffirmed his view that 'ethical practice and behaviour are fundamental to social work' (Utting, 1994, p. 4).

Employer accountability

Employment law does not currently afford explicit recognition to the potentially adversarial relationship between employer and employee unless, rarely, observation of professional ethics and obligations is written into the contract of employment.

Legal advice to the Manufacturing Science Finance Union (MSF) in 1993 on potential tensions between the Department of Health guidance on whistleblowing (National Health Service Management Executive, 1993) and the UKCC Code of Conduct states:

> One can seek to argue that any ambiguity or inconsistency between any implementation of the Guidance note must be construed so as to comply with the Code of Professional Conduct. If it were otherwise it

would make a mockery of the rules of professional conduct. Your members could find themselves in a situation where by complying with their contractual duties they were in breach of their professional obligations to the UKCC. This would put your members at risk for disciplinary action by the UKCC which could include their being struck off the register which could, in turn, lead to their losing their jobs.

(Manufacturing Science Finance Union, 1993, p. 29)

However, the courts can agree, in industrial litigation, that there are existing implied terms of contract. Included in those implicit terms are the following: 'The employer must not, without reasonable and proper cause, conduct him/herself in a manner likely to destroy or seriously damage the relationship of trust and confidence with the worker' and the employer should not 'act arbitrarily, capriciously or inequitably. An employer treating a worker arbitrarily, capriciously or inequitably without good reason will be in breach of this term' (Kibling and Lewis, 1994, pp. 2–3). It seems to me that employers are on the whole intransigent in resisting the acknowledgement of this sphere of accountability. The law would appear to set forth employer accountability quite clearly, but it usually comes to light in retrospect – at industrial tribunals, for example. This seems to establish a good case for employment law to be included in CCETSW curricula.

Public accountability

Ostensibly, social work in social services departments is publicly accountable through the elected members of the local authority. This is an illusion. The reality is that it is the members who are accountable to the public, the executive management who are accountable to the members, the middle managers to the executive, the line managers to middle management, and the social work practitioners to the line management. The practitioner is also accountable to the public by reason of the common law 'duty of care' which cannot really be fulfilled by accountability through line management. Having to try to navigate through the above extended chain before the duty of care can be met is often a ponderous and intimidating process, frequently rendered impenetrable by hierarchical policy and status barriers. All too often in practice this means getting past managers who are blind to anything other than their employee accountability to the organization and how their career may depend on this. It is easy to see that when this blindness occurs it makes a nonsense of the lattice of accountabilities and results in many practitioners backing off from even attempting the 'chicken run'.

Another worrying aspect of public accountability is the dispute about whether or not local authorities as organizations have a common law duty of care. It was reported in August 1994 that the local authority involved in the Frank Beck case of child abuse in residential care was 'denying it owed a legal duty of care to victims of Frank Beck. . . .The council argues there has never been a definition of "legal duty of care" ' (*Community Care*, 1994). Almost a year later the House of Lords ruled on the local authority duty of care:

> Social Services departments heaved a collective sigh of relief this week when the House of Lords barred children from suing them for failing in their child protection duties. . . . The Lords ruled that imposing a common law duty of care on local authorities 'would cut across the whole system' of child protection. It is multi-agency, and to enforce a duty of care on one agency would be 'manifestly unfair' and would pose 'almost impossible problems' over disentangling which body was negligent.
>
> (*Community Care*, 1995)

However, there is a ready recognition of the individual duty of care attaching to the social work practitioner – that he or she has public accountability under common law with concomitant liability – but there do not seem to be 'almost impossible problems' over 'disentangling' who was negligent when the individual social worker is scapegoated.

Statutory accountability

Statutory accountability relating to social services departments is complex and, for the purposes of illustration, I am leaving aside that pertaining to independent and charitable social work. For simplicity, I have also narrowed the focus to the field of community care, leaving aside whole chunks of children's, family, mental health and organizational legislation (Chapters 11 and 12 cover many aspects of legal accountability).

The bulk of social services activity is interdependent across several dimensions and is wholly reliant on statute for its functions. This is the case whether that reliance is through legal permission, as with Ministerial approval for the promotion of the welfare of 'old people' under the Health Services and Public Health Act 1968, or by means of a legal duty, as exemplified by that 'to provide services for the after-care of people who have been suffering from illness', under the National Health Service Act 1977. The labyrinthine state of social services statutory accountability in community care alone extends across legislation relating to community care and includes the following: Section 3 of the Disabled Persons (Employment) Act 1944; Part III of the National Assistance Act 1948; Sections 1 and 2 of the Chronically Sick and Disabled Persons Act 1970; Section 4, 8(1) and 9 of the Disabled Persons (Services, Consultation and Representation) Act 1986; and the National Health Service and Community Care Act 1990. In addition, implementation of the law often seems to be dependent on Ministerial approval or direction, and community care is largely the product of delegated legislation – the power to dictate statutory accountability lying in the hands of Government Ministers.

Employee accountability

The following are some of the statutory requirements of the employee:

- a duty to 'look after the employer's equipment and machinery';
- a duty of 'mutual trust and confidence';
- a duty of 'loyalty' to the organization;
- a duty of 'good faith and fidelity';
- a duty 'not to disclose trade secrets';
- a duty 'to obey reasonable and lawful orders';
- a requirement to 'perform the job to the standard expected by the employer' (capability);
- possession of the right 'aptitude' and 'mental quality';
- a requirement to be healthy enough to 'perform his/her contractual duties';
- a requirement not to act dishonestly in or out of work;
- a requirement not to act violently or fight;
- a requirement of good attendance and good time-keeping.

(Kibling and Lewis, 1994, pp. 2–4, 69–79)

The accountability of the social worker as employee means that the law supports an unequal balance of power in favour of the employer. Not only is there plenty of scope for employers to find some jurisdiction under which to victimize social workers who raise concerns or speak up (e.g. good faith and fidelity, organizational confidentiality and capability or mental quality), but also there is the possibility of dismissal if the social worker carries out organizational policy which is subsequently found to be wanting by a public inquiry – a not uncommon occurrence in child abuse cases. I make no apologies for referring again to the paradox of the absence of public accountability for the local authority (because they have no duty of care in child protection) and the clear public accountability vested in the individual social worker. Indeed, there is a matrix of conflicts between statutory, employer, professional, public, self and employee accountability.

Self-accountability

The philosopher Immanuel Kant provided the deepest understanding of our accountability to ourselves:

According to Kant, the ordinary moral consciousness perceives quite clearly that the ethical value of an action does not depend on its external results, but upon the interior will which gives it rise. Hence it follows that only that action is moral which springs from duty or respect for the moral law. Yielding to custom or to past experiences, however sublime, would not make an action moral. Morality therefore cannot derive from a subordination to authority.

(Benda, 1942, p. 17)

The concepts contained here are the absolute fundamentals of all accountability, and if social work education is to be at all effective it must rest firmly upon this base. The crux of the matter is that if the person has a competent awareness of self and a confidence in the integrity of self, then personal or self-accountability will have priority. The Kantian view proposes a 'moral law' which begins and ends with the self, and which does not depend on considerations external to self.

I have tried to resist turning to my own experience of social work education in 1970–1972 – the period when CCETSW took over educational regulation. However, the casework approach which was the main thrust at that time did address this moral foundation in a way that has been largely wanting in degree of emphasis in the subsequent Certificate of Qualification in Social Work and the initial Diploma in Social Work curricula. Thus one basic casework text proposed three qualities that should be present when selecting students for training. Two of them are 'intelligence and flexibility of mind' and 'imaginative sympathy and a social conscience', but at the top of the list is the following:

firstly, because social workers have to stand for social values and require high ethical standards if they are to work at professional level, we require some assurance that certain standards of behaviour and ideals have been laid down and securely founded in early life, and have been again thought out and incorporated by the candidate. ... No imposition of professional ethics later can ever be a substitute for the candidate's own integrity.

(Heywood, 1964, p. 9)

It was a substantial feature of casework training to explore self-awareness in depth as an intertwining thread throughout the whole of the training. The present curriculum (the new DipSW) does acknowledge 'knowledge of self and use of self in social work practice' in its 'key areas of knowledge', and says 'Be accountable for own behaviour and practice' as an 'evidence indicator' for the 'core competence' called 'work in organisations' (CCETSW, 1991). These are welcome improvements, but they are only separate fragments as encouraged by the NVQ-style approach – not a fundamental organic process underpinning all social work activity as was once the case.

Accountability and CCETSW

CCETSW, in its 1987 revision of the guidelines for courses leading to the Certificate of Qualification in Social Work (CQSW), made no specific reference to accountability. This is left to individual 'educational institutions'. It is stipulated:

> 5.8 (i) That students are able to demonstrate to the satisfaction of examiners, knowledge and understanding within each of the following areas of study .... (d) the social functions of law and the structure and processes of the courts; the legal context of social work, and the role of social workers in the administration of specific laws. 5.8 (iii) That students are able to demonstrate to the satisfaction of examiners ability to carry out the following tasks: .... (d) examine the moral and ethical questions confronting professional social workers as both individuals and employees and their application in practice.
>
> (CCETSW, 1987, pp. 36–38)

Nowhere in the guidelines are knowledge and understanding of professional values, obligations and accountability in the organizational and public arenas explicitly required, and in practice 'the legal context of social work' was largely confined to a portion of statutory accountability – the mandate for social services activities contained in law. Again, in practice, the task of examining 'the moral and ethical questions' (which does have a potential for exploring self and professional accountability) varied widely from course to course and was, in the main, perfunctory. Indeed, it is an untested hypothesis of mine that the middle and senior managers who are currently the incumbents in social services departments are largely products of this period of social work education – ideally suited to taking the current managerialist changes and reorganizations forward, as they have little or no appreciation of 'moral and ethical' considerations to obstruct the new health-care business and market ethos.

With CCETSW's introduction of the new primary qualification superseding the CQSW in 1989 there was a definite improvement. The original Paper 30 on the DipSW stipulated:

> 2.1 The Knowledge Base ... 2.1.2. Values, knowledge and understanding of ... the origin and justification, meaning and implication of the values of social work ... ethical issues and dilemmas, including the potential for conflict between organizational, professional and individual values. 2.1.3. Knowledge and understanding of ... individual liberty, natural justice, legal rights, human rights ... the social function of the law. 2.2.1. Competence in social work requires the understanding and integration of the values of social work. This set of values can essentially be expressed as a commitment to social justice and social

welfare, to enhancing the quality of life of individuals, families and groups within communities, and to a repudiation of all forms of negative discrimination.

(CCETSW, 1991, pp. 14–15)

Paper 30 generated a welter of criticism from Government and others, mainly focused on what is seen as its foundation of 'political correctness'. Virginia Bottomley, the then Secretary of State for Health, was reported as stating in a 1994 speech:

> That is why we have set in hand a shake-up of CCETSW, the body responsible for overseeing the training of social workers. Gone will be the notorious Paper 30 which tells us, among other things, that 'racism is endemic in the values, attitudes and structures of British society'.

She went on to say that Paper 30 would be replaced by a 'Highway Code for social workers' which would 'make clear what social work is all about, what different areas of activity social workers are involved in and what skills they must have'. That would be accompanied by 'a "national core curriculum" for social work training. ... It will set out the essential practical and down to earth knowledge and skills they must learn and apply in their difficult work' (*Professional Social Work*, 1994, p. 11).

The way ahead?

CCETSW began its review in December 1993 accompanied by firm central government pressure. The schedule was that 'DipSW programmes should be working to the new requirements from September 1995' (Pierce, 1994, p. 10). The process aroused substantial concern. In particular, the CCETSW Welsh Committee expressed seven 'major concerns', among which was 'the political context of the review and the implications and lack of definitions of words such as "control" and "risk" ', and they 'stressed that the values and principles, notably of social work within Wales, needed to be represented more effectively in future in Council documents' (Welsh Committee, 1994). The National Institute for Social Work's Race Equality Unit – an initial formal participant – withdrew from the review on 31 August 1994, expressing 'dissatisfaction with the process' (Statham and Caroll, 1994, p. 58) and 'a group of Black professionals involved in social work', including CCETSW's former 'Black Perspectives', issued a statement on 30 September 1994, which stated that:

> our views were sought less than a month before CCETSW Council is due to take far reaching policy decisions. ... There was no organised

> process for eliciting the contribution of Black people ... little or no effective face to face consultation has taken place within the profession. ... The inadequacy of the process has resulted in a poor quality document ... we are perturbed by the fact that much of the process and content that has been put forward largely reflects political ideology and opportunism, to the detriment of wider consumer consultation.
>
> (*Letter*, 1994)

Nevertheless, what seems to have resulted are some minor improvements to the framework for a single social work qualification which allow the beginnings of a modular approach and progression, through the Post-Qualifying Award and the Advanced Award in Social Work, to degree standard (CCETSW, 1990). Importantly, the DipSW review has been in partnership with the Care Sector Consortium (National Vocational Qualifications), and it is heavily 'competency' structured in line with NVQ. At the same time, the National Institute for Social Work and Mainframe (independent consultants) were appointed by the government as consultants to develop National Occupational Standards for Social Work – standards of knowledge, values and skills that social workers should be expected to possess 1 year after qualifying (CCETSW, 1994, p. 50).

The draft National Occupational Standards developed were announced by CCETSW in April 1995. CCETSW said:

> The revised requirements, which replace the existing Paper 30, follow a review involving extensive consultation conducted within a tight timetable set by Government. ... The revised Statement of Requirements for Qualification in Social Work is structured around six core competencies of social work.
>
> (CCETSW, 1995)

Those six competencies are 'Communicate and Engage, Promote and Enable, Assess and Plan, Intervene and Provide Services, Work in Organisations and Develop Professional Competence'. These changes were duly incorporated into the revised Paper 30 'approved by CCETSW Council 23 February 1995'. This document was made available in working copy form for the September 1995 DipSW student intake.

A full critique of the 'Statement of Requirements for Qualification in Social Work' is not possible here, but we can examine its view of accountability. This, in my reading, remains narrow in scope and almost entirely confined to statutory and employee elements. It should be said that there are several references to responsibilities of varying kinds, but I do not think that they address the concepts set out here satisfactorily. The accountability references are as follows. As an 'Evidence Indicator' to 'Working in Organisations' there is the requirement to 'Be accountable for own behaviour and practice and work within agency policies and procedures'. This is part of the 'Practice Requirement' to 'Demonstrate capacity to work as an accountable and effective member of the organizations in which placed'. In that context, it is clearly the old favourite accountability scapegoat – the employee's duties. There is also an evidence indicator partner, 'Contribute to development of organizational policy, procedures and provision' which, in the absence of equal consideration of employer, public, professional and self accountability, perpetuates the old familiar imbalance.

As an 'Evidence Indicator' to 'Work in partnership to develop packages of care, support, protection and control', we have 'Negotiate and confirm with service users, including those who may be reluctant service users and those subject to compulsory orders, and with carers, other professionals and providers, a combination of services, decision-making processes and accountability arrangements'. And, as one 'Evidence Indicator' to the 'Practice Requirement: Work in accordance with statutory and legal requirements': 'Identify and agree with and between agencies, the roles, responsibilities and accountability for planned action and future decision making' (CCETSW, 1995, pp. 16–20).

The latter two references could indicate a recognition of linkage of accountabilities, but the connections are, I think, tenuous. These are the only references to accountability in the 'Statement of Requirements for Qualification in Social Work', which speaks for itself.

In considering Paper 30 and its current revisions it is useful to remind ourselves about the once common arrangement of the curriculum being set by the colleges and professional associations. It is particularly relevant here because what we have from CCETSW are its prescribed requirements of the standards that need to be obtained by students in order to qualify for the practice of social work. What we do not have is the content of the teaching and experiential work that takes place within those requirements. This means, for instance, that from the evidence indicator set 'Contribute to the work of the organization' in the 1995 revision of Paper 30 for the core competence 'Working in Organisations', 'Be accountable for own behaviour and practice' is open to be demonstrated in a variety of ways and at a variety of levels of accountability. However, the simplest and most available means of evidencing this will be to show clearly that the student has been accountable as a surrogate employee of the placement agency. That can be done simply by showing positive responses to complying unquestioningly with all of the policies of the organization.

The variables in this situation are the practice teacher and the academic base, and a great deal will depend on their sensitivity and awareness of the complexity of the checks and balances of the accountability lattice and their commitment to professional values. The fact that there are current pressures to devalue and dilute the professional sphere and to avoid, seemingly for fiscal purposes, accountabilities which may be inconvenient to the organization points to a gradual diminution of the counterbalancing influences of those variables.

I think an overall comparison of Paper 30 and its successor shows, above all else, a marked difference in the language of the two documents. The revision of Paper 30 has moved towards equivocation and a blurring of the status of the professional role of the social worker. This means that there is a concomitant move towards the curriculum being one that would be preferred by the social services-employing organizations – the resulting skills, knowledge and values becoming moulded towards the needs of the organization (and the values of central government dogma). The danger is that those organizations will shed the shackles of professional practice which might get in their way.

There is the risk of a dilution of professional values, which could lead to training for qualified local government officers, rather than qualified social workers (Mrs Bottomley's 'Highway Code' perhaps). These officers would only be accountable to their employers and, by extension, to statute, and public accountability would be corporately rationalized away, as is so commonly the case in local government. I think the language of the original statements of Paper 30 was more open, honest and direct and I think that their respective statements as to what constitutes social work provide a good illustration of this. First, the 1989 and 1991 versions of Paper 30:

> Social work is an accountable professional activity which enables individuals, families and groups to identify personal, social and environmental difficulties adversely affecting them. Social work enables them to manage these difficulties through supportive, rehabilitative, protective or corrective actions. Social work promotes social welfare and responds to wider social needs promoting equal opportunities for every age, gender, sexual preference, class, disability, race, culture and creed. Social work has the responsibility to protect the vulnerable and exercise authority under statute.
>
> (CCETSW, 1991, p. 8)

In contrast, the corresponding statement in the 1995 revision reads:

> The purpose of social work is to enable children, adults, families, groups and communities to function, participate and develop in society. Social workers practise in a society of complexity, change and diversity, and the majority of people to whom they provide services are amongst the most vulnerable and disadvantaged in that society. Social workers are employed by a range of statutory, voluntary and private organisations, and work in collaboration with colleagues from allied professions and departments, as part of a network of welfare, health, housing, education and criminal justice provision.
>
> (CCETSW, 1995, p. 2)

We can see that these two statements are very different, and one wonders why a need was seen to change the statement in Paper 30 rather than add to it, unless there is some political implication. Why in particular have they removed the reference to social work as 'an accountable professional activity'? It must be borne in mind that CCETSW is an unelected, government-appointed body and open to influence by central government. It is also interesting that the whole of the revision of Paper 30 was directly monitored and approved by Government (CCETSW, 1994, pp. 49, 52).

Conclusions

Whether or not the academic centres and the practice teachers are able to use the CCETSW frameworks to produce a proper synthesis of accountabilities remains to be seen. In local authority social work the control of the *application* of any facet of social work rests with social work management. Management, in the last analysis, decides who to employ.

One of the weaknesses of BASW is that its active membership is predominantly managerial. A measure of this is that only about 5 per cent of the participants at past BASW annual general meetings were practitioners. This does have a positive side – it means that a high proportion of the membership does retain contact with professional social work management instead of being metamorphosed into county council sales executives. If we look at management training in social services departments, it can be seen that this consists mainly of training in local authority as distinct from social work administration and management. This is taking place with an acceleration of gravitation towards commercial business methods and values. That is the sort of training which emphasizes, before all else, accountability to the organization.

However, one of the few strengths of the revised DipSW requirements is their modular framework. This means that the same set of requirements can be consistently used to build on post-qualification training and education, and in this there are opportunities to pursue dedicated social work management to degree standard. This may afford some measure of preserving professional and public accountability, even if self-accountability proper has all but disappeared from the curriculum.

If it is accepted that we have social services organizations that are increasingly unhappy with traditional professional social work standards and principles which are potentially out of line with their policies, it is no surprise to see increased fudging of training for professional accountability. This is especially true where cost-cutting is involved and discrimination is part of rooted establishment policy (separate services for under and over 65 years is a pertinent example). If we now have managers who see their sole accountability as employee accountability to the organization and who are ever distanced from their own accountability to professional standards – by compromise, career rewards, lack of training (or worse), management training in business and commercial methodology and values – then a degeneration of linked accountabilities must surely result.

This is one instance in which raising concerns on the basis of social conscience will always be suppressed or deflected, whether or not we have an enlightened training framework. We need an elected regulatory body – a General Council with powers to regulate the organizations as well as the practitioners – and one which can take over the setting of the training curriculum in collaboration with the professional association.

Since this chapter was written, it has been announced that CCETSW is to be discontinued. There are proposals that social work training and education will become part of the remit of a new General Social Services Council (see chapter 10).

References

Appleyard, B. (1993) Why paint so black a picture? *The Independent* 4 August.

Baraclough, J. (1995) A hundred years of health-related social work – a cause for celebration. *Professional Social Work* **January**, 9.

Benda, J. (1942) *The living thoughts of Kant*. London: Morrison and Gibb.

British Association of Social Workers (1986) *Code of ethics for social work*, 3rd edn. Birmingham: British Association of Social Workers.

British Association of Social Workers' Conference (1995) *25th Annual General Meeting*. British Association of Social Workers, 6–7 April, 1995, Brighton.

CCETSW (1987) *Guidelines for courses leading to the Certificate of Qualification in Social Work*. CCETSW Paper 15.1. London: CCETSW.

CCETSW (1990) *The requirements for post-qualifying education and training in the personal social services*. Paper 31. London: CCETSW.

CCETSW (1991) *Rules and requirements for the Diploma in Social Work*. Paper 30. London: CCETSW.

CCETSW (1994) *Review of the Diploma in Social Work*. Paper 1: Overview Paper. Council Meeting 19–20 October 1994.

CCETSW (1995) Statement of requirements for qualification in social work. In Paper 30 (revised edn). *Rules and requirements for the Diploma in Social Work*, London: CCETSW.

Community Care (1994) Council denies duty of care to Beck's victims. News section. 10 August.

Community Care (1995) Lords rule out clients' claims for damages. News section. 6 July.

Davies, M. (1981) *The essential social worker: a guide to positive practice*. London: Heinemann Educational Books.

Heimler, E. (1967) Introduction. In *Mental illness and social work*. Harmondsworth: Penguin Books.

Heywood, J. S. (1964) *An introduction to teaching casework skills*. London: Routledge & Kegan Paul.

Kibling, T. and Lewis, T. (1994) *Employment law: an adviser's handbook*. London: Legal Action Group.

Letter (1994) Review of the Diploma in Social Work: appended letter from a group of Black professionals. *Minutes of the Council Meeting 19–20 October 1994*. London: CCETSW.

Manufacturing Science Finance Union (1993) *Freedom of speech in the NHS: A guide for MSF negotiators*. London: Manufacturing Science Finance Union.

National Health Service Management Executive (1993) *Guidance for staff on relations with the public and the media*. London: National Health Service Management Executive.

Osborn, H. (1995) Yesterday once more. *Professional Social Work* **January**, p. 10.

Pierce, R. (1994) PC or not PC: the facts behind the education debate. *Professional Social Work*, **April**, p. 10.

Pimlott, B. (1995) Early Islington man. *The Independent on Sunday*. Sunday Review Section. 16 April.

Probation Consultative Group (1994) Extract from *Unconfirmed Minutes*. Special Meeting of the Probation Consultative Group, 16 September 1994.

Professional Social Work (1994) Education focus. Extract from a speech by Virginia Bottomley to the Conservative Local Government Conference, April 1994, p. 11.

Professional Social Work (1996) Dorrell rules out a General Social Services Council. **November**, p. 1.

Pugh, E. (1968) *Social work in child care*. London: Routledge and Kegan Paul.

Royal College of Nursing (1991) *Whistleblow: nurses speak out*. A Report on the Work of the RCN Whistleblow Scheme. London: Royal College of Nursing.

Statham, D. and Caroll, G. (1994) The Report of the Consultants: Review of the Diploma in Social Work. *Minutes of the Council Meeting*, 19–20 October 1994. London: CCETSW.

United Kingdom Central Council for Nursing, Midwifery and Health Visiting (1992) *Code of Professional Conduct*, 3rd edn. London:

United Kingdom Central Council for Nursing, Midwifery and Health Visiting.

United Kingdom Central Council for Nursing, Midwifery and Health Visiting (1995) *The Council's Proposed Standards for Incorporation into Contracts for Hospital and Community Health Care Services*. London: United Kingdom Central Council for Nursing, Midwifery and Health Visiting.

Utting, Sir W. (1994) Almost a profession. *Professional Social Work* **January,** p. 4.

Welsh Committee (1994) Review of the Diploma in Social Work: response of the Welsh Committee. *Minutes of the Council Meeting* 19–20 October 1994. London: CCETSW.

10

Protecting the public:
the contribution of regulation

Daphne Statham and Don Brand

From the point of view of those who use their services, social workers and social care staff are often in positions of considerable power. Social workers can intervene in the lives of individuals and families in a variety of ways, and their assessments strongly influence the nature and scale of any support services provided. Children and adults, who may be vulnerable through complex circumstances and physical, mental or learning disabilities, and who depend on often highly personal care and support in order to cope, are looked after by social care staff working, sometimes with little supervision, in people's own homes or at unsocial hours in residential settings.

Yet, despite the impact that they can have on other people's welfare and quality of life, social workers and social care workers have no statutory regulatory body to which they are responsible for their standards of conduct and practice. They are the only remaining unregulated professional and occupational groups in the publicly funded caring services.

The argument for a regulator

Pressure has increased in recent years for the establishment of a General Social Services Council with statutory powers. A General Council for the personal social services would have two functions:

- to set, develop and promote standards of conduct and practice for social workers and social care workers;
- to hold a register for the purpose of regulation and to discipline those found in serious breach of the standards.

The people and organizations supporting the establishment of a Council are clear that it is not a panacea. The existence of a regulatory Council would not in itself guarantee that no unacceptable practice, misconduct or abuse by social services staff would ever occur again. The argument is that it is an essential component in establishing, developing and enforcing standards, and provides a vital additional route for staff, service users, carers or members of the public to use when other systems fail. Inquiries into major scandals and well-publicized examples of unacceptable practice are sufficiently numerous to show that existing systems, relying on employers to safeguard standards, regularly break down.

Anyone would have the right to take a complaint to the Council. As a statutory regulatory body, it alone would have the powers to remove the licence to practise or impose conditions on its continuance. The Council would have responsibility for the bench-mark standards against which conduct and practice could be judged by members of the public, and by colleagues within and outside the different sectors of the service who are in a position to observe misconduct and malpractice.

Arguments for a General Council are not new. Pressures have existed since the 1950s. In 1968, the Seebohm Committee, referring to its proposal for unified social services departments, noted that: 'Any organization which combines professional power with public authority is bound to involve dangers, particularly where poor, vulnerable, inarticulate and sometimes difficult people are concerned'. It went on to argue for 'safeguards against neglect and the abuse of power' (Seebohm, 1968, p. 49).

Initially the proposal was for a Council covering only social workers, but they represent only a small proportion of staff in the personal social services. Research has consistently demonstrated the importance of social care to service users and carers, and the last 15 years have seen substantial growth in the numbers of social care staff, with the major increases in the private sector. Both the feasibility study (Parker, 1990) and the subsequent Report of the Action Group to the Secretary of State for Health (Action Group, 1993) concluded that, to be effective in protecting the public, a Council has to regulate the conduct and practice of social care workers as well as social workers.

Until recently, support for a General Council came only from the professional associations and a minority of staff. In 1982, for example, a major review of the social services, the Barclay Report, recorded that it would be 'premature' to establish a regulatory council because there was little consensus in support of it among social workers or social care workers (Barclay, 1982). The professional associations produced codes of conduct and practice to which their members were expected to subscribe, but these committed only the small minorities in membership of the associations. There was general acceptance that the protection of the public was secured primarily through controls exercised by the employer. These were assumed to be sufficient to ensure that standards were met, or that where they fell below an acceptable level, remedial or disciplinary procedures would be activated.

This opinion began to change in the early 1990s. One of the first signs of this was the provision of funding by the Joseph Rowntree Foundation for a feasibility study co-ordinated by the National Institute for Social Work. The study was undertaken by Professor Roy Parker on behalf of a steering group representing the staff, employers and employee organizations, the statutory body for education and training, and professional bodies in social work, social care and health. Having begun the study as a sceptic, he argued in his report, *Safeguarding Standards* (Parker, 1990), that the changes in the social service world since Barclay made the establishment of a regulatory body both feasible and desirable. Professor Parker identified four broad factors responsible for these changes: new social policies (community care and children's legislation); the mixed economy of care; the role of service users and carers within the personal social services; and the work-force. We shall now look at these in detail.

Changes in the social services

New social policies: community care and children's legislation

As a result of the 1989 Children Act and the community care changes, 'increasing numbers of people who are frail and vulnerable are living in the community' and 'more staff are having to help support people in their own homes which do not protect them from the risks and hazards to which their dependencies expose them' (Parker, 1990, p. 49). For some service users, residential and day care and increased domiciliary support are providing opportunities for greater independence and control over their own lives. Many others, such as elderly people, are much more frail and vulnerable than they have been in the past. In child care, the emphasis is shifting away from the operation of child protection procedures in response to allegations of abuse, and towards greater emphasis on support for children and families who are vulnerable or in distress. This change is very welcome for many working with children and families, but it will also produce new risks for social workers and care staff and their managers to cope with in protecting children and supporting family life.

The mixed economy of care

Until recently, the main employers of social workers and social care workers have been local authority Social Services Departments in England and Wales, Social Work Departments in Scotland, and Health

and Social Services Boards and Trusts in Northern Ireland. Parker concluded that 'the growth in employment outside the public sector is such
that it is no longer possible to claim (and it will be even less so in the
future) that there is no need for the independent regulation of social work
and social care staff', on the grounds that most work is in the public sector which acts in the public interest and is ultimately held to account
through the democratic process (Parker, 1990, p. 58). Employment patterns now include staff in large and small voluntary organizations and the
greatly expanded private sector, the self-employed, those sub-contracted
through employment agencies, and those working in industry and commerce.

The control of standards becomes more difficult because the provision of service may be divided among a number of providers, and there
is increased staff movement between the different sectors and independent units within them. Although a member of staff may have been dismissed for unacceptable practice by one employer, there is nothing to
prevent them seeking employment with another of the many provider
organizations, not all of which apply the most rigorous selection procedures or checks on employment histories. Unsuitable staff may not be
identified unless they have a criminal record that is picked up during
police checks.

These are not criticisms of the reforms, but a recognition of their consequences. They point to the need for different systems to be put in place
which focus on the individual worker rather than solely on the agency.
The White Paper entitled *Caring for People* (Department of Health,
1989) sought to increase diversity and choice in community care by
encouraging a range of independent sector provision alongside local
authority services. This inevitably increases the fragmentation of the service and promotes a further diversification of employment opportunities.
For the vast majority of staff, this fragmentation creates no risk to the
public, but there is a minority of unsuitable staff which current systems
fail to pick up. Some form of national registration of staff is becoming a
concern for employers in all sectors, as a means of charting the status of
staff and their standards of competence.

There is a trend towards smaller units in local government. In
Northern Ireland a number of Trusts are operating social care as well
as health care. In England, Scotland and Wales, local government
reorganization is establishing smaller, unitary local authorities which
may require joint working and joint commissioning of some services.
Patterns of control and decision-making are emerging which are complex both for managers and for practitioners. It is now common for
staff to work in multidisciplinary teams in which their colleagues are
not from their own employing agencies, but include service users and
carers, volunteers and staff from other professional and occupational
groups. Operating at 'arm's length' from the direct line management of

their employer, these groupings of people working on a common task can be large enough to form a small 'agency'. Often called 'virtual organizations', these groupings can have access to substantial resources and powers to innovate, but their patterns of accountability can be complex and difficult to manage.

In work on draft national standards which the National Institute for Social Work undertook with the Eastern Health and Social Services Board, the North Down and Ards Trust, and Alyson Leslie Associates, we found that traditional definitions are no longer adequate to describe many agencies or the job structures within them (National Institute for Social Work, 1995). Diverse forms exist which have flexible and permeable boundaries. A national framework of standards is becoming essential for social workers and social care staff working in this emerging world. These could be customized by agencies in the different sectors to suit their size, focus and culture, but would serve to set authoritative minimum standards of practice across a range of patterns of contracting, commissioning, providing and inspecting services. The consistency achieved through this broad framework would enable service users and carers, social care staff and social workers, managers and employers to know what they have a right to expect and what are their responsibilities.

The role of service users and carers within the personal social services

The objective of those promoting the case for a General Council is the protection of the public, not the furtherance of professional interests. Limited resources mean that standards have to be prioritized and negotiated with all of the stakeholders on a UK-wide basis. Service users and carers have a crucial role in this process, since decisions about what should be considered to be priorities can crucially affect their day-to-day lives. The recommendation of the Action Group on the composition of the Council is that nominations representing the interests of service users, carers and the general public should be the largest single category.

This would create a distinctive Council for the personal social services. A strong degree of user and carer influence is consistent with social policy which emphasizes needs-led rather than service-led assessment and provision, with the values and ethical principles of social work and social care, and increasingly with the practice of planning, purchasing, provision, inspection and quality assurance. Work on standards for social services has shown that service users and carers are keen to be directly involved in development work and to participate in the task of negotiating what can and should be achieved (User-Centred Services

Group, 1993; Morris, 1994; Balloch *et al.*, 1995). The cogent and constructive views of user groups on standards of practice are set out in a recent publication by the National Institute, entitled *The Standards We Expect* (Harding and Beresford, 1996).

The work-force

It was estimated in 1993 that there were about 600 000 people working in the different social services sectors (Chartered Institute for Public Finance and Accountancy, 1993). Firm statistics are hard to come by, particularly for the voluntary and private sector, and it is likely that this figure has now increased to nearer one million. Part-time work is a significant employment pattern in the social services sector. The majority of employees are women, who are more likely than men to take primary responsibility for caring for children and adult dependents. There may also be significant staff turnover in some sectors. This means that the actual number of people employed in these areas of work is likely to be even higher.

Whether part-time or full-time, staff often work in isolation, have access to people's homes, give intimate and personal care, and have powers which deeply affect the lives of service users and carers.

In the past, one argument against a regulatory body for social workers and social care workers has been that the majority had no formal qualifications, and that it would be unfair to regulate them. This argument has not been accepted by the professional body representing this group, the Social Care Association, which argues that its members already subscribe to a code of practice and are daily responsible for carrying out complex and difficult work. The vast majority of social workers are qualified by the Diploma in Social Work or its equivalent.

Changes in the training and education field are also making the point less valid. Until very recently there was no means of accrediting work experience. Although the mechanisms have been slow to develop, this is now a possibility. Besides the substantial numbers now registered for S/NVQs for social care, we now have the accreditation of prior learning and new open learning opportunities. These are gradually increasing the number of people who receive an assessment of the competence they have acquired through workplace learning and have new access to qualifications.

In common with other workers, social care workers and social workers are increasingly taking responsibility for their own learning. Some research on the social services work-force has shown a surprisingly high number of staff who were undertaking courses (Balloch *et al.*, 1995).

The function of a General Social Services Council

The functions of a regulatory Council are primarily the setting and developing of standards of conduct and practice; the registration and regulation of social workers and social care workers; ensuring that the responsibilities of staff are consistent with their assessed levels of competence and experience; and providing an independent voice on matters of importance to the public and within the personal social services.

Setting and developing standards of conduct and practice

Research has established that the service user and carer are less interested in which sector provides a service than in its appropriateness, reliability and quality. A national framework of standards for conduct and practice would enable users and carers, children and families to know what to expect from social workers and social care workers. The standards established would provide staff with a bench-mark against which to test their own and their colleagues' practice, and would give employers in all sectors a framework within which to customize their own standards. In the past few years there have been a number of cases in which:

- damaging practices based on spurious theories or distortions of approaches have been accepted by colleagues, including managers;
- challenges to poor or abusive practice were insufficiently investigated by employers, so that they persisted for some time, in some cases causing considerable and lasting harm;
- standards set by employers in the different sectors were too low to meet statutory responsibilities and guidance set by central government;
- staff reporting abusive and dangerous practice have themselves been victimized.

It is easier for bad practice to become rooted in an organization when there is a lack of clear guidance (or a multiplicity of conflicting guidance), a tendency for units or sections to become isolated or inward-looking, an absence of sources of expertise in practice, or an absence of external recognized reference points to which individual staff can turn. Parker says:

> At the moment codes of conduct and guidelines for practice are issued by an assortment of organizations ... do not cover all social workers and social care staff and they differ in their emphasis as well as in the sanctions that are available.
>
> (Parker, 1990, p. 17)

Since he completed his feasibility study, there has been a proliferation of tools for setting standards. They take different forms. There are generic British Standards such as BS5750, National Occupational Standards set by the Care Sector Consortium and the Management Charter Initiative for different levels of staff competence, standards guidance developed by national voluntary organizations for specialist workers (e.g. in the alcohol and drugs fields), codes of practice which form the basis for membership of national associations in the private sector, and agency-based standards, often derived from central government guidance, which inform service management, contracting and inspection requirements. There are, in addition, the Citizen's Charter, local Community Care Charters, and the Audit Commission's performance indicators for local authority departments. These standards apply mainly to agencies, as does the operation of complaints procedures and the Parliamentary Commissioners for Administration (ombudsmen).

At national level, the Audit Commission, the Social Services Inspectorate at the Department of Health and the Scottish, Welsh and Northern Ireland Inspectorates monitor standards of service quality and value for money within agencies. The National Occupational Standards for S/NVQs set standards for the competence of individual staff. Employers have diverse approaches to the management and supervision of staff performance, and their commitment to staff training is variable. Beyond this, the system for regulating staff is through disciplinary procedures or, in extreme cases, the criminal law.

Is this collection of standards so comprehensive as to be sufficient? It is difficult to be confident that they form a coherent whole. Parker argued that variations in standards of conduct and practice did nothing to promote public confidence (Parker, 1990). Research conducted on standards confirms that there is a good deal of confusion about the proliferation of standards, and a feeling of being swamped by their number and diversity (National Institute for Social Work, 1995).

At the same time, social workers and social care workers are strongly committed to openness about what service users and carers and the public can expect, and to the promotion of standards within the different sectors of the service. A definitive code of conduct and practice standards, drawn up by a General Council, would bind those whom it registered and create greater cross-sectoral uniformity in the determination of competence and conduct .

The registration and regulation of social workers and social care workers

The case for developing standards and implementing them seems to have been established. Is the task simply to create greater coherence and clarity of purpose for the different standards that apply to the personal social services? Is there now no need to set up a General Council? On the evidence from the catalogue of scandals and inquiries showing the repeated failure of agencies in these cases to regulate themselves or the work of their staff, this is not a tenable position in a mixed economy of care. The Report to the Secretary of State from the General Social Services Council Action Group concluded that standards in themselves were insufficient to protect the public, unless they were backed up by a regulatory body with statutory powers (Action Group, 1993). This is the position in other areas of the caring professions, and there are no clear reasons why social workers and social care workers should be any different. Although the public profile of social care workers is lower than that for health care workers, the work is no less complex, it involves equally high levels of risk, and the people who use the services are often very vulnerable.

Registration of large numbers of staff, many of whom work part-time, will present some issues of logistics which will have to be resolved. The proposal to the Secretary of State showed that it was possible to introduce a requirement for registration in phases, and to identify priority occupational groups from the public, private and voluntary sectors. They would be selected on the basis of their responsibilities for protecting the most vulnerable members of the public. The following groups were recommended for registration in the first phase: all social work and social care staff working in residential child care; field social workers and seniors; fieldwork team leaders and managers; and all heads or officers in charge and their deputies in registered and local authority homes. Social workers and social care workers holding a recognized social work or social care qualification would be eligible to apply for registration in the first year.

To cope with the variety of patterns of establishing competence, three registration categories were proposed:

- full;
- transitional (for experienced staff without formal qualifications);
- provisional (for new entrants accompanied by a training plan).

After the first phase, other categories of staff would be registered in a sequence and timescale to be agreed by employers and Ministers.

There were long and heated debates about whether the General Social Services Council should depart from the traditional model of statutory regulatory bodies, in which only people who have formal qualifications are eligible for registration. The conclusion was that this was a position to work towards, but that the majority of social care workers were already operating competently within complex and demanding areas of work. It is normal when establishing a new regulatory body to have an interim mechanism for experienced competent staff. To exclude them, when they are often working with people who are very vulnerable, reduces the protection provided to the public. It would also represent a failure to recognize the dedication and competence acquired over years of experience by many social care staff. While the other statutory regulatory bodies now require formally assessed competencies or qualifications as a criterion for registration, this is not necessarily the position from which they started. The General Social Services Council Action Group agreed that the exclusion of key social care staff from registration would restrict protection for the public, and would not reflect the requirements of the whole service.

A statutory requirement for social services staff to register with the Council would be accompanied by statutory powers to investigate complaints and discipline those found in serious breach of the Council's standards. In the most severe cases, the Council could debar a social worker or social care worker from practising by suspension or removal from the register. The Council would have a range of other sanctions available, including issuing a warning, attaching conditions to continued registration, or requiring remedial measures such as further training or supervision.

Ensuring that the responsibilities of staff are consistent with their assessed levels of competence and experience

There is a tendency to see regulation as solely a means of disciplining or excluding staff who fall below expected standards. The evidence from existing regulatory bodies is that they also have a role in commenting on the practice of employers who require their staff to operate beyond their levels of competence, or use methods or procedures that are judged to be unsafe or fall below the codes of conduct or practice.

Clarity among staff with regard to national codes of conduct and practice also enables them to resist taking on work for which they are not equipped, and which could put the public at risk, and to know that they can expect the backing of the regulatory body if they have behaved responsibly in the public interest. To keep abreast of developments within the area of practice is the accompanying responsibility of the individual.

There is, in addition, evidence of employers whose standards are not high enough for their staff to satisfy practice guidance issued through central government. In any inquiry it is important to recognize the part that the employer or management has played in any failure, in order to avoid staff being scapegoated.

Providing an independent voice on matters of importance to the public and within the personal social services

Part of setting standards is learning lessons from the failures and mistakes of our work. One of the examples selected by Professor Parker is enquiries into abuse or bad practice. At the moment, the forms of enquiry in the personal social services vary widely. They are not consistent in form or membership, and they have to be set up each time from scratch. They are very expensive, and it can be difficult to compare and learn from their findings.

While it would not be possible for a General Council to carry out enquiries, it could supervise their format, promote greater consistency in their procedures and standards, and have a key role in ensuring that the implications of their findings for the practice and conduct of social services staff are disseminated widely. The Blom Cooper report on the death of Kimberly Carlile recommended that a standing group under a General Council should be set up to share and build on experience and report on its work each year in order to co-ordinate findings and their implications at a national level (London Borough of Greenwich, 1987).

The future

The arguments for setting and regulating standards of conduct and practice for social workers and social care staff are now even more convincing than they were at the beginning of the 1990s. The new mixed economy of care has created the flexibility necessary for needs-led assessments and individual packages of care. Effective mechanisms to cope with the negative consequences of the changes must be put in place for the protection of the public. Standard-setting is an important component, but it is insufficient without the mechanisms to ensure that standards are properly enforced and have a reality for service users and carers. This means establishing a General Social Services Council with statutory powers.

Following statements of support for a General Council by the Labour Party's front bench in opposition, the new government announced its intention to establish a Council in a parliamentary statement by Paul Boateng, Social Services Minister, in July 1997. In subsequent statements ministers have announced that they wish the new body to be called the 'General Social Care Council'; that they intend to link its role in regulating the workforce with arrangements for regulating training; and that a separate body will be established in Scotland. Further details are expected in a White Paper on Social Services to be published in the summer of 1998.

The features in social policy which convinced Professor Roy Parker of the case for a General Council in 1990 have become more pronounced in the intervening years. The arguments are now more about whether and how, in addition to setting standards, a regulatory body will be able to enforce them effectively. This is a substantial move forward, and one which has been reached only by building on many years of hard work by different individuals and organizations. There is still a lot to do, but the argument, that a regulatory Council for social workers and social care workers is needed to serve the public interest, appears to have been won.

References

Action Group (1993) *Final Report to Secretary of State for Health.* London: General Social Services Council Action Group and National Institute for Social Work.

Balloch, S., Andrew, T., Ginn, J., McLean, J. and Williams, J. (1995) *Working in the social services.* London: National Institute for Social Work Research Unit.

Barclay, P. (1982) *Social workers: their role and task.* London: National Institute for Social Work/Bedford Square Press.

Chartered Institute for Public Finance and Accountancy (1993) Report. In *Final Report to Secretary of State for Health.* London: General Social Services Council Action Group and National Institute for Social Work, 40–62.

Department of Health (1989) *Caring for people; community care in the next decade and beyond.* London: HMSO.

Harding, T. and Beresford, P. (1996) *The standards we expect.* London: National Institute for Social Work.

London Borough of Greenwich (1987) *A child in mind: Protection of children in a responsible society: The Report of the Commission of Inquiry into the Circumstances Surrounding the Death of Kimberly Carlile.* London: London Borough of Greenwich.

Morris, J. (1994) *The shape of things to come? User-led services.* Social Services Policy Forum Paper 3. London: National Institute for Social Work.

National Institute for Social Work (1995) *Report on Feasibility of Developing Social Services Standards.* London: National Institute for Social Work, Eastern Health and Social Services Board/North Down and Ards Trust, in association with Alyson Leslie Associates.

Parker, R. (1990) *Safeguarding standards.* London: National Institute for Social Work.

Seebohm, F. (1968) *Report of the Committee on Local Authority and Allied Personal Social Services.* London: HMSO.

User-Centred Services Group (1993) *Building bridges between people who use and people who provide services.* London: User-Centred Services Group.

11

Legal aspects of whistleblowing in the social services

Stuart Vernon

I shall discuss whistleblowing in the social services within a general legal context. I chart what I believe to be the significant transformation of whistleblowing from a vice to a virtue. Central to this transformation are changes to the language used to describe whistleblowing, and a recognition of the many positive features of the practice for employers, employees, service users and carers. The public interest in disclosure is highlighted within an argument for both internal and external systems of disclosure and for a link between such systems. An associated feature of this transformation has been the articulation of concepts such as 'a right to disclose' or whistleblow and a moral or even legal duty to whistleblow. Consequent upon this articulation is an increasing acceptance of the legitimacy of the concepts constituting this new language.

This chapter provides a brief summary of the current law on whistleblowing as it relates to social services, and a lengthier discussion of the different directions for consolidating the transformation charted, so that whistleblowing finally loses the negative implications that have historically been associated with it. Some conclusions are offered on the place of law in consolidating and guaranteeing this transformation from vice to virtue.

What is whistleblowing?

I take as my understanding of whistleblowing the definition provided by the US *Federal Whistleblower Act 1989*, which describes the concept and practice as encompassing the disclosure of information by an employee or ex-employee which they reasonably believe 'evidences a violation of any law, rule or regulation, or gross mismanagement or gross waste of funds, an abuse of authority or a substantial and specific danger to public health and safety.' It is important to make the point that whistleblowing can be internal, that is within an organization and by an employee, or external, that is about an organization to a person or body external to the organization and by an employee or ex-employee. I take the term 'the public interest' to indicate a matter which, although it originates in individual or particular circumstances, has implications for a far wider constituency of interests.

I take the definition of the term 'social services' from the British Association of Social Workers (BASW):

> Reference to Social Services includes all settings where social workers are employed, i.e. residential work and fieldwork, community teams, hospitals, hospices, clinics, residential homes, schools, colleges, universities, education services, courts, etc.; all agencies: statutory, voluntary, independent or private; Social Services Departments in England and Wales; Social Work Departments in Scotland; Social Services and Health Services Trusts, including Northern Ireland; and Independent and Private Staff Agencies.
>
> (British Association of Social Workers, 1995)

Consequently this definition includes people other than social worker practitioners.

Whistleblowing as a vice

In my assessment, attitudes to internal whistleblowing are often ambiguous, and attitudes to external whistleblowing have historically been almost universally negative. Consequently, the overriding assessment of whistleblowing is that it has been a vice – reactions to it have been hostile.

Although the internal disclosure of wrongdoing may be encouraged, it may also be subject to disciplinary proceedings or other negative employment consequences if it is perceived as inappropriate or as having taken place outside established procedures. External whistleblowing is frequently seen as reprehensible, and is often met with disciplinary measures or dismissal on the basis that such activity is both evidence of disloyalty and constitutes a breach of express terms in the contract of employment or of the implied terms of confidentiality and fidelity.

Inappropriate internal disclosure or the unauthorized public disclosure of wrongdoing in social services by employees or ex-employees is currently almost universally seen in a negative light. Why might this be so? A number of factors work together to establish such a reaction to whistleblowing. Local authority social workers are subject to national conditions for local government officers or employees which contain an express duty of confidentiality which prohibits an employee from revealing any document relating to the authority unless authorized by law or expressly by the authority. In common with most employees, social services workers are also probably subject to implied conditions of confidentiality and fidelity in their contract of employment. Increasingly, the competition and profit considerations of the private sector social services industry impose their own pressures against the public disclosure of wrongdoing. In addition, confidentiality concerning service users and carers is a basic professional principle of social work training and practice, so that a culture which militates against the breach of confidences may become the norm for concerns with practice issues and relations with employers within social services. Within such a culture it is not surprising that whistleblowing is often regarded as deviant behaviour (McHale, 1992, p. 364; Hunt, 1995, pp. 135–6, 163–4). The hostile response to external disclosure may also reflect professional and public attitudes to breaches of confidentiality owed to patients, service users or carers. The generally negative response to disclosures by Graham Pink may reflect the allegation that he breached patient confidentiality. Comparisons can be made between the Pink case and the reaction to disclosures concerning the regime and conditions at Ashworth Special Hospital (see Chapter 3). In this case the wrongdoing was so significant and serious that public disclosure was viewed positively as being entirely proportionate to the subject matter of the disclosure.

It should also be recognized that the dynamics of power that operate within social services departments may well militate against whistleblowing. These dynamics reflect the role of professionals working within a bureaucratic structure. In particular, the autonomy that professional practice needs and demands may be difficult to accommodate within such structures so that internal whistleblowing, and the structures that facilitate it, may be seen as a challenge to this legitimate realm of professional practice rather than as a means to legitimate accountability. Another aspect of these power dynamics is reflected in the observation that managers may well be discouraged from disclosing bad practice where it might be seen, rightly or wrongly, to be reflecting mismanagement on their part.

One other factor needs to be acknowledged. Historically, whistleblowing or external public disclosure has almost always been critical of the policy or practice of individual social services agencies. Consequently, it has led to investigations and inquiries which have, at best, been inconvenient, and to reports which have been highly critical of the agency concerned, and of individual officers and employees. In turn these have led to suspension, dismissal or even criminal prosecution. The Staffordshire Pin Down Enquiry is one example of the impact of the public disclosure of wrongdoing.

The coalescence of some or all of these factors creates a culture within social services which renders whistleblowing both unlikely and a high-risk activity for social workers and other social services employees. In turn, this internal culture exists within a wider societal and political structure which has no constitutional or legislative tradition of freedom of information. In fact, the governance of the UK takes place within a level of secrecy that is now both outdated and in stark contrast to other democratic societies. Given such a culture, negative attitudes to whistle-blowing are unsurprising if not inevitable. Indeed, the word itself has pejorative connotations for many people, with implications of 'sneaking' and 'telling tales'.

Whistleblowing as a virtue

It is important to challenge these perceptions by arguing that it can never, or very rarely, be legitimate to prevent, or support the prevention of the disclosure of information concerning breaches of the law, gross misman-agement, or the abuse of authority or trust. (As we shall see below, this assertion is of course conditional upon a recognition of the imperatives that flow from the primary duty of social services to the service user and carer. These imperatives include the duty of confidentiality owed to ser-vice users and carers and their right to confidentiality. Tensions between this confidentiality and duties to disclose wrongdoing, and tensions between the duty of care owed to service users and carers and the duty of confidentiality owed to employers, are therefore foreseeable.)

Within social services, appropriate private and internal disclosure should be conceived as an employee right and also as a duty consequent upon the primary duty that is owed to service users and carers. The pub-lic disclosure of wrongdoing should be seen as an important element of public accountability and as a sometimes necessary precondition to the development and consolidation of the principles and performance of good practice. From these two principles we can argue for, at the very least, protection for those who disclose such information through the recognition of rights and duties to disclose. Transformation of whistle-blowing from a vice to a virtue would see these rights and duties being accepted and protected by the law. The House of Commons Commission on Citizenship has recognized that:

> the challenge to our society in the late 20th century is to create condi-tions where all who wish can become actively involved, can under-stand and participate, can influence, campaign and whistleblow, and in the making of decisions can work together for the mutual good.
> (HMSO, 1990)

Public accountability through the law

Accountability within, and of, the social services is neither a new nor a revolutionary principle. The political process within which social services are organized and provided by local authority social services departments is subject to debate and decision-making by elected councillors. A number of structures already established within social services agencies, such as complaints and representation procedures, the appointment of independent persons, grievance procedures, and inspection and registration units, provide for an element of public accountability even if they are not expressly designed to do so. There are equivalent structures operating in other quasi-public sector social services agencies.

In addition, the 'external' legal system provides a number of procedures which impose, whether by design or implication, a not insignificant level of public accountability. Judicial review is available as a High Court procedure within which the exercise of executive power by a public body can be investigated and challenged. There is little doubt that judicial review would be available to hear a challenge to the legality of the decision-making of a local social services authority. The hearing of such an application would inevitably reveal any wrongdoing, breaches of the law, abuses of power or gross mismanagement so long as they constituted unlawful administrative action. Although an applicant for judicial review must establish sufficient *locus standi* (among other things) before leave for a hearing, thereby protecting a public body from an application from an ordinary member of the public, public accountability is an inevitable by-product of judicial scrutiny, court decisions and remedies, and the reporting of the hearing and the decision. (An applicant for judicial review must establish that they have an interest in the subject matter of the application which is at least greater than that of an ordinary member of the public.)

Although an application for judicial review by an employee of a local authority social services department is possible, the employee might be seen by their employer to be in breach of a duty of confidentiality in the contract of employment, guilty of gross misconduct and subject to appropriate penalties as a 'whistleblower'. The court might also view their application as inappropriate on the basis that their concerns could and should have been raised internally.

The Commissioner for Local Administration (local ombudsman) has a statutory jurisdiction to investigate complaints of maladministration causing injustice on an application by the person suffering the injustice. The accepted definition of maladministration, which covers 'bias, neglect, inattention, delay, incompetence, ineptitude, arbitrariness and so on', encompasses many of the matters of concern to the employees and the clients of social services organizations, and is therefore the legitimate subject of 'whistleblowing' (Wade, 1988, p. 87). The requirement that any investigation is triggered by the application of the person suffering injustice is likely to be enough to exclude, in the normal run of things, applications by employees, although the ombudsman will consider, and may investigate, complaints made on behalf of a service user or carer.

(The British Association of Social Workers has argued that 'it should also be clear that it is a function of the social worker's "advocacy" responsibilities to advise and assist with a complaint to the Ombudsman even if this complaint is against the employing authority' (British Association of Social Workers, 1995, p. 8). None the less, local ombudsman investigations and the publication of their findings will inevitably establish public accountability for local government and their social services departments.

A new and difficult challenge is to ensure that the principle of public accountability can be imposed upon the emerging and increasingly important private sector of social services. Complaints to the local ombudsman are unlikely to be entertained unless they reflect allegations of maladministration in the local authority aspect of private sector provision, e.g., in financing or contract tendering. Judicial review may be available, but only if the High Court is willing to recognize that the provision of social services by the private sector which is financed by the public purse is a matter of public law. The private provision of social services to privately funded clients on a contractual basis is more difficult to bring into public accountability, although the registration and inspection of residential and nursing homes, as required by law, may provide one avenue for such accountability.

The public interest

My discussion is premised upon the existence and legitimacy of public accountability for social services agencies working both in the public and quasi-public domain and in the private sector. Currently, and in practice, the processes of public accountability already identified are used by the clients of social services agencies rather than by their employees. From these two propositions we argue for the provision of equivalent structures for employees and ex-employees so that they are able to bring issues of wrongdoing, illegality and abuse of power into public accountability without suffering the risk of disciplinary action, dismissal or legal action.

The rationale for this argument is found in the public interest in the provision of social services, which are paid for, in whole or in part, from the public purse, and because of the vulnerability of a significant number of those who receive social services. This same public interest requires the development, establishment and consolidation of good or best standards of practice. The legitimacy of these objectives determines that the disclosure of information which enhances the likelihood that they will be achieved is valid, and it should therefore be conceived of as a duty and a right to disclose in the public interest. A shift to the positive notions of a duty and right to disclose in the public interest would mark a significant move forward; it would also encourage a shift away from the current system of what is frequently *ex-post facto* or essentially reactive public accountability. Grievance and complaints procedures, whistleblowing, judicial review, local ombudsman investigations and public inquiries are most often concerned with enquiring into things *that have already gone wrong*. Although better practice may result, the price paid is the wrongdoing in the past. Duties and rights to disclose might encourage earlier identification of wrongdoing; good practice would be encouraged and bad practice discouraged.

This argument is disarmingly attractive. However, the complexity of the situation is rather greater than has been suggested so far.

It is important to acknowledge that there may be profound disagreement over what constitutes wrongdoing in areas where decision-making involves the exercise of professional discretion. This involves the 'right' of professionals to get things wrong, or to make mistakes in the sense that only hindsight can construct such judgements. The imposition of standards, through the process of public accountability, which fail to recognize the 'space' that is an inevitable part of professional practice and within which disagreement is endemic, and attempts to impose absolute judgements are inappropriate and fail to recognize the complexities of much of social services work. Whistleblowing should not encroach on the exercise of professional discretion unless it evidences wrongdoing, illegality, or the abuse of power or trust.

This argument should also recognize that resource constraints may mean that 'best practice' is unattainable and that 'good enough' practice is all that can reasonably be expected. In such circumstances the level of available resources might determine, in whole or in part, the legitimate subject matter of internal or external disclosure. This raises some interesting questions concerning the 'whistleblowing agenda' arising from the resourcing of social services. The overall funding of such services comes from central government and is therefore the subject of established avenues of accountability through the parliamentary process, and the Parliamentary Commissioner for Administration if there is an allegation of maladministration within central government. Decisions concerning the allocation and administration of established funding by local authorities and by social services departments are themselves subject to other forms of public accountability through the local ombudsman and the district auditor, and it is clear that the courts are willing to consider the resources context of community care assessment and service provision upon an application for judicial review. (See, for example, the House of Lords decision in *R v Gloucestershire County Council ex parte Barry* [1997] 2 WLR 459.)

Such accountability might encompass allegations of mis-allocation or mis-prioritization of resources – as such they could be considered to be the legitimate subject of disclosure by a 'good faith' whistleblower. It is a matter of some conjecture whether in these circumstances current law would offer any protection against employer reprisals (see below).

The public interest in the disclosure of wrongdoing must be balanced against the public interest in confidentiality when this is appropriate and the public interest in the efficient operation of central and local government in general and, for the purposes of this discussion, in the organization and provision of social services. The rights and interests of service users and carers may need to be protected by confidentiality, and their protection may conflict with the principle of public interest disclosure.

It may be necessary to distinguish between 'low-level' problems, which should not trigger the full force of public disclosure, and 'high-level' problems, which should be subject to the full rigour of public accountability through disclosure. The principle of proportionality is both valid and necessary.

Internal disclosure

The establishment and use of internal structures for disclosure within social services is premised upon a recognition of the primacy of the duty owed by employers and employees to service users and carers. Disclosure through internal procedures is also a recognition of the other contract of employment duty owed by an employee, namely the duty of confidentiality to employers. The BASW 'Guidance' document states:

> Of paramount importance is the common law 'duty of care' which all employers and employees have. In exercising that duty, the employer and each employee has a responsibility to draw attention to any matter they consider to be damaging to the interests of a service user, carer or colleague, to put forward suggestions which may improve the quality of service and to correct any statutory omissions, or prevent malpractice.
>
> (British Association of Social Workers, 1995, p. 2)

Consequent upon the definition of these principles the BASW 'Guidance' document encourages an essentially *internal* structure for disclosure:

> 3(i) Individual members of Social Services staff have a moral obligation, a right and a duty to raise with their employer: ...
> (ii) Every Social Services manager has a duty to ensure that staff are easily able to express their concerns through all levels of management to the employing authority or Trust ...
> (iii) ... There is also an obligation to safeguard information about the employing organization which may be confidential ...
>
> (British Association of Social Workers, 1995, p. 2)

The 'Guidance' envisages that this structure has both informal and formal procedures and stresses that staff concerns should aim to be settled between the employee and his or her line manager. Only where this is impossible or inappropriate should more formal procedures be instituted. These would provide for the matter to be referred up through an employee's management line to the highest level of accountable management. An alternative to this structure is suggested in the 'Guidance', which proposes that those matters which cannot be resolved by reference to an employee's line manager be referred to an officer of the local inspection or registration unit appointed for this purpose.

The recognition of the need for such internal structures and the framing of guidance are important elements in the process of the transformation of whistleblowing from vice to virtue. However, there are a number of issues which need to be identified and which may be problematic and render this transformation less than straightforward.

First, there are tensions and possible conflicts thrown up by the duties of confidentiality that are owed by social services agencies and their employees to service users and carers. Whilst internal disclosure may be less threatening to this duty of confidentiality than public disclosure, it is nevertheless possible to conceive of circumstances in which service users or carers do not wish their confidentiality to be breached, but where such information identifies wrongdoing and should therefore be disclosed. It is impossible to identify whether, and if so how often, these conflicts frustrate internal disclosure and accountability.

There is also a more 'fundamentalist' position which needs to be acknowledged, although it may be impossible to reconcile with the issues already raised. There are those who would argue that 'violation of any law, rule or regulation, or gross mismanagement, or gross waste of funds, an abuse of authority or a substantial and specific danger to public health and safety' (Federal Whistleblower Act 1989, USA) can never be anything other than a matter of public interest. Such a position might therefore deny the relevance of internal structures, and might also wish to sacrifice duties of confidentiality owed to service users and carers in the pursuit of the public interest through public disclosure and accountability. It is probable that the current culture within social work would acknowledge situations in which the duty of confidence owed to service users and carers could and should be sacrificed to the interests served by whistleblowing. This position owes much to the principles of social work practice developed within child protection work.

Secondly, successful structures for internal disclosure may prevent important matters of public interest coming to the notice of the public through external disclosure. One way of seeking to avoid, or more realistically to limit, the chances of private disclosure frustrating public disclosure and accountability is to establish an external structure for disclosure which is available either when internal disclosure fails, or where the public interest demands or requires public disclosure, or where disclosure is made by an ex-employee. It might also be possible to construct a system in which there is a link between internal disclosure systems and an external system. Local authority inspection units or the reframing of the responsibilities of the Social Services Inspectorate provide potential models. This would allow essentially 'in-house' issues to be dealt with by an internal structure, and matters of public interest to be fed on to the external system which is concerned with the public interest. Such a system might be possible within the structures of local authority social services departments. It would be more difficult to construct such a system within what is now an important private sector of agencies and organizations providing social services, although it could be achieved through the imposition of particular contractual requirements.

Current law

A brief survey of the current legal position will establish that we are a long way from any notion of a general *right* to disclose, let alone a legal *duty* to disclose information concerning wrongdoing. Section 2 of the *Race Relations Act 1976* and Section 4 of the *Sex Discrimination Act 1975* provide for the protection of individuals who disclose information which they believe to be indicative of discriminatory practice, and the new *Disability Discrimination Act 1995* provides similar protections. The internal disclosure of immediate danger to health and safety may be a duty imposed on certain employees, and an employee complying with this requirement is protected from unlawful dismissal by provisions in employment legislation (Lewis, 1995). One might argue that external whistleblowing is protected by a provision in the *Employment Protection (Consolidation) Act 1978* that a dismissal will be considered unfair when the reason for the dismissal was that the employee alleged that his or her employer had infringed particular employment rights (Section 60A).

There is some evidence of the courts offering protection to whistleblowers, although case law has not dealt with social services specifically (Lewis, 1995, pp. 213–14). Contracts of employment contain an implied duty of fidelity which prevents employees from disclosing information which they have acquired in confidence. The Court of Appeal, in *Initial Services v Putterill [1968] 1 QB 396*, has held that there is an exception to this implied duty where the misconduct is of such a nature that the public interest requires it to be disclosed to a person who has an interest in receiving the information. In *Lion Laboratories v Evans [1985] QB 526* the court refused to grant an injunction against employees who had just cause or excuse for disclosing information which their employers argued was in breach of the duty of confidence. In *Rea Company's Application [1989] IRLR 477* it was held that an employee's duty of confidence did not extend to preventing the disclosure of information to a regulatory body which had an investigatory jurisdiction. Important principles appear to be established by these decisions, to the extent that they indicate that the courts could develop some protection for whistleblowers in the absence of generic legislation. Any sense of optimism must, however, be tempered by the limitations of employment law – protection against unfair dismissal for full-time employees arises only after 2 years of employment, and little if any protection is available to employees who suffer reprisals short of dismissal unless these constitute discrimination on the grounds of race and/or gender and/or disability.

Any assessment of the current law is likely to conclude that there is no general right or legal duty to disclose wrongdoing, established by legislation or case law, within which employees such as social workers would be protected against reprisals by their employer for doing so.

The absence of appropriate legal protections for the whistleblower acting in the public interest should have shifted responsibility on to employers, in agreement with employees, to design and establish appropriate internal structures. It is entirely likely that the failure to establish such structures within social services agencies, including local authority social services departments, has led inevitably to external whistleblowing by social workers and other social services workers.

Ironically then, the potential for whistleblowing may be seen as resulting from three factors:

- the failure of government to legislate for a structure for the public disclosure of wrongdoing where this is in the public interest, including providing the necessary protections for those who disclose such wrongdoing;
- the failure of the courts to develop through case law appropriate protections for the 'good faith' whistleblower who discloses in the public interest;
- the failure of employers, including those in the public sector, to establish internal structures which could facilitate the internal disclosure of wrongdoing. The failure to facilitate internal disclosure, or to offer appropriate protection to employees, forces whistleblowers to go public.

Confidentiality, employment and the public interest

The discussion now moves on to the ways in which a number of interests might be promoted and protected. These are:

1. the duty of confidentiality owed to service users and carers;
2. the protection of the rights of employers;
3. the protection of employees who disclose internally and employees and ex-employees who whistleblow in the public interest; and
4. the promotion of disclosure in the public interest as an entirely positive act – one that may be conceived of as a right, or even as a duty.

These interests can be employed as criteria against which suggestions for reform can be measured.

The legislative response

Until recently Parliament has shown no inclination to legislate on a comprehensive scale on this issue. The USA provides a legislative model which could form the basis of statute in the UK. The American *Whistleblower Protection Act 1989* provides that civil servants may reveal certain information not covered by the *Freedom of Information Acts*, provided that he or she reasonably believes that it shows that (a) a law, or rule or regulation has been broken, or (b) funds have been grossly wasted, or (c) authority has been abused or (d) substantial and serious danger has been caused to public health or safety. If the civil servant has been dismissed on the basis of their whistleblowing, they have a right of appeal to a Merit Protection Board on a claim that prohibited action has been taken by way of reprisal. Alternatively, an employee can file a claim with the Office of Special Counsel, which has the power to investigate the complaint and seek corrective action.

Individual states in the USA have also introduced legislation to offer further protection to the whistleblower. In Michigan, legislation prohibits an employer from penalizing an employee because they have reported or are about to report a violation of a law or a regulation having the force of law. In New Jersey, the *Conscientious Employees Protection Act 1989* forbids retaliatory action against an employee by the employer if the disclosure relates to a breach of a law or a regulation.

In the UK a private member's bill, similar to the model of federal legislation in the USA, was drafted with the help of the Campaign for Freedom of Information. *The Whistleblower Protection Bill* was introduced by Tony Wright MP in June 1995 and then followed through by Don Tuohig MP. The provisions of the Bill would have created new rights for people who have been punished for whistleblowing, whether by dismissal, reprisal or any other form of discrimination. The proposals included the right of whistleblowers to obtain an injunction to prevent reprisals and to be compensated for losses incurred. Protection against unfair dismissal for the whistleblower would have been available from the first day of employment. The protection offered by the Bill would have applied to the disclosure of information which the courts consider so significant to the public interest that the employee is released from the duty of confidence in the contract of employment. Even if disclosure was in the public interest, protection would only be available where there was no bad faith on the discloser's part and the matter had been raised internally first. The Bill, as is the way with almost all private member's legislation, failed to make any progress in the parliamentary process (see Hunt's Introduction).

Most recently a private member's bill, the Public Interest Disclosure Bill 1997, has been introduced in the House of Commons. It seems that this Bill has a greater prospect of success consequent upon indications that it will receive government support. The Bill provides limited anti-victimization and dismissal protection to 'workers' who make 'qualifying and protected disclosures' which conform to statutory requirements which themselves vary according to whom the disclosure is made. The provisions of the Bill will amend and add to the Employment Rights Act 1996.

The Bill has received less than universal plaudits. The Industrial Relations Law Bulletin concludes its review of the Bill by commenting that ... 'The convoluted structure of the protection outlined, with a variety of states of belief and awareness required of the potential whistleblower, does little to promote certainty, and gives rise to a suspicion that the only workers who will be able to take advantage of the provisions are those who are unusually well advised and informed.' (IRLB 586 February 1998, 12–14.)

Contract of employment provisions

McHale has argued, in relation to National Health Service employees, that contracts of employment could be redrafted to establish exceptions to the duty of confidentiality currently owed by employees to their employers:

> Alongside a clause providing for confidentiality to be maintained could be included a clause sanctioning whistleblowing. The clause could perhaps provide that the healthcare professional would be entitled to disclose information if it was something which it was in the public interest to know.
>
> (McHale, 1992, p. 370)

It is clear that the same arguments could be applied to contracts of employment in the field of social services. This would be easier in the public sector, but could be enforced in the private sector through the process of contract negotiation between local authority social services departments and service providers.

Professional ethical codes

Such codes may make explicit the moral obligation that many feel underpins the need to whistleblow. The United Kingdom Central Council for Nursing, Midwifery and Health Visiting (UKCC), a statutory regulatory body, includes the following statements in its *Code of Professional Conduct*:

> As a registered nurse, midwife or health visitor, you are personally accountable for your practice and, in the exercise of your professional accountability, must . . .
> 11. report to an appropriate person or authority, having regard to the physical, psychological and social effects on patients and clients, any circumstances in the environment of care which could jeopardize standards of practice;
> 12. report to an appropriate person or authority any circumstances in which safe and appropriate care for patients and clients cannot be provided.
>
> (United Kingdom Central Council for Nursing, Midwifery and Health Visiting, 1992)

This statement recognizes both the moral dimension to the work of health care professionals and the context of their practice, such as resources. In addition, it requires that disclosure is made through appropriate channels.

BASW, which is a professional association, has its own code of ethics which commits the professional practitioner to the protection of clients, to the promotion of their rights and to their enhancement as individuals. In addition, the Central Council for Education and Training in Social Work (CCETSW) has guidelines on the core values in social work, and the Social Care Association has published its own *Code of Practice* (Social Care Association, 1993; Central Council for Education and Training in Social Work, 1995).

Guidance to staff and employers

BASW has published its own whistleblowing document in the form of guidance to social services staff and employers, to which I have already referred. The rationale of its *Guidance for Social Services on Free Expression for Staff Concerns* (British Association of Social Workers, 1995) is the provision of appropriate procedures for the articulation and investigation of staff concerns, and the protection of individual staff where these procedures are followed.

Most importantly, the 'Guidance' recognizes that the primary duty of the social services is to serve the needs of service users and carers. Consequent upon this principle is a recognition of the tensions that this duty may raise between the interests of the employer on the one hand and the interests of the service user and carer on the other, the role that the individual employee may play in seeking to negotiate the consequences of this tension, and the conflicts that this may raise. The 'Guidance' seeks to reconcile these tensions by a particular definition of the common law 'duty of care'. It argues that both employers and employees have a duty to raise concerns about the interests of service users, carers and colleagues, about services provided and statutory omissions, and to prevent malpractice (see Chapter 9). This definition of the 'duty of care' is welcome confirmation of my earlier argument for the recognition of a legal duty to disclose, although I recognize that in this articulation it is a duty more in the interests of service users and carers than in the wider constituency of the public interest.

The complexities of these tensions and potential conflicts for the framing of contracts of employment in social services are recognized by the 'Guidance'. While recognizing that employees owe a duty of confidentiality to their employer, the 'Guidance' asserts that this duty is not absolute and should be balanced against the employee's duty of care. Consequently the 'Guidance' argues that disclosure in the public interest may be justified, even though it breaches the duty of confidentiality to the employer, and that any contract of employment must set out duties of confidentiality in a way that recognizes these other obligations which impinge on the social services employee.

The establishment of internal structures for disclosure is important. However, they may do little to support the legitimacy of public disclosure where such disclosure is in the public interest and does not conflict with the interests of service users and carers. Indeed, as I have said, it is entirely possible to foresee circumstances in which successful internal disclosure systems will prevent or reduce the likelihood of public disclosure. I have already identified the positive consequences of public accountability through public disclosure, and suggested that systems of internal disclosure should be linked to a 'public' system so that experiences are shared, lessons learnt and good practice encouraged. In this context I welcome recognition within the 'Guidance' that forms of external reference may sometimes be appropriate and necessary:

> 15. Local procedures should establish at which stage the local inspection/registration/standards unit should become involved and set clear steps for the referral of appropriate issues to external inspection bodies
> . . .
> 22. The local formal procedures will include a mechanism for appeal to a panel made up of representatives of the employing organization and, to ensure an independent element, representatives from a trade

union or professional association or both plus any other independent persons such as service users if available . . .

27. Where a Social Services employee has a concern about the care of a service user detained in hospital or subject to Guardianship under the *Mental Health Act 1983*, or comparable legislation, he or she can refer the matter to the Mental Health Act Commission in England and Wales or the Mental Welfare Commission in Scotland, if the problem remains unresolved after pursuing it through local procedures . . .

29. All staff should be made aware that the Ombudsman may look into complaints on behalf of a service user or carer. . . . Whilst there should be every effort to exhaust normal procedures first, it should also be clear that it is a function of the social worker's 'advocacy' responsibilities to advise and assist with a complaint to the Ombudsman even if this complaint is against the employing authority . . .

30. It is then clearly established that any person (which includes any member of staff) has the right, at any time, to consult with his or her Member of Parliament. He or she might also, as a last resort, contemplate the possibility of disclosing his or her concern to the media in the shape of the press, radio or television, and the right to pursue that course is enshrined in Article 10.1 of the European Convention on Human Rights.

(British Association of Social Workers, 1995)

It also acknowledges the fact that Article 10.2 of the European Convention stipulates limitations to freedom of speech. These limitations include the protection of the reputation or rights of others, and the prevention of the disclosure of information received in confidence.

In Section 31 there is the significant statement that 'history shows us that there is the very rare occasion when disclosure to the media in the interests of public safety is clearly justified and the only effective means of preventing tragedy.' The publication of such 'Guidance' is important in itself, and especially perhaps in its assertion that employment contracts should be framed so that their terms and conditions do not conflict with the principles of BASW's *Code of Ethics* or the 'Guidance'.

Conclusions

In many ways, and perhaps unsurprisingly, BASW's 'Guidance' provides a statement of the current level of legitimacy established by the development and continuing occurrence of whistleblowing. There is little doubt that the unconditional perception of whistleblowing as a vice is no longer sustainable, and that the protection of appropriate internal and external disclosure of wrongdoing is recognized as both legitimate and necessary. The fact that this has been slow to take place in the UK reflects a number of cultural and legal factors, including the lack of a Bill of Rights, the absence of a freedom of information culture or legislation, the importance attached to confidentiality as a condition of contracts of employment, and historically negative reactions to whistleblowing.

The principal assertion of this chapter is that there is a transformation in attitudes taking place towards whistleblowing in general that is also reflected within the social services. As whistleblowing is becoming perceived in a more positive light it is losing its label as a vice. This accreditation is conditional upon disclosure taking place within internal structures where they are established, being in the public interest where external disclosure is necessary, and with due respect for appropriate and necessary confidences. My discussion has also identified the articulation of a language of rights and duties that reflects this transformation from vice to virtue. The law in the UK has been slow to reflect these changes – case law offers equivocal protection for the 'good faith' discloser in the public interest, and as yet there is no legislation in force to protect justified and appropriate disclosure. Employers are still most concerned with enforcing contractual duties of confidentiality owed by their employees. It remains to be seen whether the Public Interest Disclosure Bill 1997 will mark a fundamental shift in the nature of this legal structure. (For a commentary on recent law developments see: Industrial Relations Law Bulletin 564, March 1997 3–11.).

These failures make very significant the initiatives of professional groups. Thus BASW's publication of the *Guidance on Free Expression of Staff Concerns*, and its content, reflect the transformation I have indicated. However, it is insufficient to establish an appropriate legal structure within which appropriate disclosure is encouraged and may take place.

This legal structure, which should be legislated for, must incorporate two elements:

- an internal procedure within which employees may bring issues of concern to the notice of employers, and which recognizes the need for an appropriate response from employers; and
- an external whistleblowing facility which provides for the public disclosure of wrongdoing in the public interest.

The confidences of service users and carers must be respected, and employees must be protected where they use internal procedures and where their external disclosure is proportionate to the issue raised, in the public interest, and made in good faith. In addition, I have argued for the establishment of some link structure between internal and external disclosure, so that issues of importance to social services in general can be identified and placed in the public domain with the objective of improving the quality of services provided and protecting the interests of all service users and clients.

My concluding contention is that appropriate disclosure, both internal and external, can be encouraged by a combination of legislation and the incorporation of guidance (and/or professional codes of ethics), such as that proposed by the BASW, into individual contracts of employment for those working in social services. The nature of the legislation has already been indicated, but I reassert my argument that some structure should be established which can receive external disclosure and which can monitor internal disclosure in the public interest. In the absence of appropriate legislative provision, the emphasis falls on the terms and conditions of individual contracts of employment and the judicial development of common-law protections for the good faith whistleblower acting in the public interest.

Acknowledgement

The author wishes to record his thanks to Suzy Braye who read drafts of this chapter and offered her advice and assistance with enthusiasm. Any errors remain the sole responsibility of the author.

References

British Association of Social Workers (1995) *Guidance for social services on free expression of staff concerns*. Birmingham: British Association of Social Workers.

Central Council for Education and Training in Social Work (1995) *Assuring quality in the Diploma in Social Work: rules and requirements. (No. 1)*. London: Central Council for Education and Training in Social Work.

House of Commons Commission on Citizenship (1990) *Encouraging citizenship*. London: HMSO.

Hunt, G. (ed.) (1995) *Whistleblowing in the Health Service*. London: Edward Arnold.

Lewis, D. (1995) Whistleblowers and job security. *Modern Law Review* **58**, 208–21.

McHale, J. V. (1992) Whistleblowing in the NHS. *Journal of Social Welfare and Family Law* **5**, 363–71.

Social Care Association (1993) *Code of practice for social care*. Surbiton: Social Care Association.

United Kingdom Central Council for Nursing, Midwifery and Health Visiting (1992) *Code of professional conduct*, 3rd edn. London: United Kingdom Central Council for Nursing, Midwifery and Health Visiting.

Wade, H. W. R. (1988) *Administrative law*. Oxford: Clarendon Press.

12

Access to information and the social services

Mike Feintuck and Caroline Keenan

Introduction

When parents are faced with an allegation of abuse concerning their child (see Chapter 3) they will invariably wish to know as much as possible regarding the investigations undertaken by agencies such as local authority social services departments. In this chapter, we consider the extent to which existing law and practice ensure that parents receive such information, and we propose principles of practice for the release of information, and mechanisms of challenge to decisions not to release information.

Reports of investigations have described social workers tending to refuse to disclose to parents information about the investigation lest the parents were the abusers of their child and would use the information in a way that would be detrimental to the child's best interests (*Re W; Re C and L; Rochdale B.C. v A and Others;* Department of Health and Social Security, 1988, pp. 36–46, 1992, pp. 251–2). We have sympathy with those professionals who are seeking to exercise their judgement in what they perceive to be the child's best interests, and we accept that responses to the growing claims by parents for greater openness in their dealings with social services should take account of the potential need of investigators on occasion not to reveal certain information to the parents during an investigation.

At the same time, however, we can also relate to the parental rights groups and individual parents who have been vociferous in their complaints about the secrecy of social services during an investigation. These complaints became particularly public after the events in Cleveland in 1987 became widely known. A letter to the Cleveland Inquiry written by two parents expressed the feelings of many: 'Once the children were removed from hospital we were left totally alone, not knowing what was happening and not having been told of any future contact with social services and when we would see our children'

(Department of Health and Social Security, 1988, p. 44, para. 2.53, Parents' Letter to Cleveland Inquiry). Especially in instances when investigators had removed the child from home (immediately a suspicion that the child might have been abused came to light) parents could be left without any knowledge of what was happening to their children (Department of Health and Social Security, 1992, p. 252, para. 14.58).

In this chapter we seek first to set out the general legal position on access to information in relation to local government's role in the social services, before looking specifically at the position of those involved in child sex abuse investigations, especially the parents of children at the centre of investigations. Clearly, this area involves a congeries of complicating factors, not least significant of which is the complex interplay of a variety of agencies (social services, health, education and police), and the fact that the parents are often seeking information relating not so much to them as to their child. Such factors render this area far from typical and raise particular confusion for parents seeking to complain about their treatment.

Despite these complications, we none the less choose to focus on this area as an example, not only because of its topicality, but also because of Stevenson's observation that the parents of children involved in such investigations 'frequently endure multiple deprivation: they are often financially and materially in poverty; their difficulties are overwhelming and they seem unable without help to fight or manipulate the system to their benefit' (Stevenson, 1989, p. 155). This raises a series of important questions regarding the extent to which legal rights are relevant, and the ability of parents to encash such rights in practice. We focus on parents rather than the position of other carers, teachers, or indeed the children themselves, because while the protection of children seems quite properly to be the focal point of discussions of child abuse, it needs to be remembered that parents have a particular and especially strong case for being involved in decisions regarding their children's welfare, unless or until they have been authoritatively determined to have lost such a legitimate interest by virtue of their past conduct. The potential or actual conflict of interests between parents and their children makes this a particularly interesting, if difficult, area for legal research.

Amphlett (see Chapter 3) highlights the nature of the questions and complaints raised by parents in such situations, including the following.

- Are 'they' allowed to do this?
- What will happen during this investigative process?
- What tells them how they must carry it out?
- What rules must they abide by?
- What are my rights while this is going on?
- What can I do if I am not being treated properly?

(Amphlett, 1994)

Such questions essentially concern the process of investigation rather than the nature of the evidence being found, and it is the thrust of this chapter that *there is no good reason why parents should not receive answers to this kind of question.* Our aim is to discover to what extent this claim is currently supported by the law, and to consider how it might offer further assistance.

We suggest at the end of this chapter that guidance regarding the investigative process rather than legal rules, and investigation via an ombudsman rather than redress via the courts, may in practice provide the most suitable means of structuring discretion, increasing transparency, and therefore improving the accountability of the process. While we focus on a narrow area, the issues raised, especially that of accountability, are of broader, indeed fundamental, democratic and constitutional significance, and our considerations and proposals may be of relevance in other comparable contexts.

The secret state opened up?

The themes of openness, accountability and responsiveness are, of course, familiar to anyone who is aware of the Citizens Charter initiative and the many subject-specific charters it has spawned. The rhetoric associated with these developments has emphasized the empowering of individual users of public services in their role as 'citizen consumers', and has acknowledged, if often only implicitly, the crucial need for access to information if individuals are to be able to exercise their 'rights' as consumers. Although the whole charter movement may be criticized on the grounds that it fails to recognize the wider concept of citizenship (Feintuck, 1994), it remains significant for our inquiry in so far as it establishes a climate in which an active role for individuals in relation to the provision of services by the state is being emphasized, with access to information as a prerequisite.

Perhaps of more direct interest to us here, and closely connected with the Charter movement, is the government's 1993 *White Paper on Open Government* and the resulting *Code of Practice on Access to Government Information* (HMSO, 1993; Office of Public Service and Science, 1993). Although applicable directly only to those bodies which are part of, or connected to, central government, the White Paper and Code of Practice, in claiming to provide major advances in opening up government, serve as a clear indication of the government's stated aims, which we must presume to be of general applicability in the modern context.

It is now our intention to discuss the extent to which recent developments have in practice enhanced the ability of those affected by the activities of a local public body, such as a social services department, to access information in which they have an interest.

Access to information and local government: the legal framework

Birkinshaw has stated that, 'Local government has been subjected to legally imposed processes of open decision-making which have invited judicial intervention in a way that other areas have not ... in stark contrast to the position of central government' (Birkinshaw, 1988, p. 129). While this observation is undoubtedly true, it is equally true to say that the existing legal provisions have failed to resolve satisfactorily the complex tension between access to information and confidentiality, nor in many cases have they met the expectations and demands of service users. This is true generally of local government – the key provider of social services – but is highlighted especially in the sensitive and often high-profile area of child abuse allegations.

The Local Government (Access to Information) Act 1985 goes some way towards opening up the activities of local government to public scrutiny. The Act requires that meetings of local authority committees and their subcommittees should be publicized and open to the public, and papers associated with their business published. There are, understandably, exceptions to these requirements, which include information relating to the adoption, care, fostering or education of any child, and information relating to the prevention, investigation or prosecution of crime (Birkinshaw, 1988, pp. 91–2).

The Data Protection Act 1984 is also relevant to local authorities in so far as name-linked, personal data is held by them on computers. Under the terms of this Act, data users (i.e. those holding personal, computerized information) must register with the Data Protection Registrar, stating the purposes for which they hold information. Information may only be held for specified and lawful purposes, and must be adequate, relevant to the stated purpose, accurate and up to date. An individual is entitled to be informed, on request, whether any data user holds information about them, and to have access to the data without undue delay or expense and, if necessary, to have it corrected or erased. Data users are required to implement sufficient security measures to prevent unauthorized access to, or alteration or disclosure of personal data.

The utility of the Act's provisions is limited not only by it being restricted to computerized records, but also by the onus being on the subject to be aware of the provisions and to make enquiries of any body they think may hold information about them. In addition, predictably, substantial exemptions to the provisions exist, including records relating to the prevention or detection of crime. Under the Data Protection Act, the relevant Secretary of State is empowered to exempt or modify the Act's provisions regarding information relating to the physical or mental health of data subjects (Data Protection (Subject Access Modification) (Health) Order, 1987).

The key exemption here embodies the same principle as can be seen in the Access to Health Records Act 1990 (which applies to 'paper', i.e. non-computerized, records), involving the exclusion of access of a subject to information about them the release of which would be 'likely to cause serious harm to the physical or mental health of the data subject' (Access to Health Records Act 1990). Under the 1990 Act, where information is withheld, the applicant must be informed of such a decision, and of their right to challenge the decision, ultimately through the courts but initially via the relevant health authority.

A further, limited extension of openness applicable to certain local government functions is achieved by the Access to Personal Files Act 1987 – in many ways a framework Act which must be read in conjunction with specific regulations (Access to Personal Files (Social Services) Regulations, 1989, p. 1587: SI 1989: 206, as amended by Statutory Instrument 1991). These measures are based on the principle of subject access established in the Data Protection Act, but extend it to manual (i.e. non-computerized) personal files relating to local government housing and social services functions.

A local authority is exempted from the requirement to give access to information, if:

- under Regulation 9(2) 'the carrying out of the social services functions of the local social services authority would be likely to be prejudiced by reason of the fact that serious harm to the physical or mental health or emotional condition of the individual who is the subject of the information or any other person would be likely to be caused'; or
- under Regulation 9(3) 'the identity of another individual (who has not consented to the disclosure of the information) either as a person to whom the information or part of it relates or as the source of the information, would be likely to be disclosed to or deduced by the individual to be the subject of the information or any other person who is likely to obtain access to it'; or
- under Regulation 9(4) the information is held by the local authority for the purposes of 'the prevention or detection of crime or the apprehension or prosecution of offenders', and if these purposes would be prejudiced by the disclosure of the information.

In addition, Regulation 8 provides exemptions for information provided by a health professional or health authority where similar circumstances exist.

These exemptions are clearly intended to reflect the sensitive functions of social services departments, and their dependence upon confidential reports from and co-operation with other agencies and individuals in areas such as child abuse.

A further complication in such areas is that in the case of children, an authority should only grant the child access to such records where it believes that the child understands the nature of the request. Where a parent seeks access under the provisions, access should only be granted where the authority is satisfied that the application is made in the *child's*, and not in the parent's, interest (Birkinshaw, 1990, pp. 233–4), and clearly Regulation 9(2) (above) must be considered.

While the foregoing establishes a general background for access to information in relation to local authority social services functions, and already demonstrates some of the difficulties encountered in establishing a balance between the principle of access to information, privacy and confidentiality, and the protection of children, it is also necessary to consider the law and practice specific to child protection functions.

Child protection and access to information

Legal rhetoric in this area now supports the concept of the centrality of a child's family in the promotion of that child's needs and interests. The legislation and policy of the 1970s were characterized by a belief that the state was the ally of the child, which acted to protect him or her from abuse or further abuse at the hands of his or her parents (Parton, 1985, pp. 100–28; Fox Harding, 1991, pp. 59–97).

However, the mid-1980s saw a definitive change in attitudes. The *Review of Child Care Law* in 1985 made it clear that 'a distinction is often drawn between the interests of children and the interests of their parents. In the great majority of families, including those who are for one reason or another in need of social services, this distinction does not exist' (Department of Health and Social Security, 1985, p. 4).

Children Act 1989

As can be seen, the law has now allied the concept of the support of the family primarily with the idea of support of the parent. The overall principle which should now underlie any work undertaken by professionals on behalf of any child is that of partnership with the parents in achieving any goal for the child. In the *Working Together Under the Children Act*, the guidance for professionals involved in a child abuse investigation states clearly that 'local authorities must work in partnership with parents' (Home Office, Department of Health and Department of Education and Science, 1991, p. 1, para. 1.4).

All of the work undertaken in the late 1980s and early 1990s has been guided by what has been described by Fox Harding as a belief that 'state intervention is legitimated, but this intervention is seen as ideally of a supportive kind, helping to defend and preserve birth families' (Fox Harding, 1991, p. 10). To this end, Section 17 of the Children Act 1989 has imposed a duty upon local authorities to:

> 1(a) ... safeguard and promote the welfare of children who are in need; and
> (b) so far as it is consistent with that duty, to promote the upbringing of such children by their families, by providing a range and level of services appropriate to those children's needs.
>
> (The Children Act 1989, Section 17)

However, although the rhetoric relating to children may be bursting with soundbites stressing the importance of the family, the concrete rights that parents may exercise to find out what is happening during the course of an investigation into whether their child has been abused may be written, if not on the back of a postage stamp, then certainly on the back of a small index card. It seems that parental privilege is derived from a belief that state support of parents is in the best interests of their children. Thus where the child's interests can be clearly seen to be at variance with those of his or her parents, should the privileges accorded to parents also correspondingly decrease?

In order to understand the legal rules that exist in this area it is important to be aware of two underlying facts. The first is that the majority of 'rules' which social services must follow, violations of which could possibly be upheld in a court of law, are not contained in legislation. Principles are contained in guidance issued by government departments, such as the document *Working Together Under the Children Act*. However, 'rules' also derive from departmental circulars, which often accompany guidance, and from criminal and civil case-law. Interestingly, some of the most important principles have been laid down by public inquiries into investigations either where children have not been adequately protected (Department of Health and Social Security, 1974; Brent, 1985; Greenwich, 1987; Lambeth, 1987) or conversely where investigators have acted in a way which was felt to be over-zealous (Department of Health and Social Security, 1988, 1992).

The second underlying issue is that any rules issued by national bodies, in whatever form, are intended only to act as guidance, to be developed and enforced by the local Area Child Protection Committee (ACPC). This a body made up of senior members of the agencies with an interest in child protection. Those writing the national principles have given each ACPC discretion to interpret the principles in developing local practice (Home Office, Department of Health, and Department of Education and Science, 1991, p. 5, para. 2.4).

The central statute governing matters relating to children, namely the Children Act 1989, does not consider the rights of parents to know what is happening during an investigation, nor indeed does it give parents the right to know the contents of any other file about their children. The Act does expect that the local authority will allow parents to retain contact with their children when those children are being cared for by the local authority, although this is seen in terms of the right of the child to maintain links with his or her family when at all possible, rather than the right of the parent to know about the health and welfare of their child (Children Act 1989, Section 34(1)a).

Thus we observe that the most important rules for this purpose are contained not in legislation but in inquiry reports and guidance and procedures issued by government departments.

Inquiry reports, guidance and procedures

Work in this area has echoed the growth in openness which has been prevalent in the overall approach to local government. The first acknowledgement of a general concept of openness towards parents during an investigation is contained in the Cleveland Report. The Inquiry concluded that those investigating a case of sexual abuse should be open to parents at all stages of the investigation, irrespective of how the parents had acted. This was seen as being a right of the parents: 'Whether the parents were abusers, possible abusers or ordinary people caught up in the result of a misdiagnosis, this situation of isolation and lack of support was a most worrying feature in the Cleveland Crisis' (Department of Health and Social Security, 1988, p. 246, para. 2.65).

The Family Rights Group stated in their evidence to the Cleveland Inquiry that 'parents and other family members unhappy with a service should not have to wait on the goodwill of those who provide a service.' The Cleveland Report responded to this type of complaint by trying to set down rights that parents should enjoy during the course of an investigation. Among the Report's recommendations were that 'Parents should be informed and where appropriate consulted at each stage of the investigation. ... Parents are entitled to know what is going on and to be helped to understand the steps that are being taken' and that 'Social Services should confirm all important decisions to parents in writing. Parents may not understand the implications of decisions made and they should have the opportunity to give the written decision to their lawyers.' The Report specifically recommends also that 'Parents should always be advised of their rights of appeal or complaint in relation to any decisions made about them or their children' (Department of Health and Social Security, 1988, p. 246, *Recommendations* 3b).

The lead provided by the Butler-Sloss Report was followed 2 years later in the Report by the Social Services Inspectorate into Child Protection Services in Rochdale. This was instigated as a result of the highly criticized investigations into satanic abuse in the area which had taken place the previous year (*Rochdale B.C. v A and Others* and *Re C and L*). This Report recommended, in the interests of 'good practice and natural justice' that 'information is prepared for parents outlining what will take place under the child protection procedures, informing them how they will be kept involved and informed and advising them of their legal rights' (Social Services Inspectorate, 1990, p. 26, para. 7.4, 7.5).

The Orkney Report, published 4 years after Cleveland, recommended in addition that parents should be given some case-specific information. In this particular instance the Report suggested that parents should be told the whereabouts of their children when the children had been removed from home to a place of safety, and that they should, where possible, be invited to child protection conferences. This was seen as important not because parents had a right to be given certain information about their children, but because it was felt to be an essential step in improving the relationship between the parents and social services (Department of Health and Social Security, 1992, p. 252, para. 14.58).

Working Together Under the Children Act, consistent with the Children Act itself, closely interlinked the interests of children with those of their parents, and expected that professionals would be 'working in partnership with parents and with other family members' in child protection work. The culmination of such work was seen to be the child protection conference, which was described as the forum which 'brings together the family and professionals to exchange information and plan together' (Home Office, Department of Health and Department of Education and Science, 1991, p. 41, para. 6.1). The parent has no absolute right to attend, although there is a presumption that they will do so: 'exclusion should be kept to a minimum and needs especially to be justified' (Home Office, Department of Health and Department of Education and Science, 1991, p. 43, para. 6.15). Although *Working Together* speaks in terms of 'sharing information', parental attendance at conferences has not generally been justified in terms of access to information, but rather in terms of the right of parents to have their arguments heard. Thus where parents have had the opportunity to express their views to social workers prior to the child protection conference, but have not been invited to the child protection conference, the courts have not quashed the decision made by the conference (*R v East Sussex County Council*). Furthermore, advocates of parental attendance at conferences have often stressed the importance of the conference as a forum for gathering further information from the parents, rather than parents gathering information from investigators. For example, it has been suggested that if parents attended the conference they could correct any factual inaccuracies voiced at the conference (Lambeth, 1987, p. 107, para. 7; see also Monk, 1988, p. 3).

However, in order to underpin the work of the child protection conference, *Working Together Under the Children Act*, like Cleveland before it, supported the concept of openness in professionals' dealings with parents. In its chapter on child protection conferences it states that:

> it cannot be emphasized too strongly that involvement of children and adults in child protection conferences will not be effective unless they are fully involved from the outset in all stages of the child protection process and unless from the time of the referral there is as much openness and honesty as possible between families and professionals.
>
> (Home Office, Department of Health, and Department of Education and Science, 1991, p. 43, para. 6.11)

The guidance has established, if not a norm of openness, at least a principle that openness in dealings with parents should be supported where possible. However, we suggest that what it has failed to do is to elucidate this concept in a way that would help investigators to exercise it and parents to enforce it. We feel that questions about what exactly parents can expect to be told and what practitioners should be expected to tell them have not been sufficiently answered. It is vitally important that a code of best practice is established within this principle. *Working Together Under the Children Act* fails to distinguish between different categories of information to which parents might wish to have access. Furthermore, it has not acknowledged that investigators may be much more reluctant to let parents have access to what may be described as 'case-specific' information than they would for what may be described as procedural information. We discuss possible changes to this position in the section below entitled 'The way ahead?'.

Grievance redress

> A grievance . . . connotes a sense of wrong or injury to one's interests, dignity or rights, either felt personally or on behalf of another and which sense of injury has not been rectified or assuaged through any process or procedure. It clearly does not include a simple request for information, though obviously where a request is refused, that may well become a grievance.
>
> (Lewis and Birkinshaw, 1993, p. 16)

We believe that complainants have different reasons for seeking redress for their grievances. Some may wish to receive a specific 'legal' remedy, such as the consequences of an action being undone, or cash compensation being paid, while others will pursue a grievance primarily to rectify a sense of injustice, and perhaps with a goal of receiving an explanation, an acknowledgement of the rectitude of their claim and/or an apology. For the first category, complainants may ultimately need to use the court process to achieve their goal, but for the second, a variety of alternative mechanisms may prove more appropriate. We wish now to consider a range of mechanisms which may be relevant to parents who have been denied access to information in the course of investigations into child abuse.

Complaints procedures under the Children Act

Unfortunately, in the interests of clarity, we need to raise this potential avenue of redress only to dismiss it as largely irrelevant to the situations we consider.

The complaints procedure under s.26 of the Children Act requires local authorities to establish a mechanism to examine complaints from the public regarding the operation of Part III of the Act. This Part relates to the provision of services for children by local authorities, but does not include the duties of the local authority to investigate suspicions of child abuse, which arises out of s.47, in Part V of the Act. Although some local authorities may take it upon themselves to go beyond the strict requirements of s.26, and review via this procedure their activities under other parts of the Act, this is exceptional. The inconsistency and lack of clarity and certainty as to the availability and suitability of this process to the kind of situations we are considering is in itself a fundamental problem.

Courts

The courts have considered at length in a number of cases the question of whether parents have a right to enforce disclosure of information gathered during an investigation. However, all of the requests for information which have been considered by the courts have been made after an investigation had been completed, again apparently too late to allow parents any scope to inform or influence the outcome. These requests have been made in the context of mounting a defence in a criminal court or to counter the allegations made in a civil court case to decide about the future care of a child. Where judgements in these cases allowed certain information to be disclosed, this was because it was decided that the public interest in enabling parents to answer the charges against them outweighed the public interest in maintaining the privacy surrounding records, particularly those compiled by the social services (*Re M*). This has been justified particularly in the terms that it is in the best interests of the child, as:

every child has an interest, as part and parcel of its general welfare, not only in having its own voice sympathetically heard and its own needs sensitively considered but also in ensuring that its parents are given every proper opportunity of having the evidence fairly tested and preparing themselves in advance to meet the grave charges against them.

(R v Hampshire C C ex parte K, p. 133)

This is not a right *per se* to receive information, but a right to gather information to prepare a defence. The broader claim to information does not, as yet, seem to have been litigated.

European law

Appeals to the European Court of Human Rights have concentrated upon the rights of parents to be involved in decision-making about their child, rather than freedom of information issues. *R v The United Kingdom* found that parents should be involved in decision-making about their children. This aspect of the appeal to the European Court had been based on Article Eight of the European Convention of Human Rights, which states, *inter alia*, that 'Everyone has the right to respect for his private and family life'. The judgement found that respect for such rights required the local authority to find out the views of the parents and take them into account in any decisions that it made. Although the court found that 'The relevant considerations to be weighed by a local authority in reaching decisions on children in its care must perforce include the views and interests of the parents' (*R v United Kingdom* [1988] 2 FLR 445, p. 465), this judgement was not primarily focused on the rules surrounding case conferences, and did not support the principle of parental attendance *per se*. In fact, the opinion of the court was that 'regular contacts between the social workers responsible and the parents often provide them with the requisite protection of their interests' (*R v United Kingdom* [1988] 2 FLR 445, p. 466).

Commissioner for local administration

While the courts have sought on occasion (although apparently with only limited success) to establish clear legal principles on parental access to information in cases of child abuse allegations, an alternative avenue of redress available to aggrieved parents is to the Commissioner for Local Administration (CLA), otherwise known as the 'local government ombudsman'.

Created under the Local Government Act 1974, the CLA's remit parallels that of the Parliamentary Commissioner for Administration (PCA, the 'parliamentary ombudsman') in relation to the activities of central government departments and connected institutions. Three regional offices of the CLA cover England. Under the terms of the Act the CLA can investigate complaints from members of the public who allege that they have 'sustained injustice in consequence of maladministration' in connection with the exercise of administrative functions by a local authority. 'Maladministration' is a broad, and in many ways ill-defined, concept which is heavily dependent for definition on the interpretation of the ombudsman, but it certainly extends to cover a range of matters beyond the scope of the courts' powers in actions for judicial review. Although the extent of the CLA's remit is therefore broader and more flexible than that of the courts, it should be emphasized that, like the courts, the CLA's jurisdiction, in theory at least, provides only for review of administrative practice, rather than a review of the merits of administrative decisions.

In 1988, the requirement for complaints to the CLA to be addressed via a local councillor was removed, and complainants may now contact the CLA directly. The CLA may, in general, only act in response to a complaint from a member of the public, and not on their own motion, although in 1993 the CLA published a guidance note, entitled *Good Administrative Practice*, which sets out general principles which local authorities should follow in carrying out their functions. Although not legally binding, such guidance is likely to prove highly persuasive. In addition to providing redress for complainants, CLAs' reports of their investigations into allegations of maladministration frequently make recommendations that the local authority in question should review its procedures in relation to the matter in question.

Like the PCA (although unlike the CLA's counterpart in Northern Ireland), the CLA's findings cannot be enforced via a court of law. Instead, the CLA makes recommendations as to redress, and where a local authority refuses to take action which satisfies the CLA, the ombudsman can now require a local authority to publish a statement on the case in a local newspaper, at the authority's expense. The potential expense of publishing such a statement often outweighs the cost of implementing the CLA's recommendations, which in terms of cash compensation for victims. of maladministration are generally small.

Although the absence of legal enforceability of CLA's recommendations may appear to be a weakness, in practice only a handful of cases each year result in the CLA requiring local authorities to publish statements (14 in 1991/1992, 13 in 1992/1993 and 9 in 1993/1994), and in the vast majority of cases where the CLA finds injustice and maladministration, the local authority concerned complies with the recommendations issued. Indeed the CLA's reports are often of substantial influence in respect of local authority practice and procedure.

In 1993/1994 over 14 000 complaints were received by the CLA for England as a whole. These resulted in 391 reports being issued, of which 330 revealed maladministration causing injustice. Complaints regarding social services departments have consistently accounted for approximately 5 per cent of the total number of complaints received by the CLA over the last 4 years – a small figure when compared with the number of complaints regarding local authority housing, planning and poll tax/council tax issues, which between them in 1994 accounted for two-thirds of all complaints received (statistics compiled from the *Annual Reports* of the Commissioner for Local Administration).

It has been suggested to us that in practice the CLA will refuse to act in the kind of situation we are considering here until such time as all internal redress mechanisms within the local authority have been completed. Section 26(5) of the Local Government Act 1974 states that before proceeding to investigate a complaint, the CLA must be satisfied that the local authority concerned 'has been afforded a reasonable opportunity to investigate, and reply to, the complaint'. The following subsection, 26(6), provides that the CLA shall not conduct an investigation either where a remedy is available through the courts, or where a right of appeal, reference or review to a tribunal exists. However, the impact of this restriction is lessened by the express grant of discretion in the same subsection, stating clearly that 'a Local Commissioner *may* conduct an investigation notwithstanding the existence of such a right or remedy if satisfied that in the particular circumstances it is not reasonable to expect the person aggrieved to resort or have resorted to it' (emphasis added).

This clause clearly allows the CLA to investigate even where a legal remedy exists, while the clause in Section 26(5) requires the CLA only to ensure that the local authority must have a 'reasonable' opportunity to reply to the complaint. Neither of these clauses impose any legally binding limitation on the CLA preventing investigation where a local authority has failed to reply to a complaint within a reasonable time or where it would not be reasonable for a complainant to have recourse to legal redress. Indeed, many of the reports of both the CLA and the PCA identify delay on the part of the public body as the principal cause for a finding of maladministration. Thus, where a local authority repeatedly fails to respond to correspondence in a timely manner, or exhibits undue delay in implementing its procedures, this in itself can form the basis for a complaint to the CLA.

We wish to consider two examples of recent cases where the CLA has found maladministration leading to injustice regarding the treatment of parents in cases involving social services departments' investigations regarding their children. The first, relating to a failure to allow a parent to attend a case conference, arose in the context of the earlier (1988) edition of *Working Together*, (Department of Health and Social Security and Welsh Office, 1988), and serves primarily to demonstrate that ombudsman processes can at times offer effectively the same ability to challenge a public body's actions as pursuing legal action, although without the expense and formality. The second case, in considering a requirement that the local authority social services department is effectively under a duty to act properly in relation to provision of information to parents *throughout* the period of investigation, seems to go further than the law presently does, and indeed appears to seek to impose standards on local authorities approaching those recommended in the Cleveland Report.

In the first report, into a complaint against Humberside County Council, the 9-year-old child in question, a ward of court, was in the care of the Council. (*Complaint against Humberside County Council.* Commissioner for Local Administration, Investigation No. 91/C/2587). The child's mother received a written invitation to a case conference at which discussions were to be held regarding contact between her and her daughter, and child protection issues were to be discussed. The conference subsequently decided that the child should remain on the child protection register and recommended that the child be found a long-term foster placement with no plans for rehabilitation with her mother, and also that access between mother and child be supervised. When the mother arrived at the conference, she was not invited in, and after the conference had finished the council officers told her of the decisions reached, and also that one of the papers she had prepared for the conference had not been circulated. The relevant guidance in *Working Together* at that time stated that 'Parents should be invited where practicable to attend part, or if appropriate the whole, of case conferences unless in the view of the Chairman of the conference their presence will preclude a full and proper consideration of the child's interests.' The Humberside Area Review Committee guidelines stated that it was not appropriate for parents to attend the whole of a case conference, but that they might be invited to attend the latter part of the conference to discuss its outcome. The mother had expected to be invited in at least at the end of the conference, and when she was not invited in at all became suspicious as to what had taken place, feeling that she had been denied an opportunity to comment on her child's progress and to give her views on any plans for the child.

Although the CLA doubted whether the decisions eventually reached at the conference were substantially affected by the mother's exclusion from the meeting, she did find that the mother had not received the consideration which she was entitled to expect, and found that maladministration had occurred. By the time the CLA's report was published, the Council were in the process of undertaking a review of their practices in such circumstances. The recommended remedy of a payment of £350 and an apology may not seem much in terms of 'compensation', but for complainants in such a situation an apology and acknowledgement of fault often seem more significant. Furthermore, the CLA's investigation contributed to the Council reviewing its practice.

The second relevant CLA's report. (*Complaint against the London Borough of Lambeth.* Commissioner for Local Administration, Investigation No. 93/A/0429), into a complaint against the London Borough of Lambeth, concerned a complaint by parents about the manner in which the Council dealt with suspicions of sexual abuse regarding their 5-year-old daughter. In particular, the parents claimed that the matter had not been properly investigated and that, after an initial contact from the social services department, they had not been kept informed of the progress or outcome of the enquiries (which resulted in no further action being taken), as a result of which the family as a whole suffered a long period of uncertainty and anxiety.

Although Schedule 5 of the Local Government Act 1974 excludes the CLA from investigating 'Action taken by any authority in connection with the investigation or prevention of crime', this case clearly establishes that the CLA considers that maintaining adequate contact with families involved in child abuse allegations, and following proper procedures in such situations, remains within their remit. There is a history of broken appointments and unanswered correspondence in this case, and substantial questions over the effectiveness of liaison between the Council's education and social services departments. However, perhaps most significant for our purposes is the mother's complaint, as described in the CLA's report, that:

> Social Services seemed to drop the matter without making it clear what was happening. They walked in, accompanied by the police, upset the family, and then just walked away. Some families might have been destroyed by such actions and she feels her family will never get over it completely.
>
> (CLA, 93/A/0429, p. 13)

The Council's *Children and Families Manual* stated that, 'Following any investigation of a family in respect of possible sexual abuse, and regardless of the outcome, assessment is needed of post-investigative therapeutic/counselling needs of the family.'

It is difficult to imagine a more stressful situation than that in which the family found themselves in the 15 months between concerns first being expressed to the social services department and the parents finally being assured by a social worker that no further action would be taken. The CLA summarizes the parents' anxieties: 'There had been the constant fear that someone would turn up without warning and take [the daughter] away. It had been like a never-ending nightmare.' The CLA found that failures to answer correspondence (including a failure to allow the mother access to her file), last-minute cancellation of meetings, and effectively dropping the case without informing the parents, combined with the failure to consider whether post-investigative therapy or counselling was necessary, caused unnecessary distress to the family and amounted to maladministration. The CLA recommended that the council pay £2000 to the parents, in recognition of the distress and anxiety caused, plus £250 in relation to the time and inconvenience the parents had been put to in referring the case to the CLA, and recommended that the Council should review its procedures.

These two cases illustrate not only the potential for the CLA to provide remedies in individual cases, but also the potential for the inquisitorial approach of ombudsman techniques to recommend and instigate more far-reaching and proactive inquiries to prevent a recurrence. This prophylactic effect is perhaps the most under-rated part of the CLA's achievements, but the effect is limited by the relatively small number of complaints received and the still smaller number investigated. This is almost certainly to a large extent a consequence of a lack of public awareness of the CLA's existence.

Amphlett (see Chapter 3), notes that by the time that families have exhausted the potentially confusing array of local authority review mechanisms relating to child protection functions, they may have little energy left to pursue a complaint via the CLA. We understand this point, but would note that in so far as such exhaustion derives from unreasonable delays on the part of the local authority, the process can be short-circuited by early reference to the CLA on the grounds of delay itself. Frequently, the threat of reference to the CLA, or failing that an initial contact from the CLA following receipt of a complaint, provides sufficient impetus to prompt an apparently inert local authority into action. Here, greater publicity for the existence and role of the CLA seems crucial.

The cheap, relatively informal and accessible grievance redress mechanism provided by the CLA appears to offer significant potential both for resolving immediate disputes, and for recommending reviews of future action, in addition to offering substantial advantages over potentially protracted and costly adversarial court processes. The CLA's brief focuses clearly on the procedures and practices of the authority concerned, avoiding consideration of the relative merits of the positions of local authority and parents on the substantive issue in question. Particularly in respect of cases where a complainant primarily wants their sense of justice to be restored, rather than hard legal remedies such as large sums of compensation, the ability of the CLA to investigate a complaint, and to obtain an acknowledgement from the local authority of their failings, perhaps combined with an apology, and to make recommendations about future policy and practice, seems far more relevant to the motivation and needs of such complainants than the traditional legal process.

The way ahead?

In reviewing the rules surrounding the availability of information for parents, we have identified two categories of information that they might require during the course of an investigation. These are, on the one hand, information about the progress of the particular investigation and, on the other, information about the procedures which should be followed in investigating any case of child abuse. We do not believe that improvements in parental access to either of these categories of information necessarily require or would be best achieved via legislation.

Why not legislation?

Legislation granting 'rights' of access to information is inconsistent both with recent rhetoric in the field of child protection (and more generally in relation to public life in the UK), and with existing practice which is substantially based upon procedural guidelines. It might also serve to inhibit unnecessarily the exercise of professional discretion, which appears desirable, beneficial and ultimately relatively unproblematic provided that it is exercised, structured and checked in an adequately public manner. We also believe that the unequal ability of parents to encash such rights would lead to disadvantaged parents, those to whom Stevenson refers, benefiting only marginally from any such enactment.

As our consideration of the CLA's role has sought to demonstrate, there is no problem in general with providing scrutiny via procedural requirements, and indeed this can contribute substantially to the accountability and hence legitimacy of decision-making, provided that scrutiny mechanisms are sufficiently accessible and well publicized to ensure that they are utilized. In many ways, *safeguards in the form of procedural requirements* are the crucial element here, because it is the effective granting of an ability to access information and the decision-making process with which we are concerned, rather than the content of the information or the substance of the decision that is in question.

We have doubts as to the effectiveness of legislation in bringing about the kind of procedural openness which we seek. Not only does the likelihood of such legislation seem remote, given the obvious preference of government for informal, discretionary mechanisms rather than statutory requirements, but it also runs counter to the co-operative spirit espoused by recent legislation, guidance and rhetoric in the area of child protection. In addition, given the track record of the courts in attempting to develop principles adequate to deal with problematic cases such as those discussed above in relation to disclosure of information, the introduction of legislation on access to information, with the likelihood of resulting litigation, would be unlikely to produce helpful developments. More-over, the relative formality and potential cost of court proceedings would be likely to restrict significantly the number of families able to utilize them.

Enhancing legal rights via legislation can have the effects of strength-ening the position of those best able to utilize the system (typically the well educated, articulate and relatively affluent), while offering little to the less advantaged, thus contributing to the legitimation of existing inequalities through the application of a spurious veneer of legal equal-ity. Rights which cannot be effectively encashed are really not rights at all.

We also believe that legislation, unless carefully drafted, may unnec-essarily reduce the discretion of those professionals working within the social services, undermining the scope for the exercise of professional judgement. We consider the objective in providing greater access to information not to be the removal of all professional discretion, but rather to ensure accountability, via the provision of meaningful access to information, and to ensure that where discretion is exercised it is on an open, structured and checked basis.

Thus we suggest that positive outcomes in terms of enhanced access to information might be more likely to be brought about by a combina-tion of the adoption of existing best practice by local authorities in con-junction, crucially, with greater publicity of their procedures in fields such as child abuse investigations, combined with effective grievance procedures, such as those pursued by the CLA, for investigating allega-tions of maladministration. We feel that these steps, namely the develop-ment of published procedural standards, embodying the principles that we have set out above, combined with a well-publicized grievance redress mechanism such as the CLA, would provide the most effective system for furthering access to information.

We have considered the possibility of the introduction of a specialist agency, independent of local authorities – perhaps an expanded version of the 'Office for Child Protection' considered in the Cleveland report – to provide independent investigation of allegations of unreasonable denial of access (Department of Health and Social Security, 1988, *Recommendations* 11(5)(a); see also Gieve, 1989). However, we believe that it would duplicate unnecessarily the current activities of the CLA, who appears to be perfectly well equipped, if at present inadequately publicized and perhaps somewhat under-funded, to deal with such cases.

The existing legal provisions constitute only a partial and incomplete framework for access to information for users of social services – an *ad hoc* assembly of provisions with no central organizing principle of open-ness. Although in places detailed provisions such as the Data Protection Act provide specific and enforceable rights, and although the legal posi-tion on access to information is somewhat better than that relating to central government, significant gaps exist in relation to the provision of access to information, highlighted by the position of parents involved in allegations of child sexual abuse.

Despite the 1993 White Paper and the resulting Code of Practice applicable to central government, the dominant norm of secrecy in British public life continues to contrast markedly with the position in other Western democracies, and is perhaps so all pervasive that there is little likelihood of dramatic changes being brought about via legislation, at least in the absence of broader constitutional reform. Indeed, there is a significant risk that any legislation in this area would be likely to prove tokenistic in the absence of broader constitutional reform reversing the norm.

Case-specific information

During an investigation a parent may wish to know a great deal of case-specific information. This could include, for example, who made the allegation in the first place, what evidence investigators have that the child has really been abused, the possible abusers of the child, and what the child has said about the allegations.

It would be wrong to assume that it is necessarily in the best interests of a child for his or her parents to be told this information at the time when they request it. Guidance, in responding to the understandable concerns of parents, has tended to gloss over the fact that at present data suggests that parents are the most likely perpetrators of child abuse. A nation-wide study conducted by the National Society for the Prevention of Cruelty to Children (NSPCC) found that 58 per cent of cases of sexual abuse reported between 1983 and 1987 were perpetrated by the child's father or father-substitute (National Society for the Prevention of Cruelty to Children, 1989, p. 21, Table 16). The same survey found that 39 per cent of reported cases of physical abuse in the period were perpetrated by the child's father or father-substitute, and 34 per cent by the mother or mother-substitute.

Where investigators are not certain that the parent is *not* involved, it seems proper that the parents should not be given information which they could then use to cover up signs of abuse or to blackmail the child emotionally. Investigations are not undertaken for the benefit of parents – they are meant to be undertaken in support of the interests of the child. Present child protection procedures have linked the best interests of the child with the conduct of an effective child abuse investigation, which must on some occasions include the concealment of information from suspects. As *Working Together Under the Children Act* warned, 'failure to conduct child abuse investigations in the most effective manner may mean that the best possible protection cannot be provided for the child victim' (Home Office, Department of Health and Department of Education and Science, 1991, p. 16, para. 4.11). The decision to conceal information should, however, be made within the context of a norm of openness which ensures that parents are given information at the earliest possible opportunity.

In practice, in some areas of the country, where investigators are almost certain that a parent has not abused the child they will keep a non-abusing parent closely informed of the progress of the case. This is seen partly as a courtesy and partly as a way to encourage a non-abusing parent to protect the child from an abuser. Where it is possible and does not interfere with the protection of the child, this practice should be extended and routinized. A situation of antagonism and distrust between investigators and the child's parents is unlikely to be helpful to the child, and should be avoided wherever reasonably possible.

We accept that there will be circumstances in which the investigation, and the child's best interests, will legitimately require the withholding of information from parents. However, we believe that those taking decisions to withhold such information should be obliged to record meaningful reasons for their decision, in order to allow subsequent investigation as to the propriety of their decision, and that even in such cases the reasons for denying access to information should be made available to the parents. In addition, we believe as a general principle that all information should be made available to parents as soon as is consistent with effective investigation although, provided that a reasoned case is made out, the continued withholding of information may be justified by reference to complex inter-agency issues (e.g. relating to medical evidence) and/or potential or actual prejudice to necessary future relationships between the agency or the child and the parents.

The key element here is requiring decision-makers to give reasons for their decisions, which can subsequently be subjected to review by an external body such as the CLA – but also, crucially, ensuring that the norm is one of openness, with only reasoned and justified exceptions to this norm.

Information about procedures

In relation to this second category of information we feel no need for equivocation. We can see no reason why parents – even those who have abused their child – should not know the content of the procedures which investigators are expected to follow, such as the meetings that investigators would be expected to have, and what should happen at each stage of the investigation. We can see no reason why this would prejudice an investigation or be contrary to a child's interests – rather we feel that this could actually improve relations between investigators and parents.

Working Together Under the Children Act 1989 recommended that Area Child Protection Committees should make copies of local child protection procedures available to the public through, for example, local libraries. However, a study completed at the end of 1994 found that only 50 per cent of the ACPCs in the sample had done this, while one ACPC had made their annual report available in local libraries, but not the actual child protection procedures (Keenan, 1994, pp. 204–6).

We suggest that the most appropriate way for parents to encash rights to know the content of local child protection procedures is in the form of a leaflet designed for parents and accompanied by explanations from investigators. In view of the highly emotional situation in which parents find themselves, this seems of infinitely more use than the opportunity to wade through the unfamiliar and lengthy Area Child Protection Procedures.

The adoption of existing best practice is essentially what we are advocating here, in order to ensure that, without exception, parents are adequately informed about investigation procedures and avenues of complaint, be they internal or external, formal or informal. We can see no good reasons for exceptions to this principle. Parents, whether or not they are guilty of abuse, should be informed both of the progress of the case (although not necessarily the details of evidence if this would prejudice effective investigation or future relationships) and of how they can complain if procedures have not been followed.

We advocate increased publicity of the existence of the CLA as the primary external mechanism of scrutiny, but believe that local authorities should develop detailed internal review processes, with a maximum degree of separation from the original decision-maker, in order to avoid any possibility of a flood of complaints being directed to the CLA.

A framework for access to information

Birkinshaw states that 'Information is inherently a feature of power. So too is its control, use and regulation' (Birkinshaw, 1988, p. 20). This being the case, access to information is crucial for ensuring that an individual is able to challenge the actions of the state effectively.

We conclude by reiterating that it is possible that the problems associated with lack of access to information may best be implemented with the active consent and involvement of those presently in control of information. This would be an example of 'structuring' discretion through 'internal rule-making' (Davis, 1971, Chapter 4) and operating within the pattern established by central government in recent reforms. It seems to us that if a regime of access to information is to be effective, while at the same time allowing effective executive discretion to be utilized in providing social services and investigating matters such as child abuse, it must be introduced within the dominant cultural scheme, rather than seeking to impose alien concepts via legislation. Temperate plants rarely flourish in a desert, and thus unless climatic change is brought about via constitutional reform, there seems little hope that legislation on openness will prove effective if it is planted in an unfavourable environment.

In any case, we are concerned about the likelihood that many parents, such as those identified by Stevenson above, will experience severe difficulty in encashing such rights.

Thus we advocate the development of published codes of practice, seeking to establish to the satisfaction of both service users and service providers a balance between adequate access and effective professional activity. The obvious criticism, we are well aware, is the absence of legal enforceability. However, in so far as practices are published, there is some hope that the courts may on occasion be called to aid in enforcing their continued application, notwithstanding their lack of legal status. In addition to the generally better track-record of enforcing procedural rather than substantive rights, UK courts have recently been actively developing a concept of 'legitimate expectation' under which an individual or group that has previously received a benefit, or has been promised it by a public body, may expect that a court will enforce appropriate procedural requirements prior to such a benefit being denied, even if such procedural claims extend beyond existing legal rights. One case, *R v Brent LB ex parte Gunning*, even appears to suggest that parents (of schoolchildren, in that particular case) may acquire procedural rights simply because of their special and particular interest in the matter under consideration.

Although the courts may have a place in disputes in this area, in general we do not wish to see the law courts used as a primary mechanism of challenge to decisions regarding access to information. Rather, we suggest that transparency in decision-making, and hence accountability and legitimacy, can best be achieved by the public structuring of professional discretion, combined with effective and accessible avenues of challenge which avoid whenever possible the formality and expense of courtroom process. However, this will require substantially increased publicity to be given to alternative grievance redress procedures such as the Commissioner for Local Administration.

The existing position presents us with a risk of system abuse of parents involved in child abuse allegations, and while we have no problem in affirming the centrality of the child's interests in such proceedings, we cannot ignore the very real and reasonable interests and expectations of parents relating to decisions regarding their children, at least until such time as they are proved to have been guilty of abuse.

In essence, the model we propose is intended to achieve two objectives:

- the establishment of a norm of openness, subject only to reasoned exceptions; and
- the availability of accessible and effective avenues of challenge.

In concrete terms, we recommend that a clearly elucidated concept of *openness* should be widely and prominently put forward in material relating to child protection, with a clear distinction being made between the types of information that parents might expect to receive. At the same time, a practice should be established whereby investigators should be expected to record their reasons for withholding certain information from parents in order to enhance their accountability, if necessary through subsequent review.

If existing redress mechanisms are not adequate, alternatives must be considered, although we consider that substantial potential – at present under-utilized – exists for the CLA to act as an effective means of external scrutiny.

We believe that the implementation of such proposals would go some way towards ensuring that the constitutional and democratic promise of accountability is fulfilled, and will ensure the recognition and protection of parental interests alongside those of children.

Acknowledgements

We wish to acknowledge the assistance given by Sue Amphlett (PAIN), David Nice (Commission for Local Administration) and Helen Jordan (University of Sheffield), but we accept full responsibility for all views expressed and any defects contained in the text. We point out that this article does not cover any legal developments beyond April 1995.

References

Amphlett, S. (1994) *Secret suffering or false allegation?* Stansted: Parents Against Injustice.

Birkinshaw, P. (1988) *Freedom of information.* London: Weidenfeld and Nicholson.

Birkinshaw, P. (1990) *Government and information.* London: Butterworths.

Creighton, S. J. and Noyes, P. (1989) *Child abuse trends in England and Wales 1983–1987.* London: National Society for the Prevention of Cruelty to Children.

Davis, K. C. (1971) *Discretionary justice: a preliminary inquiry.* Illinois, IL: University of Illinois Press.

Department of Health and Social Security (1974) *Report of the Committee of Inquiry into the Care and Supervision Provided in Relation to Maria Colwell.* London: HMSO.

Department of Health and Social Security (1985) *Review of child care law.* London: HMSO and Department of Health and Social Security.

Department of Health and Social Security (1988) *Report of the Inquiry into Child Abuse in Cleveland 1987.* London: HMSO.

Department of Health and Social Security and Welsh Office (1988) *Working together: a guide to arrangements for inter-agency co-operation for the protection of children from abuse.* London: HMSO.

Department of Health and Social Security (1992) *The Report of the Inquiry into the Removal of Children from Orkney in February 1991.* Edinburgh: HMSO.

Feintuck, M. (1994) *Accountability and choice in schooling.* Buckingham: Open University Press.

Fox Harding, M. (1991) *Perspectives in child care policy.* London: Longman.

Gieve, K. (1989) Where do families stand after the Cleveland Inquiry? In Riches, P. (ed.), *Responses to Cleveland – improving services for child sexual abuse.* London: National Children's Bureau.

Greenwich Health Authority and Borough of Greenwich (1987) *A Child in Mind: Protection of Children in a Responsible Society. Report of the Commission of Inquiry into the Circumstances Surrounding the Death of Kimberley Carlile.* London: Borough of Greenwich and Greenwich Health Authority.

HMSO (1993) *White Paper on Open Government.* London: HMSO.

Home Office, Department of Health and Department of Education and Science (1991) *Working Together Under the Children Act 1989.* London: HMSO.

Keenan, C. (1994) *The development of the law and its implementation in the investigation of child sexual abuse.* Unpublished Doctoral Thesis, University of Sheffield.

Lewis, N. and Birkinshaw, P. (1993) *When citizens complain.* Buckingham: Open University Press.

London Borough of Brent (1985) *A Child in Trust: The Report of the Panel of Inquiry into the Circumstances Surrounding the Death of Jasmine Beckford.* Brent: London Borough of Brent.

London Borough of Lambeth (1987) *Whose Child? The Report of the Public Inquiry into the Death of Tyra Henry.* London: London Borough of Lambeth.

Monk, D. (1988) Freeing information. *Social Work Today* **19**, 3.

Office of Public Service and Science (1993) *Code of practice on access to government information.* London: Office of Public Service and Science.

Parton, N. (1985) *The politics of child abuse*. London: Macmillan.

Social Services Inspectorate (1990) *Inspection of Child Protection Services in Rochdale*. London: Social Services Inspectorate and Department of Health.

Stevenson, O. (ed.) (1989) *Child abuse: professional practice and public policy*. London: Harvester Wheatsheaf.

Cases

In re M (a Minor) Times 4.1.90

KS v GS [1992] 2 FLR 361

R v Brent London Borough ex parte Gunning (1985) 84 LGR 168

R v Hampshire County Council ex parte K [1990] 2 All ER 129

R v United Kingdom [1988] 2 FLR 445

Re C and L [1991] F.C.R. 351

Re M [1987] 1 FLR 293

Re W [1987] 1 FLR 297

Rochdale B.C. v A and Others [1991] 2 FLR 192.

Index